D0820181

DOES SOCIALISM LIBERATE WOMEN?

DOES SOCIALISM LIBERATE WOMEN?

EXPERIENCES FROM
EASTERN EUROPE

HILDA SCOTT

BEACON PRESS BOSTON

Beacon Press books are published under the auspices
of the Unitarian Universalist Association

Published simultaneously in Canada by Saunders of Toronto, Ltd.

Printed in the United States of America

9 8 7 6 5 4 3 2 1

Library of Congress Cataloging in Publication Data

Scott, Hilda
  Does socialism liberate women?
  Includes bibliographical references.
    1. Women in Europe, Eastern.   2. Women and
socialism.   3. Discrimination in employment.
  I. Title.
HQ1587.S36   301.41′2′0947   74–212
  ISBN 0–8070–4162–9

Dedicated to the Memory of

DOROTHY W. DOUGLAS

CONTENTS

INTRODUCTION

My own upbringing and education inculcated in me a naïve belief in the equality of men and women. I marveled at stories of suffragettes marching for the vote in the streets of New York City. Among my childhood recollections are memories of old-fashioned photographs of the kind that used to appear in the rotogravure sections of the Sunday paper, showing Soviet women in white uniforms bending over infants in *crèches,* as they were then called. This solved everything, it seemed to me then, and I resolved to have many children and combine them with a career. Later I discovered that there was something wrong with this plan, and later still I had an opportunity to find out for myself over an extended period how motherhood and employment were combined in a country which earnestly believed that it was making equality for women a reality.

The two early visions of mine reflect the two lines of development which the fight for woman's rights has taken: one, emancipation as we have known it in the United States and England, the other growing out of the socialist labor movement in Europe. The first has had high moral principles but little theory, and only sporadically its own organizations. Taking the path of gradual legislative reform, it has improvised its way through history, sometimes becoming inactive, at other times militant, opening its arms to radicals or conservatives as long as they supported the goal of the moment. The other adopted

Marxism as its guiding principle, and found the origins of women's inferior position in the private property system. Organized and disciplined, it adhered to a cohesive and clearly defined program. As everyone knows, the first attempt to put this program into practice was made in Russia, and after the Second World War the Soviet example was followed by other countries of Central and Eastern Europe.

It is not easy for women in capitalist countries to visualize the socialist solution in action. It has been hailed as a tremendous victory and condemned as betrayal. There are impressive facts regarding women's legal rights, employment, nurseries, and other benefits which still represent a maximum program in other countries. Yet it is suspected that women in socialist countries have not achieved the degree of liberation which their program promised, and that they are still victims of discrimination. Since the renewed interest in women's liberation in Western countries in the 1960s, a number of writers have made the point that neither the first nor the second approach to emancipation seems to have brought about real equality, and that more theoretical work is necessary to arrive at a complex solution capable of developing as society develops. For this purpose it is important to know as much as possible about how existing answers work and where they have disappointed their advocates.

For many reasons it is discouraging to try to answer these questions on the basis of Soviet experience in terms that are applicable to our own lives: the Soviet Union is too vast, too varied, too remote; and it is too difficult to obtain firsthand knowledge, too hard to draw the right conclusions from statistics without it. Fortunately for the purpose of such an investigation, although all the socialist countries differ, seven of them — Czechoslovakia, the German Democratic Republic, Hungary, Poland, Bulgaria, Rumania, and the Soviet Union — have in common the fact that they are attempting to apply the same interpretation of Marxist theory. This makes it possible to draw some general conclusions from the experience of one country about this way of putting Marxist ideas about the emancipation of women into practice.

Czechoslovakia, where I lived for many years, is uniquely suitable for this study. Because of its geographical position and its historical evolution, Austrian, German, French, and British influences have provided a counterweight to its naturally Slavic allegiances. Politically it has a democratic tradition which none of the other socialist countries shares. Although its area (49,370 square miles) is only about the size of the state of New York, with a somewhat smaller population (14.4 million), it presents all the problems and advantages of life in an industrialized country in miniature. It has all the major industries, and it became the first country in the world to embark upon a socialist program when it already ranked among the first ten in total volume of industrial production and per capita production. The standard of living is generally acknowledged to be lower than Austria's but higher than Italy's, while Soviet sources put Czechoslovakia's per capita consumption at about 40 percent greater than that of the Soviet Union. Czechoslovakia is a federated state of two nations, Czechs and Slovaks, speaking separate languages; but these two peoples are closer in their outlook and understanding of each other than are the inhabitants of most other multinational states of Europe, or the residents of Massachusetts and Alabama or Scotland and England, for example. Minority nationalities make up only 6 percent of the population. This reduces the danger of specious generalizations.

Because every reader will approach this book with certain well-established prejudices, more so than if it were about any country in the capitalist or third world, I should like to emphasize that it is not an exposé; not is it a personal story, although most of it is backed by personal experience and observation. I have tried, insofar as my own prejudices permit, to record objectively what happened in a particular part of the world at a particular time when certain ideas were applied under certain conditions, and to attempt to explain why certain things happened as they did, on the basis of publicly available evidence.

The story is necessarily incomplete, as it is obviously impossible to bring all aspects of woman's life into one book and do justice to them. It deals with the outer mechanics of living rather than with the inner mechanics of people's relationships. One reason for this is that the Marxist movement has always frankly put heavy emphasis on the tangible, material, economic, and political at the expense of the more ephemeral personal and psychological. To examine the development under socialism of personal relationships between men and women, among adults, among children, in school, on the job, and so on, would require a totally different study by an investigator with different qualifications, of different material, much more difficult to come by and to evaluate.

In spite of this, I have permitted myself some conclusions and speculations in the hope that they will provoke others into a more fundamental discussion of socialist experience with women's emancipation than we have had in the past.

I take this opportunity to thank many friends in several countries who have helped to make this book possible.

Hilda Scott

Vienna, October 1973

CHAPTER ONE

IS THERE ROOM AT THE TOP?

By 1972 the image of the beautiful tractor driver as heroine had receded so far into the distant past that a top official of the Czechoslovak Communist Party, on a visit to a cooperative farm at harvest time, was captured on the TV screen expressing astonishment when he was introduced to two young husband-and-wife combine-operator teams. "And do you let them drive?" he inquired of the husbands. "They know the job," came the terse reply.

These young girls, now the exception, would have been described fifteen or twenty years earlier as typical of the new woman. As late as 1963 it was possible for the Women's Committee to present the situation of women, in a book published for the information of foreign visitors, as completely transformed:

"

Socialist society has done away with the difference between physical and mental work, a difference so typical of the past and characterized by the humiliating position of the working class. Mental work was the privilege of the propertied class, while working men and women were condemned to tiring physical work. Formerly women were usually given unskilled jobs. . . . Eighteen years ago women who had formerly been enrolled for war work began learning to handle machines serving peaceful needs. They often succeeded better than men in getting rid of old survivals and habits and they became pioneers of new methods. The problem was to raise productivity not by working overtime and harder, but by improved working methods, better organization of work, economies in material, a reduction in the number of rejects . . .[1]

"

This kind of socialist optimism, in which the goal was confused with reality, was not uncommon; and the authors in this case were undoubtedly personally convinced that what was then the exception would someday soon become the rule. To others who at that time were following events on the factory floor it was already clear that, while some women were being trained for men's jobs, the dominant trend was not one in which women and men would soon be working side by side at the same machines for the same pay.

Between the years 1948 and 1958, while there were women who went to work in heavy industry and took jobs considered unconventional for their sex, there was still room in the traditional occupations — light industry, office work, teaching, health — to absorb most of the women who entered the labor force. After that time, as the share of women in the total manpower picture grew, efforts to recruit them for other fields to ease the shortage of manpower there, or release men for heavier work, met with greater success simply because most of the familiar women's fields were becoming saturated. While in 1948 women made up a majority of workers in only two of the seventeen branches of the economy (agriculture, and health and social welfare services), by 1966 they accounted for more than half of workers in ten out of eighteen branches.[2]

The law guaranteed equal pay for equal work, but at the bottom of the scale were the branches where women made up the majority and where the average wage was 1,000–1,200 crowns monthly, while at the other end were the jobs where women were the exception and the average wage was around 2,000 crowns. Within any given branch the same was true: women were at the bottom, men at the top. As early as 1960, women made up 37 percent of all workers in the general engineering industry; 78 percent earned less than 1,200 crowns monthly, while 83 percent of men earned more than this. It was the rule not only for women at the lathes and milling machines but in other branches of engineering: electrical engineering, radio engineering, precision engineering, and optics, where women were sought after because of their nimble fingers, patience, and willingness to put up with tedium. At the Tesla-Pardubice electrical engineering plant making TV sets and tape recorders, where women outnumbered men by better than three to two, in 1965 only 0.3 percent of women earned more than 1,200 crowns monthly compared to 70 percent of men. The investigators who uncovered this fact commented: "The plant for the production of television sets is a classic example of the modern division of labor: a large development and design department employing chiefly men with secondary school or higher vocational training, and a preproduction and assembly division employing women with on-the-job training, that is, with a low level of skill." [3] The foremen of these women's divisions were men.

A major reason for this state of affairs was certainly the inferior skills and more limited experience of women who were new to the industry and often new to work outside the home. Theoretically they could improve their standing in factory-run courses, but in practice women were much more reluctant than men to do so, for obvious reasons. In a study made in six engineering plants of men and women workers between eighteen and forty-nine years of age who had come to the job without special training, it was discovered that girls either improved their ratings by the time they were twenty-three or they usually did not do so at all. Once children arrived, women found little time for study. In one factory where motivation for raising qualifications was investigated, men and women gave the same reasons for doing so: money and interest in their work. However, 70 percent of the women were not interested in improving their position, and of these almost half explained that they had too much work at home.

It was expected that a new generation of workers, in which boys and girls had equal access to jobs of all types and education of all kinds, would eventually tend to equalize the difference; but this hope proved illusory. The engineering industry, the spearhead of the country's economic drive, in spite of its need for labor soon began to demonstrate its reluctance to accept girls for its apprentice-training program. While in 1960 women made up almost 26 percent of workers in heavy engineering, these plants allotted only 16 percent of their places for incoming apprentices to girls. In general engineering 25 percent of places went to girls, although women made up 37 percent of the work force. A decade later only 5 percent of all apprentices in engineering and metallurgy were girls. The leaders of the industry justified this approach to women's training by the fact that the girls they did train did not stay in the field. "Our enterprise threw out three million crowns between 1952 and 1962 training girls who left to work in entirely different occupations from those for which they had been trained," complained a director of the apprentice training program at ČKD, the country's largest engineering complex.[4] Only 9 percent of the girls trained in the ČKD-Stalingrad plant in Prague during that decade, for example, remained in engineering.

In 1967 twenty-four heavy-industry plants looked back over the records and discovered that of all the girls trained as apprentices between 1955 and 1961, only a little over 8 percent were still there as workers. A big Brno engineering plant had lost all but six of its original six hundred trained girl apprentices; two engineering plants in Prague did not have a single one. This information, published in the trade union daily, *Práce,* was accompanied by the conclusion that the plants had not created the kind of working conditions that would keep women satisfied, and that apparently they were not very anxious to do so.

Women who did acquire suitable training did not find themselves welcomed with open arms. Younger women, especially, were often discovered at jobs for which they were overqualified, and their training was thus wasted. Or, if they did get ahead, they were more likely to be held to the minimum for the category while the men rose to the maximum. This was true, for example, even in the predominantly female ready-made clothing industry. In 1964 the Communist party committee at one of the most important plants of the industry in Prostějov, employing 70 percent women, found that where women were employed in the better-paid medium grade jobs — technical controllers, norm-setters, foremen, technologists, planners, and designers — in almost every category a much higher percentage of women than of men had the necessary qualifications as far as training and experience were concerned. When it came to pay, however, women foremen earned less than men foremen, women controllers less than men controllers, and qualified male workers earned more than qualified women on the same job. Various reasons were advanced: women themselves were not eager for more demanding work; management tended to regard the man as the head of the family whose pay was decisive; foremen favored men in the distribution of work; men were stronger, tired less easily, had a higher output. None of these seemed adequate to the Communist daily, *Rudé právo,* which commented: "The facts discussed here are a reflection of a much deeper social process which has been very little investigated in its full complexity and concrete aspects." [5]

In a study made of the earnings of workers and technical and administrative personnel in industry, retail trade, and public agencies in 1968, women workers were found, on a national average, to earn 27.9 percent less than men. Similar relationships prevailed in all industries and professions — including those in which women predominated — from the building trades where women's pay was 48 percent of men's to the textile industry where it averaged 71 percent and the health services where it was 80.4 percent of men's earnings. In several light-industry plants, women's earnings were as much as 24 percent less than men's for the *same* job. When it came to positions requiring training and responsibility, women were required to fulfill all the necessary conditions to qualify, while lack of education and experience was often overlooked in men. "The facts which I have presented," wrote the author of this study, "are shocking from the point of view of the economic equality of women. They show that economic equality does not exist in practice. In reality in a socialist state wage policy has the same consequences as in a state in which women's equality has not received even *de jure* recognition." The reasons? "Unfortunately there is not even the most primitive evidence available. Unfortunately no serious analysis has been made from the economic, sociological, or psychological point of view." [6]

In an investigation of nearly five hundred medium-level technical and administrative personnel in two textile plants, published in 1971, men averaged higher pay and higher bonuses in every category, even though the women were equally and sometimes better qualified. Some women who had been promoted to these jobs pointed out that when the posts had previously been occupied by men they had had their own secretaries, "and for the most part attended conferences and meetings while their work was done for them by this subordinate. When they were replaced by a woman, however, she had to do all the work including that which had been done for the man by someone else." [7] A majority of these women acknowledged that men were objectively more desirable workers than women because they were not burdened by home worries, and one third added that many women themselves preferred less responsible jobs which left them more time and strength for their household duties. Observers have commented on another aspect: women have much less time for public office-holding, and therefore must put much more work into the job itself to receive the same recognition as a man. If a man undertakes various voluntary public functions it becomes known that he is capable, gets around, is a leader; and he is more likely to be considered when important positions are to be filled.

Government statistics published in 1968 dispelled any illusion that women had an equal chance with men in industry by relating average monthly earnings of men and women throughout the economy to the level of education attained, without regard to the field or type of job held. From this it was clear at a glance that a man with only nine years of compulsory schooling earned almost as much, on the average, as a woman with a university degree, and that while a man could expect to find a decent job as a technician or administrator if he had what corresponds in the United States to a high school education, a woman could arrive at this salary level only if she had been to college. [8]

This helps to explain the nature of the female education explosion which occurred in Czechoslovakia in the 1950s and

60s. It was expected that there would be a spurt in enrollment, but it was not anticipated that girls would not only catch up with boys but surpass them. In the 1957–67 decade, the number of male university students increased by 47 percent; but the number of women grew by 212 percent, and by 1971–72 made up 40 percent of the total. While there were six times as many male college graduates as female in the population in 1950, by 1970 the ratio was only two to one. By 1965 girls made up 66 percent of all students at academic secondary schools and 55 percent of all those at vocational secondary schools, compared to the prewar figure of 21 percent. These are the schools which provide the college population. Obviously, women have one incentive to study which men do not share. A man can make a relatively good living at almost any educational level, and in fact if money is his main concern he will become a qualified worker in heavy industry. The difference between the opportunities for higher earnings of women workers in industry and those of professional women with university degrees is much greater than between the corresponding groups of men. "The only type of education which has an effect on the earnings of women is a university education," one team of investigators concluded.[9]

Behind the unprecedented rise in the proportion of educated women a more familiar trend is apparent. The girls choose the arts and humanities and medicine; they prefer biology to physics and mathematics. At the secondary school level they monopolize the schools for nursing (98 percent), office work (87 percent), teaching (98 percent), and library work. While there has also been an increase in the percentage of girls studying technical subjects (they account for 23 percent of students at vocational secondary schools of the technical type and 17 percent of enrollees at technical colleges), this could not be otherwise in view of the extraordinary demand by women for higher education. Many candidates are turned away from the liberal arts schools and other traditional women's fields and must take what they can get. These figures, therefore, do not reflect women's actual inclinations. When, in 1970, as part of a study on job satisfaction and fluctuation, the State Population

Commission questioned one thousand 21-year-old girls in cities and another thousand in country villages, they learned that only one-third were satisfied with the field of study they had chosen, whether they had learned a trade, completed secondary school, or were at college. In the apprentice training program, where 60 percent of all youngsters are prepared for life after they finish their compulsory nine years of schooling, girls have also increased their numbers: from 20 percent of places in 1955 to 30 percent in 1970. However, the same kind of polarization has occurred. Half of these girls prepare for jobs as salesgirls, cooks, and waitresses, or for service occupations like dress-making and hairdressing; one quarter go into the textile and clothing industry; and only one quarter train for less conventional occupations like electrical engineering, the printing trades, the food industry, or transport and communications. Meanwhile, one-third of all boy apprentices are being trained in Czechoslovakia's most highly favored industry, machine building and metallurgy. This division into girls' occupations and boys' occupations is intensified by the reluctance of most industries to take their quota of girls; and by the fact that of the 288 available types of apprentice training courses, most of them lasting two or three years, 95 are now reserved exclusively for boys, 20 exclusively for girls, while 173 are open to both but not in equal numbers.

So there has been created at both ends of the ladder a new problem which has been known since the mid-sixties as "feminization." This blight — for that is how it has been viewed — struck whole professions (especially medicine and teaching), whole occupations and branches of industry. Women made up 40 percent of doctors, and the proportion was growing, since they already accounted for 60 percent of medical students (and 90 percent of all pharmacology students). Had they reached this preeminence because they were recognized to be better than men? Unfortunately not. The fact was (and is) that in the nationalized health service the average doctor's pay was lower than that of a worker in heavy industry who, in addition, could be earning a substantial wage at eighteen instead of a meager one at twenty-four. The best male graduates of secondary schools went on to study physics or mathematics, entered research institutes to pursue other professions, or went directly into industry where the pay was higher. This left the medical field free to women, for whom a doctor's pay was about the highest to which they could aspire. Belatedly it was discovered that in the early years when a doctor's professional level is decided, many of these medical women were at home having babies. And when they were at home on maternity leave or taking care of ill children they increased the load on other women doctors. They found it difficult to keep abreast of the literature in their fields because they had to do the shopping, cooking, and laundry. Due to the exacting nature of their profession, they felt the burden of their "second shift" more than other women. In the Slovak city of Bratislava, where the percentage of women among doctors (44.2 percent) was already greater than the overall percentage of women in the work force (43.3 percent), two medical sociologists questioned a representative sample of men and women physicians in 1970. They found that women took their specialization exams later than men and that a smaller percentage rose to the higher posts: only 3 in 117 had become head of a hospital department or clinic compared to 13 out of 81 men. Although they had fewer children than average, only 18 percent said that they combined their roles as physicians and homemakers without difficulty. Forty-one percent had to exert "extraordinary effort," 16 percent felt their professional level suffered, 6.7 percent thought their children lost out, 5.5 percent felt that the housework was neglected.

Soon an unwritten but clear change in admissions policy was noted, aimed at halting the "feminization" trend in the universities and secondary schools by applying less exacting criteria to male candidates. Since girl applicants heavily outnumbered boys, this shift inevitably froze a considerable number of girls at the secondary-school level. Girls who had gone to academic high schools with the idea of going on to college now found themselves stranded without any real profession or skill. The new policy also cut off a considerable number of girl graduates of elementary school who had hoped to go to a secondary school, but now could not even find a place in an attractive apprentice training course. At the same time, at the very bottom there was created a pool comprising some 18 percent of all girls of school-leaving age (compared to 4.5 percent of all boys) who, like their mothers before them, were going straight to work at fifteen without any training whatsoever, or who were having difficulty in finding employment. "What Shall We Do with Them?" was the headline which appeared over interviews with learned sociologists, educators, and statisticians, and over many an indignant contribution from parents in the daily press. No one needed to be told that "Them" referred to these hard-to-dispose-of female children. Typical was the comment of a woman economist published in the women's weekly, *Vlasta,* in 1966. Charging that stricter standards were applied to women than men in entrance examinations for medical schools, and not only at medical schools, she wrote:

"

And so another campaign is born. And as in the case of so many other campaigns, it is being conducted with enthusiasm, without looking to right or left, and it runs from wall to wall. The apparition of feminization has emerged suddenly in horrible guise, stalking the colleges and secondary schools, the relevant organs of government and institutions. And horrifying everyone. Thy name is woman, and therefore know thee that thou must relinquish any desire for medicine, teaching, philology, sociology, and I don't know what else. Some years ago we were carried away by the number of callings which had been invaded by women and in which they had proved worthy. Now we are carefully, pedantically weighing and choosing one occupation after another which women must not be allowed to enter.

At the end of this year, tens of thousands of fifteen-year-old and eighteen-year-old girls received their first knock-out blow in the course of their first step into life. . . . Like a slap, the words "girls not accepted" were thrown into their faces. What bitterness and disappointment will a fifteen-year-old girl with top marks carry away with her into life who is now placed before the dilemma: either you study aircraft engines or you don't study at all. No one is interested in whether she has any particular feeling for engines. . . . What is important is that this particular vocational school should fulfill its quota. Its unusual interest in girls is explained to their parents without mincing words. Graduates will step up to the drawing board in the factory for 900 crowns monthly, something no man would do. . . .

It's an endless circle. On every possible occasion we criticize the low qualifications of women, disproportionate to the high percentage of women employed. And now we are taking measures which are by no means simply a brake on the tempo of feminization; we are preparing the ground for a numerically strong army of cleaning women and workers' helpers ten years from now. . . .[10]

"

A spokesman for the ever-realistic State Population Commission pointed out that the number of women in the already feminized fields would continue to rise anyway, and added, "If we are going to talk openly about undesirable feminization, so far no one has established scientifically for individual fields just where the borderlines of desirable feminization are located, and where undesirable feminization leads." [11]

The conflicting interests of various groups could be seen at work: the growing aspirations of girls, the desire of planners for the rational long-term development of manpower, and the immediate interests of the captains of socialist industry who were quite content to have a reservoir of inexpensive labor power which did not offer any real competition with men in the labor market. Since these three elements were allowed to fight it out on an equal footing, the results were foreordained. One might have hoped for a vigorous campaign to counteract the traditional feminine upbringing of girls and direct their interests and possible talents along less conventional lines, as well as a drive to tell parents, who were also employers, that new and interesting possibilities were opening up for their daughters. That nothing of the kind occurred must be explained in part by the complete absence of vocational guidance in the socialist countries, in the modern sense of the word.[12] The mining and steel industries sent recruiting officers into the schools to attract boys to these two preferred fields. Otherwise boys and girls were left to their daydreams and, most of all, to their parents' preconceived notions and the traditional pressures of society; until, at the end of the ninth grade, they went before a local vocational guidance committee which hastily tried to encourage each child in a direction that would suit him, his parents, and the national economy. The impossibility of this task may be judged from the applications for apprentice-training courses in 1971. Among girls there were ten applicants for every place available to learn jewelry-making, and ten for every apprenticeship in glass-painting. In order of popularity there followed photography, window arrangement, hairdressing, pastry-making, porcelain-painting, dressmaking, and switchboard-operating. Boys wanted to be housepainters, electronic mechanics, automobile mechanics, butchers, cooks, and waiters. "We must be aware," wrote the trade-union daily, *Práce,* "that the interests of pupils in the ninth grade represent . . . more often the wishes and calculations of their parents and relatives concerning easy work, quick earnings, opportunities for making money on the side. . . ." [13]

The vocational consultation services which are now slowly being introduced come at a time when the division of occupations into those suitable for boys and girls has become fixed. In school the division begins in the ninth grade, where girls learn cooking and child care while boys receive manual training. With the new emphasis on education for parenthood it is quite probable that it will begin much earlier, in nursery school. In order to relieve the pressure on other vocational secondary schools, a new type of four-year vocational school was established in 1967–68 to prepare girls for work in the service industries and at the same time to train them in domestic science. In addition, two-year vocational schools were introduced to train fifteen-year-old girls in such subjects as administrative work, farming, fashions, mechanical drawing, and the beginnings of a foreign language, as well as domestic science.

Under the circumstances it is not surprising that in industry there is so little room at the top, or even in minor positions of authority, for women. So far it has been sufficient to pay lip service to women's good qualities ("It is generally known that the majority of women are outstanding for their industriousness and discipline and their deep sense of responsibility"); to admit that little has been done to advance them ("Women in leading economic posts are still the exception"), and that prejudice still prevails ("Some men obviously still believe the old saying 'long on hair, short on brains' ") ; and to promise to do better ("We in management, together with the Party organization, are trying to improve things"). The general director of the Czech Shoe Trust, who made these statements in an interview on the occasion of International Women's Day in 1972, acknowledged that women made up 64 percent of his employees and 68 percent of his manual workers, and that of these only 25 percent were qualified, the rest having received only on-the-job training. When management vacancies arise no real effort is made to find a woman for them, he admitted. "We are literally marking time," he told his interviewer.

Although he said nothing concerning steps being taken to increase women's participation in the management of a predominantly female industrial branch, this executive, Mr. Kadlec, did indicate he was aware that by the time a woman enters industry — a milieu dominated by men even when the majority of workers are women — she is equipped by nature and nurture with a rather different set of needs and values than the average male worker. "The high employment of women in our plants," he said, "requires a study of the difference in the psychology of women and men, especially from the point of view of the management of work teams. We must gradually begin the education of foremen and all management workers in these questions." [14]

So general is acceptance of the fact that management jobs belong to men that the trade union paper saw nothing incongruous in publishing, as one of their International Women's Day human interest stories that same year, an interview with a Mr. Veselý, the head of Prague's central telephone exchange, whose main worry was how to congratulate all 760 members of his all-female work force in one day. There is no doubt that women themselves help to create an atmosphere in which a male head of a women's collective is a natural thing. When women have an opportunity to elect a work-team leader from their midst, it has been observed that they usually choose one of a minority of men.

A male executive in the food industry explained: "Just as in nature females can't stand each other, so in human society women can't stand a woman boss. . . . A woman can only hold a top job in a collective of men, because men don't go in for rivalry of that kind." Another told the same interviewer: "A woman in an executive post is an anomaly. Matriarchies exist only in primitive society." In this industry, half of whose employees are female, only 5 of 579 plant directors were women in 1973.[15]

Official statistics do not provide detailed figures on the number of executive posts or responsible government jobs occupied by women, although the figure of 4–5 percent is usually given. It is known that in agriculture, where 52 percent of all workers are women, only 20 of the country's 5,800 farm cooperatives are headed by women. There are no women ministers or vice ministers or ambassadors or members of the Presidium of the Central Committee of the Communist Party of Czechoslovakia. The Slovak party has one woman on its presidium. There are no women members of the Academy of Sciences and only two corresponding members. Only two of the more than three hundred district national health centers are directed by women, in spite of the "feminization" of medicine.

In contrast to their reluctance to share real authority with women is the willingness of men to vacate lesser functions in local government and the trade unions. In response to directives calling for greater participation of women in public life, the percentage of women was increased in a single election in 1971 from less than 20 percent, on a national average, to nearly 24 percent in local national committees; to 30 percent in district and regional national committees; and to 26 percent in the national and federal parliaments. The percentage of women serving on trade union committees at the factory or office level rose from 21 percent to 40 percent in that same year. Apparently men regard these as positions that carry little real power — since there is a parallel Communist party organization at every level whose decisions take precedence — but that require patient, plodding, day-to-day administrative work of the kind women are supposed to be good at.

In view of her "two roles" and her education in this atmosphere, even the talented and educated woman is subjectively prepared in advance to give up her ambitions at the half-way mark. Her dual responsibilities divide her physical and mental energy, divert her attention from major goals to a hundred petty details, fix her to a schedule, make her less mobile. At the same time deeply rooted traditional thinking enforces the conviction in both men and women that certain occupations are suitable for her, particularly those which are an extension of women's "mothering" role (teacher, nurse) and those which require her "nimble fingers." When they can do so anonymously, men will admit that they do not want to see women get ahead. Thus in a UNESCO research project conducted in 1967 to discover how the people of various countries view the future, only in Poland and Czechoslovakia — of eight countries polled on this particular question — did a majority of men hope that *fewer* women would occupy leading posts in the future than do today. Reporting these results in 1972, a Czech sociologist commented, "Yet it is the socialist countries where the greatest emphasis is laid on the equality of men and women, where conditions are consciously created for the comprehensive self-realization of women, and where leading statesmen and other public figures emphasize that more women in leading posts are needed." [16] The other countries were Yugoslavia, Holland, Finland, Norway, Spain, and Japan. When men must go on record as individuals, bows are made in the direction of equality; but the results of "feminization" are deplored, and woman's right to devote her time to her "natural function" in which she is "irreplaceable" is defended. Somehow this natural function of motherhood and postnatal care expands in time and space to occupy four to five hours a day, down through the years, until the children leave school and even beyond. Describing an election meeting of a Communist party group in a farm cooperative (the average age of women workers in agriculture is over 45), a reporter noted that while more than half of those present were women, not one of them had been nominated for the executive committee, nor did they take part in the discussion:

" 'Oh, they know how to say what they think when something is really at stake,' I was assured by one of the newly elected officials. 'But nominate them for the committee? It's tough. Women get up early, they're always busy, and give them a function on top of it? We can't really ask that of them.'" Such consideration may seem very appealing, the reporter went on, but it would be still more gallant of the men to give the women more help in the household and in caring for the chidren.[17]

Although women's household tasks are theoretically to be lightened by various conveniences and services and even, as the writer of this editorial suggests, by the assumption of some duties by men, steps to bring about this utopia move with glacial slowness. This is because the system of priorities rests on a concept of equality according to which men and women are equal but different, and it is woman who deviates from the standard. Therefore the work she performs in the outside world is worth less; and if anyone is going to do the work in the home, which is obviously worth less too (even though it consumes more hours per year than are worked in all of Czechoslovak industry put together), she should do it. No matter what the professed aim, such equality can only permit most women to take up some kind of low-grade or medium-grade employment which she can combine with her role in the home.

This has, in fact, been admitted recently, and a kind of justification found for it, in a special issue of the Slovak journal of sociology published in 1973 and devoted to problems of women's advancement as a contribution to "carrying out the demanding tasks in this sphere outlined by the Fourteenth Congress of the Communist party of Czechoslovakia." [18] In this issue one woman author recalls Lenin's statement (quoted in this book near the beginning of Chapter Seven) that equality calls for women's active participation in the life of society, but not necessarily on the same job or under the same conditions as men. What actually happens when different values are placed on men's and women's work comes to light in another article in the same issue, this one on increasing the participation of women in management. The author, again a woman, points out that the protection of woman's reproductive function eliminates her a priori from certain types of work and therefore from certain types of executive work. Further, because a woman's maternal functions require her frequent absence from the job, while an executive should be in constant contact with the workplace, "a woman of reproductive age has an objectively smaller chance of achieving a management position." Consequently, "woman's biological specificity can . . . be considered as an objective obstacle to the greater participation of women in management." Although authorities do not agree, she says, on how many years a child should be in close contact with its mother, "in real life, as a rule, popular opinion connects the rearing of younger children, roughly up to the age of fifteen, primarily with the woman and also with her maximum physical presence in the family." [19] Research shows, she says, that the majority of men and women believe that a woman can more easily manage an executive function when her children are over fifteen. In her opinion society should make it easier for women to assume responsibility even when they are still of reproductive age, but she acknowledges that the conditions which would make this possible are being created very, very slowly.

What this suggests is that women can think about advancement when they are forty or forty-five, and only in those fields from which they are not a priori excluded. The path of retreat from the naïveté of the 1950s, when women were urged to take up men's tools, has been paved by the increasing delimitation of men's and women's occupations, the introduction of special girl's schools, and finally by elaborate legislation designed not only to protect women for potential maternity but to cushion her against the impact of her dual role.

There have been two opinions about the efficacy of special legislation to protect women at work since the middle of the nineteenth century. The organized feminist movement in England began to intervene against special legislation affecting women's labor in 1873, when it lobbied successfully against the reduction of women's hours from sixty to fifty-six. The feminists also attempted without success to force amendment of the Ten Hours Act to exempt women from the hours' provisions which applied only to them. They later helped to defeat both an attempt to prevent employment of women miners at the pit head, and legislation designed to limit the weight of hammers which could be wielded by women nail and chain makers. The feminists' argument in all these struggles was that such legislation placed women at a disadvantage in the competition for jobs and played into the hands of men who wanted to force them out of industry entirely. Women could protect themselves more effectively by organizing, just as men did, they said. The feminist view of protective legislation has lived on, for example, in the Open Door International, an organization dedicated to the economic emancipation of women, which was founded in 1929 and has its headquarters in Brussels. This organization opposes all limitations on women's right to work, including special legislation to protect her in childbirth and maternity; these, it holds, should be treated like all other cases of incapacity to work. Its stand is that a woman should be free to work and be protected as a worker on the same terms as men, and that all regulation of conditions should depend upon the nature of the work and not upon the sex of the worker.

This "idealistic" view, as it has been called by its opponents because it assumes that women will act in their own best interests, is supported by a few governments — notably those of Sweden, Denmark, and Norway. Sweden, for example, takes the position that labor legislation should not make a distinction between men and women apart from rules relating to childbirth; but should promote the entry of both sexes into the labor market without discrimination. Its government argues that the differences which exist among women and among men are as great as those which exist between women as a group and men as a group, and that there are no jobs which are not dangerous to some men or which cannot be performed without harm by some women. Supreme Court decisions in the United States have recently invalidated protective legislation on the grounds of sex discrimination, and the thinking of the British government seems to be moving in the same direction.

The opposing "realistic" view, which still motivates the policy of most governments and of the International Labor Organization of the United Nations, is that in this imperfect world it is necessary to protect women if only in the interests of future generations. Although Marxists have always supported protective legislation, the socialist countries actually began to enforce it only recently. While the Soviet Union had considerable protective legislation on the books, from the beginning of the 1930s until well into the 1950s it was never consistently enforced. Overtime, night work, and work underground for women was general; and studies were published showing that this was not harmful. Czechoslovakia, for example, ratified the international convention on work underground before the war, and on night work for women immediately afterward. Since the interests of management and labor were believed to be in complete harmony under socialism, however, it was expected that plant managements and trade unions would cooperate in enforcing safe and agreeable working conditions; and these problems were left to them to solve on a local basis. It was not until the mid-sixties in Czechoslovakia that official note was taken of the fact that rules governing work safety and industrial hygiene were being widely violated, and further, that it requires considerable know-how and investment to design and install machines and production processes that are in maximum harmony with the psychological and physiological needs of workers. Indeed, a whole scientific discipline known as human engineering had grown up around this subject in other parts of the world. As this new awareness coincided with widespread concern over the unexpected effect of women's employment on the birthrate, the Labor Law of 1965 attempted to make good the damage at one fell swoop, for women at least. It was felt necessary to take into consideration woman's reproductive function primarily, but also her lower nervous resistance and inferior physical strength, as well as her increased burden — in employment, in the household, and in bringing up her children.

The resulting catalog of jobs forbidden to women (not merely to pregnant women, who are protected by a much longer list) fills several pages. It aims to protect women from radiation, mechanical vibration, electromagnetic waves, extreme heat and cold or changes in temperature, substantially increased or lowered pressures, exposure to infection which might lead to chronic illness, work involving poisons or harmful substances in any substantial amount, hand-lifting of weights heavier than thirty-three pounds, jobs involving danger of injury except where appropriate safety measures are insured, and night work after 10 P.M. These regulations effectively ban women from any but office jobs in the building, iron-and-steel, chemicals, and mining industries, and limit their usefulness in a score of others. They may, for instance, be excluded from driving a farm tractor or working in a photographic darkroom.

In view of the high employment of women, all of these regulations cannot be enforced everywhere. Exceptions are made in the case of the health service, communications, and other fields where work would otherwise be brought to a standstill. Other exceptions, for which trade union approval is required, are often sought. Where desired, however, these rules provide "objective" reasons for not employing women.

Under the heading "We Want Youngsters But Not Girls," the Slovak newspaper *Práca,* in March 1970, published interviews with half a dozen personnel men in heavy industry. The following statement by the representative of a large rubber factory is typical:

"

We work three shifts, which women are not supposed to do, and yet 320 of them are doing so. They don't want to leave; they like the work. There is a good deal of turnover with women, however, and in general we don't have enough work for them. The conditions for women's work are stricter. . . . Therefore we do not want and cannot take on more girl apprentices. We are already paying for the fact that we gave in to pressure and tried to help solve the problem of what to do with the fifteen-year-olds.[20]

"

The experience with the ban on night work is particularly instructive. The ruling forbidding women to work after 10 P.M. was adopted in 1965, with exceptions permitted under certain conditions up until the end of 1967. The ban affected, for example, 27,400 women in the Ostrava coal and steel region — primarily an area of heavy industry — where it was extremely difficult to find substitutes for the women, particularly in the poorer-paying jobs. It was also almost impossible to find comparable employment for the displaced women, since there was a scarcity of light industry; and almost all of them were thus faced with a reduction in pay. As one crane operator declared at a protest meeting at the Klement Gottwald Iron and Steel Works:

"

All of a sudden there's talk about the Geneva Convention . . . but it's nothing new. Why wasn't it observed ten or fifteen years ago? . . . I went to work then, the children on my neck, the youngest only a few months old, and no one asked me whether I minded being in a steel mill or whether I could work at night. . . . It's an injustice, a great injustice. As long as you needed us, we were good enough for you. And health conditions were much worse then than they are now, when the cranes have air-conditioned cabins. . . . Now you offer us employment in quiet surroundings, when our hands are used to rough work and our eyes have lost their keenness. . . .

"

The situation is just as complicated in the consumer goods industry, where women make up the vast majority of workers and where many plants, born in the industrial revolution, are badly in need of modernization. In some of these the goals cannot be fulfilled without working night shifts, because of the low productivity of the equipment. Exceptions to the ban on night work were permitted by the government in 1968, in 1969, in 1970, in 1971; and the law continues to permit exceptions in agreement with the trade unions.

Exceptions to the prohibition against women lifting weights over 33 pounds by hand and over 110 pounds by hand-truck, which were supposed to end at the latest in December 1970, were extended first to March 1972, and then to the end of the Five-Year Plan in 1975; not long ago it was admitted that it will probably be impossible to meet this deadline. This is a problem which affects the predominantly female-staffed retail shops; and industry has simply been unable to find ways either to pack goods in lighter, smaller containers which could be manipulated easily by women, or to attract more men to retail trade.

When technology is introduced to make jobs more productive and less tiring, this does not automatically increase women's chances for job equality, as some optimists expect. It may "open all doors" to women only in the sense that women are pushed out through them. Consider a study of women in agriculture published by a farmer's daily in 1969. In it the work of Czechoslovak farm women is described as seasonal, unqualified, poorly paid, and, for the most part, heavy manual labor.

"

The women can achieve top earnings only by extreme physical effort or by tremendously lengthening the working day. Efforts to limit the participation of women in work using highly productive machinery pushes them from the most highly qualified and best-paid work into manual work, often more tiring and always worse paid. It is usually work which men do not want to do. . . .

In view of the importance of mechanization, the opinion has arisen that we may permit a decrease in agricultural manpower to the level of the most advanced capitalist states. In this connection it is claimed that women need not play an important role in our farming. Care of the house and children will again become their domain. At the same time they will form a kind of reserve for peak work. . . . In this connection a *numerus clausus* has been set for girls applying for specialized training in agriculture, and various types of schools are being established for village girls to train them to manage the household. . . .[21]

"

Even General Secretary of the Communist Party Gustav Husák, in his speech to the Eighth Congress of Agricultural Cooperatives in 1972, pointed out that women made up only a small percentage of graduates of secondary- and university-level schools of agriculture.

Complaining about the effect of transferring women to lighter work in the Třinec Iron Works in 1968, a woman trade union official pointed out that many women had been working at the plant for twenty years under very rough conditions; now, just when automation and air conditioning were being installed, they were being reassigned to jobs with lower pay — over their objections and their insistence on their right to have a say about the work they did — because it was the law. Some philosophers of women's liberation comfort themselves with the thought that soon the differences between men's and women's work will become academic as a result of general mechanization and automation. This is really still in the realm of science fiction, even in the most advanced socialist countries like Czechoslovakia. In the favored engineering industry whose modernization receives priority, only 1 percent of workers are employed on fully automated processes, and in the next fifteen years this figure will rise to only 2–3 percent.

The special health risks of women are not eliminated by assigning them to industries considered suitable for them. National insurance statistics for Slovakia for 1971, based on the number of days of work lost through medically certified illness, showed that women workers suffered from anemia and iron deficiency fifteen times more often than men; from neurotic tendencies twice as often; and from migraine five times as often. While the higher incidence of circulatory disorders and varicose veins among women is attributed to the effects of pregnancy and childbirth, the higher incidences of neuroses and migraine are found to be connected with conflict situations resulting from women's dual responsibilities. Dr. Jaroslav Černý, a physician working in the administration of health insurance, reports a higher national incidence of illness in women than in men workers in all age groups except those under twenty and over sixty. Various studies of workers in the consumer goods industries show that women experience a greater feeling of weariness than men, suffer more frequent and more intense headaches, use more analgesics, drink more coffee, and visit the plant doctor more often; and that their headaches and weariness correlate closely with the amount of sleep they get. Strong or very strong neurotic tendencies are found regularly in more than one-third of women in the textile, shoe, and clothing industries. This is apparently related to the stereotyped movements, the tempo and the intensity of the work (stand-by time being only 5–8 percent in clothing and shoes as compared with 25–30 percent in engineering). In a group of loom-operators a correlation was found between neurotic tendencies and length of employment, number of children, and family status (whether married, widowed, or divorced); this suggests an obvious connection with the demanding regimen of most of the women.

Neurotic complaints of women in the consumer goods industries increase with age and also as the week progresses, and are felt more intensely in the afternoon shifts. They are manifested in feelings of overwork and weariness, in the appearance of ulcers and hypertension, and in difficulties connected with menstruation and pregnancy. These last are also aggravated by the working position: long hours sitting bent over a machine. Almost all women textile workers, who spend most of the day on their feet, suffer from varicose veins, cramps, and back pains. In one sample of wool and cotton workers, 14 percent reported that they were so tired after work that they had to rest before doing anything else, while 34 percent forced themselves to work at home with difficulty. In the thirty to thirty-four-year-old category this second group represented 47 percent of the total.

These are the women near the bottom. To return to those who are competing for responsible jobs, the reluctance with which women are admitted to positions of this kind is also found in other socialist countries. In Hungary, for instance, women now occupy 50 percent of all trade union posts; but in the clothing industry, where they comprise the majority of workers, women head only two out of forty-two enterprises. The feeling is general that it is not practical to put women between the ages of twenty and thirty-five in leading posts because of their absenteeism, and it is not worthwhile investing in the training of a woman over forty. The number of qualified women in Hungarian industry has actually fallen, and now amounts to only 14 percent of the total.

It would seem that in the Soviet Union, where women account for 75 percent of doctors and more than one-third of lawyers and engineers, women have a better chance of getting ahead. Women there have advanced further in many fields usually reserved for men than they have anywhere else. It should be remembered, however, that they have achieved this under conditions which are not likely to be reproduced in other countries. Beginning with the first Five-Year Plan in 1929, the need for manpower was such that it was necessary to recruit a constantly increasing number of women not only into traditional occupations but also into heavy industry. The war, in which every able-bodied man was engaged, accelerated the pace. Afterward the high representation of women in occupations that in other countries would not have been considered suitable for women was maintained, not only because so many men had been lost, but also because so many women remained the sole support of the family. As it became a commonplace for women to work in heavy industry, it became common for their daughters to study subjects related to industry, and for many of them to rise to semiprofessional and professional jobs. Nevertheless, according to the 1959 census, four-fifths of Soviet women were still engaged in physical labor.

In 1959 there were ten million more Soviet women than men in the thirty-five to fifty age group from which executives are usually chosen; but in spite of the high employment of women throughout industry, three-quarters of women administrators and specialists were employed in the nonproductive sectors of the economy. They made up 6 percent of factory directors in 1963. And in spite of the overwhelming majority of women in medicine, education, and culture, only 11 percent of university professors, 5 percent of directors and deputy directors of universities, and 16 percent of top personnel in scientific institutes are women. The Soviet Union has one woman minister, and one deputy chairman of the Council of Ministers is a woman. There is no woman department head at the ministry level.

It is sometimes forgotten that over half the employed women in the Soviet Union are still found in agriculture, and that more than 70 percent of these are engaged in unskilled work. While during the war many Soviet women worked as tractor drivers, there was a mass exodus of women from machine and tractor stations when the war ended. In 1959 women made up only 0.8 percent of tractor drivers and combine operators, compared to 17.4 percent in 1947.

In general it holds true everywhere in the socialist world that there is at present very little room at the top for women, and even on the middle rungs of the ladder the footing is slippery. This situation is a tribute to the strength of certain deeply ingrained patterns which are both economic and psychological. The economic pattern results from the established structure of the economy, which favors heavy industry over light industry and the "nonproductive" services — that is, traditional men's jobs over traditional women's jobs — in spite of the fact that the primary sphere is of no use without the secondary and tertiary spheres. The psychological pattern is based on the myth that this division into men's and women's occupations, along with the social and monetary values assigned to these jobs, correspond to actual differences between the sexes: that men do the heavy work, which since the Stone Age has been more important for man's survival, while women, with their gentleness and skillful fingers, do the light work. One need only watch women washing down railway cars on an open siding in winter, or unloading sacks of potatoes into a farm wagon while the driver (a man) supervises, or take note of the fact that while 42 percent of Czechoslovak doctors are women, they comprise only 19 percent of surgeons — to realize that this is a stereotype which does not correspond to reality. The fact is that women move into a job or profession when it is relinquished to them by men.

The socialization of the means of production was expected to break down the barriers between men and women in the employment field by putting brains ahead of brawn and creating conditions for relieving women of the major part of their family and household burdens. When this did not happen, society fell back on its stereotypes. From the inherited division of jobs into men's and women's, and the traditional values assigned to different types of work, there developed the need to divide education at some point into men's and women's and to formalize the division in certain employment practices. Although this has been done in recognition of women's "natural function," the permanent extension of this function to include the lion's share of the housework and child care is really the result, and not the cause, of the present division of labor in the employment field. If women had ever really been accepted as equally valuable members of the work force, if the jobs they did had the same social and monetary value as men's, it would have been deemed worthwhile to invest in the redistribution of some of their household burdens and to modernize the industries in which they work. This would, of course, have required a substantial amount of reeducation and retooling.

Since it was not economically possible to dispense with or even reduce the participation of women in the labor force, their "overloading," became evident not only in their subjective complaints but in their objective state of health and their disinclination to have children. The result was legislation to protect them, but this does not really relieve them of their double burden even when enforced; at the same time it reduces their employment opportunities still further. At this point, improved technology and larger and longer maternity grants, whatever their intention, cannot have the effect of giving women the same opportunities as men to realize their talents, to work for the public good, or simply to earn money outside the home. When women make up nearly half the work force and are excluded from or accepted on sufferance in a large number of fields, they are bound to crowd into others where their preponderance will cause difficulties, real or imagined. Some of them will necessarily remain on the fringe of the work force as cheap labor. If improved technology should make some of women's work more attractive, more productive, and better paying, these jobs will attract men, who will be welcome as a counterbalance to excessive "feminization." If at the same time society is willing to pay women to stay at home for several years with their children, all but the most ambitious and independent-minded women will see this as a way out. They will return to the labor market in their thirties or forties with a much lower level of skills than men of the corresponding age. Meanwhile some of the pressure will have been taken off the demand for services to take housework out of the home.

How did this situation come about within a socialist framework? To understand the conflicts we must step back into history and look at the way socialist ideas about the emancipation of women developed.

CHAPTER TWO

ENGELS AND THE RISE AND
FALL OF THE FAMILY

Two essays provided the theoretical armory of the movement for women's emancipation in the nineteenth century: John Stuart Mill's *The Subjection of Women,* written in 1861 but first published in 1869; and Frederick Engels's *The Origin of the Family, Private Property and the State,* published in 1884. Mill supplied the philosophical basis for the woman's rights movement in the English-speaking world; Engels was the prophet of revolution as the key to women's freedom, an idea realized for the first time in Eastern Europe.

For socialists, Engels introduced a new way of looking at the family and at women. His description of the position of women in the societies of recorded history was (and is) an eye-opener, and the goals he set became the declared program of the left socialist labor movement, which ultimately formed communist parties and subsequently established socialist governments. Although Engels's work remains virtually unread in the Western world, the major demands of the women's liberation movement in Western countries today are found to be formulated in it. His fundamental thesis, so radical in his day — that the family is not static but reacts to changes in the way people earn their livelihood — has become a basic assumption for most people interested in the study of the family (although they may not have reached it by Engels's route).

Mill built on a foundation laid seventy years earlier by

Mary Wollstonecraft's *A Vindication of the Rights of Woman,* written under the impact of the French Enlightenment and the idea of mankind's natural right to liberty and equality to which it gave currency. He based his plea for women's rights on principles of morality and justice. Woman's subordination by man was both wrong in itself and an obstacle to human improvement. Mill hoped for advances in psychology which would illuminate the real and imagined differences between men and women; without proof it was presumptuous for one sex to declare another inferior, he said. He put his ideas into practice in his personal and in his public life, sponsoring the first attempt to introduce an amendment on women's suffrage in the British Parliament in 1867 — an action which he considered his most important contribution as a member of the House of Commons. His name is linked to the fight for women's legal rights — the right to vote, to own property, to receive an education, to choose a vocation, to make decisions in domestic matters, and to end an unsatisfactory marriage without being deprived of one's children. This is a struggle to whose history in Great Britain and the United States we are now being gradually reintroduced, thanks to the revival of the movement for women's liberation in the second half of the twentieth century.

Both Karl Marx, to whose ideas Engels gave shape in *The Origin of the Family, Private Property and the State,* and Engels himself concerned themselves very little with problems of the individual's psychology or self-realization; it was basic to their thinking that these considerations were secondary to society's main problem, which arose from the way wealth was created and the way it was distributed. As long as one class of men worked and another appropriated the fruits of that labor, there could be no talk of right or justice in general, they reasoned. There was only right exercised by one class at the expense of the other, and justice used to protect the rights of one class against encroachment by the other. Marx made his life work the study of man's relation to production and the relation of men to each other in the production process: the way, as he and Engels saw it, the development of the productivity of labor had made it possible for mankind to produce an ever-increasing quantity of new values; the way this had in turn affected men's ideas and institutions; and the way this dialectical interplay throughout history had divided mankind into antagonistic propertied and propertyless classes whose character had changed through a series of revolutionary clashes until, in the nineteenth century, the Industrial Revolution had ushered in what they believed was to be the final conflict. This would end, Marx and Engels predicted, in a society where the class that produced the values would, for the first time, own the tools — the means of production.

Within this concept, the relation between the sexes for the reproduction of the species was first of all part of the whole process of production in which man had already engaged long before history began to be written. "The first division of labor is that between man and woman for the propagation of children," Marx and Engels wrote in 1845–46 in *The German Ideology*. The family, dominated by the male, had obviously existed in some form from the beginning of recorded history, operating as a production unit to secure its members' existence and the future of their children. Now, in the nineteenth century, this economic unit — as Marx and Engels argued — was being atomized by the introduction of machine manufacture, and the antagonism between man and woman had taken on a new aspect. Woman was exploited as an unpaid worker in the home and a wage laborer outside it, and her inferior status made her an instrument for the intensified exploitation of the working class. At the other end of the scale, the loveless bourgeois family jealously guarded its integrity and its myths, for it represented a union for the consolidation and expansion of property stolen from the workers. In this family the wife was wholly owned by her husband, and fidelity was demanded of her to insure the legitimacy of his heirs.

This contrast (between the fractured working class home and bourgeois ties cemented by money) occupied Marx and Engels in their earliest writings. Engels, in *The Condition of the Working-Class in England,* published in 1845, burns with indignation at the conditions under which women work and the effect on their health. These conditions were even then coming to be the subject of government reports and the recommendations of reformers. Engels, however, went further, noting the way the family as the basic unit of the society suffered. He observed that of 419,560 factory workers in the British Empire in 1839, 242,296, or more than half, were women. "The employment of women at once breaks up the family," he wrote, "for when the wife spends twelve or thirteen hours every day in the mill, and the husband works the same length of time there or elsewhere, what becomes of the children? They grow up like wild weeds." As an example, he quoted testimony presented in Parliament in favor of the Ten Hours Bill: "H. W. has three children, goes away Monday morning at five o'clock, and comes back Saturday evening; has so much to do for the children then that she cannot go to bed before three o'clock in the morning; often wet through to the skin . . ." and added:

"

The employment of the wife dissolves the family utterly and of necessity, and this dissolution, in our present society, which is based upon the family, brings the most demoralising consequences for parents as well as children. The children who grow up under such conditions are utterly ruined for later family life, can never feel at home in the family which they themselves found, because they have always been accustomed to isolation. . . . In many cases the family is not wholly dissolved by the employment of the wife, but turned upside down. The wife supports the family, the husband sits at home, tends the children, sweeps the room and cooks. . . . It is easy to imagine the wrath aroused among the working-men by this reversal of all relations within the family, while the other social conditions remain unchanged. . . . We must admit that so total a reversal of the position of the sexes can have come to pass only because the sexes have been placed in a false position from the beginning. If the reign of the wife over the husband, as inevitably brought about by the factory system, is inhuman, the pristine rule of the husband over the wife must have been inhuman too.[1]

"

Marx and Engels returned to this subject more than once. "All family ties among the proletarians are torn asunder, and their children transformed into . . . instruments of labor," they wrote in *The Communist Manifesto* in 1848. They predicted that "the bourgeois family will vanish as a matter of course when its complement" — the practical absence of the family among the proletarians and public prostitution — "vanishes, and both will vanish with the vanishing capital."[2]

And in Volume I of *Capital,* characteristically finding the seed of the new in the outworn social relationships, Marx wrote optimistically:

"

However terrible and disgusting the dissolution, under the capitalist system, of the old family ties may appear, nevertheless, modern industry, by assigning as it does an important part in the process of production . . . to women, to young persons, and to children of both sexes, creates a new economical foundation for a higher form of the family and of the relations between the sexes.[3]

"

The lines along which they were thinking were already clear. It remained for Engels to set them down systematically after Marx's death (in 1883) as "the fulfillment of a bequest" which he offered as "a meager substitute" for what Marx himself might have written about that "false position," noted earlier, in which the sexes had been placed "from the beginning." The result was *The Origin of the Family, Private Property and the State* (1884), which was based, as Engels tells us in his preface, on Marx's abstract of Lewis H. Morgan's *Ancient Society* (published in the United States in 1877), which Engels found among Marx's papers after his death. Marx had been attracted to this work, Engels says, because Morgan's researches into prehistory substantiated Marx's hypotheses about the way property and social institutions — culminating in the modern state and the bourgeois monogamous family — had grown out of conditions of primitive communism which must have preceded all other forms of social organization in the early dawn of man's existence. Morgan's work seemed to Marx and Engels to provide factual substantiation for their belief that class antagonisms were not a "natural," preordained state of affairs but that they must have originated at some point in mankind's history as a result of concrete conditions. Their study of contemporary society and recorded history had convinced them that these irreconcilable antagonisms were caused by the appropriation by the few of the labor of the many — that is, by private property. In their view, the patriarchal family was an institution for the accumulation of property in the hands of the ruling class; and the state was neither divinely ordained nor a matter of social contract in which the ruled agreed to be governed, but an instrument with which the ruling class protected its properties. Morgan's discoveries have made a complete revolution in the conception of prehistoric society, wrote Engels in his preface to the fourth edition of *Origin*. The historical development of these institutions could now be traced back to the point of their birth, and the connection between property, classes, the state, and the bourgeois monogamous family could actually be demonstrated, he said.

Lewis H. Morgan, America's most important anthropologist until his death in 1890 and a pioneer field worker among American Indian tribes, had come to the conclusion that mankind had passed through a series of stages each of which was characterized by the level of its skills in producing the means of subsistence. From the kinship terminology which Morgan had collected among preliterate peoples, he had deduced a kinship system, that is, a type of family appropriate to each stage. At first, he wrote, group marriage prevailed and kinship could be traced through the female line only, since in conditions of promiscuity the father of a child could obviously not be determined. Thus status and possessions were inherited through the woman's line of descent and remained in her tribe. This, added to the dominant position of women in the household given by the natural division of labor, gave women considerable prestige and authority. Only when man's skills enabled him to produce substantially more than he consumed did it become important to him to be able to identify his children and to pass his property on to them. To do this he had to break up the primitive communist household based on women's supremacy. This was the argument defended and expanded by Engels in *Origin,* and which was used to support the controversial concept of matriarchy.

It was important to Marx and Engels to have scientific

proof for the existence of matriarchy as the universal earliest form of social organization; it made it possible to argue that the manifest injustices of the nineteenth-century patriarchal monogamous family and the extreme exploitation of women were not eternal, but had been born out of private property relationships together with class conflict; that these had had a beginning and therefore could be expected to have an end.

Monogamy was not the product of a higher form of morality; not the reconciliation of the sexes, which distinguished "civilized man" from the savages; not the victory of sexual love between individual man and woman over the indiscriminate carryings-on of native tribes. "It was the first form of the family based not on natural but on economic conditions, namely, on the victory of private property over primitive, natural, common ownership." [4] "The first class antagonism which appears in history," writes Engels, referring to slave society, "coincides with the development of the antagonism between man and woman in monogamian marriage, and the first class oppression with that of the female sex by the male." Monogamy was a great historical advance because it introduced the possibility of modern individual sexual love; but at the same time it inaugurated, along with slavery and private wealth, "that epoch lasting until today, in which every advance is likewise a relative regression, in which the well-being and development of the one group are attained by the misery and repression of the other." [5]

Sexual love at first played no part, continues Engels. Marriage contracts were concluded without the consent of those involved, to perpetuate property and power. Sexual love was enjoyed outside marriage, by men almost openly — giving rise to the institution of public prostitution — by women in secret. Only after the Reformation and the rise of capitalist production did the idea that the validity of a contract depends on the free will of the participants arise to give an aura of romance to bourgeois marriage. Marriage, runs Engels's argument, remained an economic affair nevertheless. The husband continued to exercise supreme power over his wife and her property. The myth of marriage for love was established, but in reality personal in-

clination, at least on the part of the woman, remained a very
secondary consideration. Unlike the prostitute, she does not
"hire out her body like a wage worker on piecework, but sells
it into slavery once and for all." [6] Only among the proletariat
can sexual love between husband and wife become the rule,
declares Engels, because there is a "complete absence of all
property, for the safeguarding and inheritance of which monogamy and male domination were established."[7]

When man's work began to produce a surplus, the new
wealth in his hands allowed him to occupy a dominant place
not only in his own domain but in the household previously
controlled by woman. Consequently, Engels argued, the "division of labour remained unchanged and yet it put the former
domestic relationship topsy-turvy. . . . The very cause that had
formerly made the woman supreme in the house, viz., her being
confined to domestic work, now assured supremacy in the house
for the man: the woman's housework lost its significance compared with the man's work in obtaining a livelihood; the latter
was everything, the former a negligible auxiliary."

As a result, "the emancipation of women becomes possible
only when women are enabled to take part in production on a
large, social scale, and when domestic duties require their attention only to a minor degree. And this has become possible
only as a result of modern large-scale industry, which not only
permits of the participation of women in production in large
numbers, but actually calls for it and, moreover, strives to con-
vert domestic work also into a public industry." [8]

The enemy was defined. It was not the male sex but the
institution of private property: capitalism. Engels closes his
book with Morgan's hopeful prophecy:

"

A mere property career is not the final destiny of mankind, if
progress is to be the law of the future as it has been of the past. The
time which has passed away since civilization began is but a fragment
of the past duration of man's existence; and but a fragment of the ages
yet to come. . . . Democracy in government, brotherhood in society,
equality in rights and privileges, and universal education foreshadow

the next higher plane of society to which experience, intelligence, and knowledge are steadily tending. *It will be a revival, in a higher form, of the liberty, equality and fraternity of the ancient gentes.* [The italics are Engels's.][9]

,,

The Origin of the Family provided a program for the socialist women's movement which has remained virtually unmodified down to the present. First the complete equality of man and woman before the law; then woman's economic independence through employment outside the home, this to be made possible through the assumption of household duties by society. For all of these things the abolition of capitalism was a necessity:

"

. . . The peculiar character of man's domination over woman in the modern family, and the necessity, as well as the manner, of establishing real social equality between the two, will be brought out in sharp relief only when both are completely equal before the law. It will then become evident that the first premise for the emancipation of women is the reintroduction of the entire female sex into public industry; and that this again demands that the specific feature of the individual family of being the economic unit of society be abolished.[10]

,,

In the old communistic household, said Engels, the administration of the house and the care of children had been a "public function," a "socially necessary industry." In the monogamous individual family it had become a private service; and the wife had become "the first domestic servant," pushed out of social production. Capitalist society is arranged in such a way that when a woman "fulfils her duties in the private service of her family, she remains excluded from public production and cannot earn anything; and when she wishes to take part in public industry and earn her living independently, she is not in a position to fulfil her family duties. What applies to the woman in the factory applies to women in all the professions, right up to medicine and law. The modern individual family is based on the open or disguised domestic enslavement of the woman; and modern society is a mass composed solely of individual families

as its molecules." [11] But "with the passage of the means of production to common property, the individual family ceases to be
the economic unit of society. Private housekeeping is transformed into a social industry. The care and education of the
children becomes a public matter."[12]

This is the prophecy. The anthropological argument presented in *Origin* is another story. It is by now scarcely known in
the West, yet it is important to appreciate the positive contribution of the discussion concerning whether the original form of
society was matriarchal or patriarchal in drawing attention to
the fact that women occupy very different positions in different
cultures, that their roles and status vary considerably, and that
what is "typically female" for one society is not typical for
another. Further, one must be aware of the special position
which Engels's work has occupied in its entirety in the socialist
women's movement and in the socialist countries of the world.

The controversy between the matriarchal and patriarchal
camps within the evolutionist school of social theory (the first
represented in Engels's time by J. F. McLennan, for example,
and the second by Sir Henry Maine — both leading British anthropologists) continued "with mounting acrimony" well into
the twentieth century "and is not quite dead even yet." [13] In the
United States the German-born anthropologist Franz Boas, himself originally a believer in the evolutionary development of
human society through set stages, started anthropologists thinking along new lines in the first decades of the twentieth century
when he pointed out, on the basis of his own field work among
Indians on the Northwest coast of America, that man's institutions do not develop in accord with the same laws as those that
govern man's physical life, and do not always pass from the
simple to the complex. Societies are not collections of fossils, but
living entities; seemingly remote tribes undergo change through
contact with other societies, and traditions handed down from
earlier generations are modified by the culture of the moment in
a complex way which does not fit any universal evolutionary
pattern. Contemporaneous civilizations cannot be arranged in
"historical" sequence; furthermore, primitive societies do not
represent mankind's childhood and will not grow up to be just

like us. They exist parallel to Western civilization and have their own developmental history. "Once the 'one grand scheme' of evolutionism was rejected, the multiplicity of *cultures* which took the place of the cultural *stages* of savagery, barbarism and civilization were not more easily to be brought within one standard of evaluation than they were within one system of explanation." Each was an integrated way of life, and although based on different traditions might be no less valuable than our own.[14]

As for the kinship relationship that Morgan and Engels used to conclude that matriarchy was primary: the great expansion of fieldwork in the twentieth century has brought to light such a variety of kinship systems existing in tribes that could be said to be at the same stage of technological knowledge, that no direct correlation between kinship and economic factors — such as Engels tried to establish — can be agreed upon. No evidence of a true matriarchal society has been found. Nor has it been possible to show that the matrilineal system, as a supposed vestige of matriarchy, everywhere preceded the patrilineal system — a sequence essential to Engels's argument that patrilineal descent arose as a result of man's desire to pass his property on to his son, and is associated with the emergence of the monogamous family (required to establish paternity) and the transition of woman from freedom to oppression.

There is not just one type of matrilineal system that can be studied today. There are matrilineal systems in which a man inherits his name or property or position from his mother's brother; and there are matrilocal societies in which the land and household are handed down in the female line, and husbands move in and out. There are matrilineal systems that are also matrilocal, meaning that the children live with the mother's clan; there are others that are matrilineal and patrilocal. There may be two lines of descent, with land and ancestors being patrilineally determined and money passing through the mother's line; or any one of numerous variations. Some give more importance to women, and some less. Patrilineal societies are more common than matrilineal, but this is not necessarily because they are at a "higher level." At least one of the reasons seems to be that the other types promote conflict between a woman's husband and her brother, since most power or wealth even in matrilineal societies is inherited by men.

The tracing of patrilineal-patrilocal and matrilineal-matrilocal systems and their permutations among hunting and food-growing societies has become an extremely sophisticated science, relying on statistical methods and the use of computers. An example is the study made by David F. Aberle, who used a sample of 565 societies — including 84 matrilineal cases — classified with reference to thirty variables (subsistence base, sexual division of labor, etc.), in an attempt to discover the circumstances under which matrilineal reckoning of kinship is likely to arise and to survive or disappear. He concluded that matriliny is associated with horticulture, tends to disappear with plough cultivation, and vanishes with industrialization. He makes the point, however, that matriliny is a feature of specific evolution but not of general evolution. That is, it makes it possible for a particular society to adapt to certain conditions, as certain protective coloring makes it possible for an animal to adapt to his environment; but it is not a stage universally connected with a particular level of complexity or advancement. On the contrary, various levels of organization are found among matrilineal, patrilineal, and bilateral systems. "Even if we could assert confidently that matriliny first arose in conjunction with horticulture, or that it is an invariant feature of first adaptive horticulture everywhere, it would still not be a stage in general evolution. For some hunters and gatherers, some fishers, and some pure pastoralists would belong to the same stage as some horticulturalists. . . ." Therefore, says Aberle, "I abjure efforts to decide whether matriliny preceded patriliny, or vice versa, since these efforts assume that the question is one of general evolution." [15]

To sum up, it has gradually been recognized that, since preliterate peoples living today are not our ancestors but our contemporaries, we cannot learn anything about social relationships 50,000 years ago simply by projecting observations concerning these people into the past together with our own system of values. Further, we cannot even learn much about such peoples as contemporaries unless we try to get inside their minds and view their institutions through their eyes; moreover, instead of studying isolated phenomena, like kinship terminology, it is more useful, as Margaret Mead says, "to work always with a whole society as a backdrop." [16] Reconstructions of the past today are attempted by archaeologists and anthropologists on the basis of concrete evidence, and even here opinions differ on how to interpret their finds and how much "reconstruction" can be allowed.

If this seems obvious now, it was not so in the years when the socialist movement underwent its important formative development. Engels's work, with its convincing hypotheses about the connection between the origins of property, the family, and the state, had a profound effect on the thinking of the new socialist movement in nineteenth-century Europe. August Bebel, the leader of the German Social-Democratic Party, the largest in Europe, gave it wide circulation in his book *Woman Under Socialism,* which went through fifty editions in his lifetime.

"The reign of the mother-right implied communism; equality for all; the rise of the father-right implied the reign of private property, and, with it, the oppression and enslavement of woman," wrote Bebel.[17] Communism and women's equality had been the rule in the dawn of human society; equality would be restored, on a higher level, of course, when private property was abolished. This seemed eminently logical and gave both communism and women's equality a legal claim, so to speak, while joining them firmly together. Mother-right, or matriarchy, thus became a necessary starting point in the socialist scheme of the evolution of mankind. Long before the erudite discussions of anthropologists had trickled down to a more or less indifferent public in Western countries, matriarchy had become dogma in the Soviet Union. The advances made in the methodology of the study of preliterate societies between the wars did nothing to shake this concept because they were not studied or discussed, and matriarchy entered the history books and political science texts of the socialist countries after the Second World War. Only now is it slowly and unobtrusively fading.

These postwar works, by an almost imperceptible shift in emphasis, went further than Engels in attributing great power to women in the primary stage of society. Engels refers to the "complete rule of women" as Johann Jakob Bachofen's conception. (Bachofen, a Swiss scholar, argued there had been an epoch of rule by women general to all mankind, in a work published in 1861). But Engels is satisfied with the supremacy of woman in the house (p. 70) and the esteem accorded her. He considers Bachofen's use of the word mother-right an unhappy choice, although he uses it "for the sake of brevity"; for no such things as rights in the legal sense could have existed at this social stage, in his view. He believed with Bachofen that a "predominancy of women" was generally prevalent in early times, but at the same time he visualized that society as one in which "there was no place for rulers and ruled." Labor was divided between men and women and "each was master in his or her own field of activity, the men in the forest, the women in the house." His emphasis was not on women's dominance but on why men later became dominant. It remained for Stalin to explain the source of women's power in terms of pure economic determinism. "History tells us that the class or social group which plays the main role in social production and fulfills the main function in production necessarily becomes, with the passage of time, the master of that production. There was the period of matriarchy, when women dominated production. How can this be explained? In the production of the time, in primitive agriculture, women played the main role in production, they fulfilled the most important function, while men hunted animals in the woods."

Although Stalin wrote these words in 1906 in a work called *Anarchism or Socialism*, they are quoted here from the introduction to the Czech translation of a book entitled *Matriarchy* by a Soviet professor of ethnography, Mark Osipovich Kosven, published by the Soviet Academy of Sciences in 1948 and in Prague in 1952.

The theoretical inadequacy of the Marxist approach to the "woman question" which some writers have noted can no doubt be traced in part to "the original weakness in the traditional discussion of the subject in the socialist classics," as one British writer on women's liberation, Juliet Mitchell, suggests.[18] A more important reason is that in the countries where socialist theory has been applied in practice, real theoretical work on the woman question has never been carried forward. The contribution of Marx and Engels was that they emphasized the historical character of the family and its importance as a basic social institution which could not be studied in isolation from its social context. The fundamentalist interpretation of their writings encouraged the belief that women would be "returned" to a position of equality by the destruction of the private property system, as part of a kind of natural history process.

This may originally have given women self-confidence and disposed of their detractors quickly, but it diverted attention from the importance of overcoming the barriers to equality created by centuries of historical development. The legislative and social program for the emancipation of women introduced in the socialist countries, with all its virtues, has stemmed essentially from this approach. If women's inferior position can be traced directly to the emergence of private property there is no need to search for the answers to questions about whether women today are really men's equals, physically, mentally, and psychologically; to try to define equality; to inquire whether men as individuals or as a group actually treat women as equals or whether, in fact, women regard themselves as equals to men, and according to what criteria — in other words, no need to unwrap people's minds and souls or air their misconceptions and prejudices. If patriarchal beliefs then continue to lie just below the surface in men and women, these are likely to determine the kind of equality that is set as the goal. If, however, anthropological research has provided reason to question a direct and simple connection between economic change and a crucial reversal of woman's position, then there may be other roots to women's troubles which cannot be found by consulting the classics as though they were a home medicine library. The discussion which such an admission would provoke would inevitably have to deal with the reality that some of Marx's and Engels's ideas have been corrected by time; and doubt cast on one part of a doctrine may lead to reassessment of others. Although this is something that inevitably happens to the ideas of all the greatest scientists, and although it is a process implicit in the Marxist idea that there is no such thing as abstract and permanent truth, it is something that no socialist country has yet felt able to allow.

The persistence of the matriarchy theory (although its tenacity cannot, of course, be compared to that of the patriarchal view) serves, interestingly enough, to confuse issues for women's liberationists in the West as well. An example is the widely read work by the psychoanalyst Wilhelm Reich, *The Sexual Revolution,* written in its presently available form in 1935. In it Reich presents a dramatic and impassioned plea for the "sex-affirmative" society; for the liberation of the normal sexual urges of children and adults from the bonds of conservative morality; and the destruction of the compulsive patriarchal family — "a factory for authoritarian ideologies and conservative structures" — and its replacement by the socialist collective. His book contains what is probably the most influential account in the English language of the experiments in the abolition of the family which took place in the Soviet Union immediately after the revolution, as well as the reintroduction of restrictions on abortion and divorce and the reemphasis of conventional morality and the family unit in the 1930s. His ideas are to be found, with modifications, in some of the most popular works of the women's liberation movement, where the cry for the abolition of the family is raised.[19]

However telling Reich's other arguments in favor of sexual revolution and his criticism of its suppression may be, it should be recognized that his proof of the necessity of replacing family life with the commune, as a prerequisite for the success of the sexual revolution, is based on Engels's reconstruction of primitive society (although Engels is not mentioned), which he accepts as fact. From it he deduces a "definite law which governs the relationship between the sexual forms and the forms of organization." According to this, primitive society "has a collective and work-democratic organization" which is matriarchal, and for the free clan member "there is no other marriage than the loose ties of a sexual relationship." When patriarchy supplants matriarchy, the clan disintegrates, economic power rests in an authoritarian chief, and the clan member becomes a suppressed family member. After the social revolution the process is reversed: primitive work-democratic conditions on a more civilized, higher level are reestablished, and the family is replaced by a new organization bearing a certain similarity to the old clan of primitive society — the socialist collective. *"Just as in primitive society the family destroyed the clan, so does the economic collective destroy the family."* From this, according to Reich, flows the inevitability and necessity of replacing the patriarchal family or compulsory family by the collective, with its *"sex-affirmative striving toward sexual independence."* [20]

Since the first half of this proposition cannot be shown to be true, the second half cannot be held inevitable by this argument, even if we accept the doubtful necessity for history to rewind itself backwards like a reel of motion picture film.

Some socialists have found in Engels confirmation of the necessity of destroying the family as an institution from the ground up; others have used his hypothesis that there is a form of the family to correspond to every socioeconomic formation to support the conclusion that socialism strengthens the family, and that "under socialism the family is a totally new type of family which expresses the nature of the new social relations." [21]

Engels himself was much more modest about drawing a blueprint for the future. He did not foresee a return to group marriage; on the contrary he speculated that the elimination of the economic justification for marriage opened the way to true monogamy based on an historically new element — individual sexual love.

"

What will most definitely disappear from monogamy, however, is all the characteristics stamped on it in consequence of its having arisen out of property relationships. These are, firstly, the dominance of the man, and secondly, the indissolubility of marriage. . . . If only marriages that are based on love are moral, then, also, only those are moral in which love continues. . . .

Thus, what we can conjecture at present about the regulation of sex relationships after the impending effacement of capitalist production is, in the main, of a negative character, limited mostly to what will vanish. But what will be added? That will be settled after a new generation has grown up; a generation of men who never in all their lives have had occasion to purchase a woman's surrender either with money or with any other means of social power, and of women who have never been obliged to surrender to any man out of any consideration other than that of real love, or to refrain from giving themselves to their lovers for fear of the economic consequences. Once such people appear, they will not care a rap about what we today think they should do. They will establish their own practice and their own public opinion, conformable therewith, on the practice of each individual — and that's the end of it.[22]

,,

This is a restatement of the belief that the family changes to meet historically determined needs, and at the same time a warning against simplistic and antihistorical solutions.

CHAPTER THREE

THE ENEMY IS CHALLENGED

Are all women natural allies against men, or can women achieve emancipation only in a joint struggle with men against injustice? Can women be free without a change in the social system? These questions have divided the women's movement into feminists and revolutionaries since women began to organize in the early decades of the nineteenth century, and they continue to divide it today. Of course the line has not always been clear. In some countries at some times there has been considerable overlapping and cooperation between the two camps — represented generally by the woman's rights movement on the one hand and women organized in trade unions and political parties on the other — in other places at other times there has been inability to communicate or even open hostility. In the United States and Britain, where the feminist movement in the late nineteenth century was relatively militant and the trade unions, operating under conditions of parliamentary democracy, were on the whole politically uncommitted, the differences were never as sharp as on the European continent. Both camps aimed at improving women's position within the existing system.

In Europe trade unionism arose under the influence of socialistically oriented political parties; women as well as men had tasted fire on the barricades. There was an audience for a different approach to women's rights, one which emphasized that women's enemy was not man but capitalism. This was especially true in Germany, until 1871 a decentralized collection of semi-feudal states, where trade unions came into being comparatively late. When they did appear, however, they were products of the Marxist Social-Democratic party, for the most part; while the early feminist movement was timid and vacillating under the stern eye of an autocratic monarchy. Here in the mid-1860s, under the influence of two of Marx's and Engels's disciples — Wilhelm Liebknecht and August Bebel — there appeared the first labor movement dedicated to the emancipation of men and women through revolutionary struggle.

As the German Social-Democratic party grew in strength and assumed the leadership in the international organization of socialist workers' parties, it also took the lead in pressing for an international socialist women's movement. After the socialist parties split over the question of support for their national governments in the First World War, this movement found its second home in the Soviet Union. It is associated with the name of Clara Zetkin, who dedicated herself to a revolutionary concept of women's emancipation from the time she joined the Social-Democratic party of Germany in 1881 to her death in the Soviet Union in 1933. Though it cannot be said that the movement was ever wholeheartedly supported by its sponsor, the Second International Workers' Association of socialist parties and trade unions, it played an important "consciousness-raising" role among both men and women — especially in central and eastern Europe just before the First World War and in the period between the wars. Like its militant founder, it eschewed cooperation with feminist campaigns dedicated to women's suffrage, women's education, equal pay, the right to divorce, and other legal and political rights; not because it did not believe in the causes but because it did not trust the benevolence of middle-class women. Experience had convinced its adherents that even those ladies who were ready to speak out against low wages, long hours, bad housing, and miserable working conditions were usually on the other side of the argument when the police were called out.

Why had Germany, in its revolution of 1848, produced no fighting women like the women of France who in 1792 took up arms and demanded bread and freedom? Clara Zetkin posed this question when, in 1905, she tried to piece together the beginnings of the proletarian women's movement in Germany for the paper which the edited in Stuttgart, *Die Gleichheit (Equality)*. Why did Germany produce no woman leader like Flora Tristan of France, exotic and passionate follower of Saint-Simon, who believed it was her mission to convince the working class of its revolutionary role? In her book *The Workers' Union*, which she published in 1843 without ever having heard of Marx or Engels, Tristan called upon the workers to unite in an international union and set up their organizations in the main cities of Europe. Why had the German bourgeoisie, Zetkin inquired, created no movement for the complete emancipation of women like that in the United States headed by Elizabeth Cady Stanton — a movement which produced the Seneca Falls Declaration of 1848 and which had the physical as well as the moral courage to campaign against slavery?

Her explanation was the one given by Marx and Engels for the failure of the German bourgeoisie to press its gains in the revolution of 1848. In the period between the French bourgeois revolution of 1789 and the German bourgeois revolution of 1848, she said, capitalism had developed and the class conflict ripened to such a degree that the bourgeoisie could no longer afford to raise general slogans about man's natural and universal right to freedom for fear of arousing the proletariat to a struggle which would not stop with a bourgeois revolution, but would demand a working-class victory. Rather than rally the workers or support them, it preferred to withdraw from the field with its own demands half won. This conservative bourgeoisie, so unlike the leaders of the French Revolution, Zetkin wrote, could only produce hesitant and halfhearted feminists whose campaigns were part of the last battle for the "natural rights of man" against feudalism. Although their movement was, in her opinion, historically outdated, the feminists refused to see that real emancipation could be won only by a movement in which working women would liberate themselves by the side of working men.

There was — as two angry young men, Marx and Engels,

had written in a document which appeared in London only a few days before the revolution of 1848 broke out in France — a spectre haunting Europe — "the spectre of communism"; a statement which received dramatic confirmation when, after the overthrow of the monarchy of Louis Philippe, the French workers forced the establishment of a republic and imposed revolutionary reforms which lasted from February to June 1848. The document was the manifesto of the newly formed Communist League, the first international communist organization, established by German workers and intellectuals living in exile. It had been intended to serve as a statement of principles to guide the proletarian party when the anticipated bourgeois revolution in Germany was transformed into a workers' revolution. The revolution of 1848 failed, however, and in the period of repression that followed, German revolutionaries again went into exile — many of them in the United States — while the League fell apart in factional quarrels. The *Communist Manifesto* remained, however, as the single clearest statement of the new doctrine — the liberation of the workers by their own political action; not the unity of the nation for "human rights" but the unity of the working class across national boundaries for the rights of the disinherited. In it, the League's views on the family and the position of women were not expressed as a program but as a series of answers to the charges of their opponents: that communists intended to abolish the family, to destroy the home by taking over the education of children, to introduce community of women.

The *Manifesto* declares that the bourgeois family, based on property, will vanish as a matter of course when capitalism vanishes. It points out that communists did not invent the intervention of society in education, but that they do seek to alter the character of that intervention and free it from the influence of the ruling class; and finally it states that the communists "have no need to introduce community of women; it has existed almost from time immemorial." It adds provocatively that the bourgeoisie, having misused the wives and daughters of their workers and encouraged public prostitution, "take great pleasure in seducing each other's wives." It is self-evident, the *Manifesto* continues, "that the abolition of the present system of production must bring with it the abolition of the community of women springing from that system, i.e., of prostitution both public and private." Although the aim, clearly stated, "is to do away with the status of women as mere instruments of production," no concrete plan is suggested.[1] Of the ten measures proposed by the *Communist Manifesto* only one, free education for all children in public schools, relates in any way to the family.

The ideas about the family expressed in the first communist credo are in general those to be found in the writings of the French utopian socialists of a generation earlier, Henri Saint-Simon and Charles Fourier, whose works were widely read in Germany and influenced Marx when he was still a student. It was only many years later that Marx in *Capital* pointed to the positive aspect of woman's employment as the economic basis for her liberation, and Engels in *The Origin of the Family* enumerated what he believed to be the essential steps leading to emancipation. Both Marx and Engels frequently acknowledged their debt to the utopians in this sphere. Engels pointed out that Fourier was "the first to declare that in a given society the degree of the emancipation of women is the natural measure of the general emancipation."[2] Fourier's formulation so pleased Marx and Engels that they frequently rang changes on it. Thus, in 1868 Marx wrote to a correspondent in the United States, praising the short-lived National Labor Union for adapting a resolution in favor of equal pay for equal work (the first such resolution by a national labor federation in American history): "Anybody knows, if he knows anything about history, that great social changes are impossible without the feminine ferment. Social progress can be measured exactly by the social position of the fair sex."[3]

The fierce vocabulary of the *Communist Manifesto* had to be put aside when, in 1864, a second attempt was made to form a world organization of socialist workers, the International Workingmen's Association, with Marx again as the theoretical and practical leader. A different kind of organization was needed this time to weld the many political trends which had taken root in the growing working-class and trade-union movement that had spread all over Europe in the sixteen-year interval. Although Marx was given the task of writing the inaugural address, there were only a handful of Marxists in the I.W.A. (retrospectively to become known as the First International) at the start. If the organization was to be effective, it had to achieve unity for the overthrow of capitalism, unity among these diversified groups: the British workers with their pure-and-simple trade unionism, dedicated to daily practical aims; the followers of Louis Blanqui, who believed in armed insurrection and conspiracy and cared nothing for trade unions; the Proudhonists who put their faith in consumer cooperatives which were eventually to put capitalism out of business; the Lassallists who believed that an "iron law of wages" prevented workers from ever rising above the subsistence level and thought trade unions futile; and finally the anarchist followers of Bakunin, who called for the destruction of the state without wasting time on political reform. Sentiment among workers generally at this time was for excluding women from industry altogether because of the competition they represented, and only the most politically conscious among them were coming to think of women as possible allies who should be organized. Added to this, Proudhonists and anarchists were totally opposed to women's employment on the grounds that they were the guardians of the hearth and belonged at home.

Consequently the statement of principles which the I.W.A. adopted was vague. The supporters of the right of women to work eventually had their way, however, and the organizations' congress in Geneva in 1866 rejected the call for a ban on women's employment. It also took a stand in favor of special legislation protecting the "weaker female organism" from working conditions harmful to it. This was a victory for the concept worked out by Marx who, while he viewed the participation of women in industrial production as of revolutionary significance for the working-class movement, maintained that women, at least — for their own sakes and for the future of relations between the sexes — should be protected from the extreme effects of capitalist exploitation which led to the further deterioration of

the position of workers and their families. Equally important
from the point of view of the working woman's growing class
consciousness was the fact that the I.W.A. permitted women's
trade unions to affiliate — among them the French silk workers
of Lyons, whose strike in 1869 was brought to a victorious conclusion with I.W.A. support.

While in France the I.W.A.'s influence was reflected in the
mentality which produced the Paris Commune of 1871, wrote
Clara Zetkin in her history of the proletarian women's movement in Germany, "it was different in Germany, where the proletariat had first to discover itself as a class before it could
organize as a class and act as a class." [4] The process of self-dis-
covery began in workers' education associations organized by
liberal-minded capitalists. While British and American labor
had had their militant trade unions from the early years of the
nineteenth century, these clubs were the only places where German workers could meet for self-improvement and discussion.
When in some of these groups the need for independent political action by the workers began to be felt, supporters of
Ferdinand Lassalle, Liebknecht, and Bebel broke away and
finally, in 1869, formed the Social-Democratic Workers' party
of Germany.

There grew up under this influence the first German trade
unions, of which the most radical were organized from the beginning according to the guidelines of the I.W.A., the First
International. They included in their aims not only the defense
of workers' rights but the overthrow of capitalism, and they accepted women members as a matter of course. The unions fell
victim to the political and economic crisis which followed the
Franco-Prussian War of 1870–71, but the party survived. At the
time Chancellor Bismarck introduced his antisocialist emergency laws in 1878, the Social-Democratic party was already
polling half a million votes, and had elected August Bebel, a
wood turner by trade, to the Reichstag, where he remained a
deputy almost uninterruptedly until his death in 1913. In
spite of the emergency laws, the party continued to gain followers; and after the laws were abrogated in 1890 it received a
million and a half votes, one-fifth of the total. The rapid in-

dustrial expansion which followed Germany's unification in 1871 and soon gave her the status of a first-rate power, was accompanied by the growth of the German proletariat and of its trade-union and political activity. The center of the European workers' movement shifted from France to Germany.

Under the pressure of general reaction following the Franco-Prussian War and the defeat of the Paris Commune, and again rent by dissension between anarchist and Marxist members, the First International moved its headquarters to the United States, where it quietly disbanded in 1876. When the Second International was founded in Paris in 1889 by nearly four hundred labor and socialist delegates from twenty countries on the one-hundredth anniversary of the fall of the Bastille, political leadership found its way immediately into the hands of the German Social-Democratic party, the strongest party with the strongest Marxist orientation. While Britain had no workers' party and its new socialist movement was of the gradualist Fabian variety, and while American labor leaders were avowedly antisocialist, the Germany party, just emerging from illegality, had not yet developed the urge to become respectable. Two events of note for the growth of the socialist women's movement occurred during this period. One was the publication of August Bebel's book, *Woman Under Socialism*. The other was the appearance on the scene of Clara Zetkin, who joined the Social-Democratic party as a young teacher of twenty-four, and for half a century thereafter remained identified with the effort to organize women for socialism on an international scale.

The fact that Bebel was the acknowledged leader of the party, and its most popular figure, made his book worthy of serious notice outside as well as within labor circles, and gave prestige to the cause it was intended to forward.

Bebel began to write his book in prison, and the first edition was published illegally in 1879 in Leipzig under cover of the imprint of a Swiss publishing house. A second edition was published in Zürich. This was followed by another six editions of 2,500 copies each, also distributed illegally. Following the repeal of the emergency laws, Bebel completely revised the book, incorporating new material (Engels's *Origin of the Family* had

appeared in the meantime, for instance); and he continued to
revise it up through the fiftieth edition, which appeared in 1909.
by which time it had been translated into fifteen languages.

No such book had ever come before the reading public,
and no such book has gone into battle for the working woman
on so many fronts since. The pain it caused to various sections
of the Establishment may be judged from the debates Bebel
carried on with learned professors in his prefaces and in his
revisions of successive editions. In spite of its scientific errors,
its crude use of statistics, and some of its naïve conclusions, the
book deserves to be read with respect today. It took up aspects of
the "woman question" never discussed at that time in polite society or in popular literature — women's sexuality, for example,
and prostitution — and it presented a mass of data and arguments in favor of woman's economic and personal independence
and in support of her capabilities.

The first section of the book, "Woman in the Past," sum-
marizes Morgan's and Engels's arguments according to which
the original prehistoric organization of society, matriarchy, was
replaced by patriarchy and the growth of the monogamous family to meet the needs of private property. Bebel goes further
than Engels in the imaginative picture he gives of gynecocracy,
or the supposed period of woman's rule, deduced from legends,
the Bible, and the writings of ancient Greek poets and histo-
rians; and in the weight he gives to Bachofen's view that women
possessed real power and fought like the legendary Amazons to
preserve it. In subsequent chapters he deals with woman's need
for a satisfactory sex life, and demonstrates the inability of modern marriage to meet this need either in loveless property-based
unions or in families undermined by poverty and by women's
long hours in industry combined with work at home. He dis-
cusses the way women were penalized, in the face of the inability
of many men to marry (a result of financial hardship), by the
conventions which withheld from them the sexual freedom
granted to men. And he condemns the hypocrisy which permitted men to seek sexual satisfaction with prostitutes while
making outcasts of the women who were forced to earn a living
by selling themselves.

Bebel declared it ridiculous, in view of the fact that the majority of new workers in expanding German industry were women (the female work force had increased 35 percent between 1875 and 1882, the male by only 6.4 percent), that women should be considered fit only for the kitchen. Instead, he said, they should be enabled to compete with men, for which they needed equal access to education. He pooh-poohed the idea of women's inferiority. "If the conditions for social development are equal to both sexes, if to neither there stands any obstacle in the way, and if the social state of society is a healthy one, *then woman also will rise to a point of perfection in her being, such as we can have no full conception of, such conditions having hitherto been absent in the history of the development of the race.*" [5] Women's suffrage, women's participation in public life, universal public education of both sexes in coeducational schools (following the example of the United States), with the program including training for a useful occupation — in support of all these he cites contemporary facts and figures and quotes authorities to demolish supporters of the status quo.

Bebel was a worker and a practical politician with an understanding of the workers' aspirations, rather than a theoretician. He took the ideas of Saint-Simon and Fourier, Morgan and Bachofen, Darwin and Engels, John Stuart Mill and Marx, Krafft-Ebing, Richard Wagner, George Sand, and several dozen lesser minds, and added to them his own analysis of late nineteenth-century social conditions to produce a kind of Marxist utopia, the vision of the future which Engels had hesitated to define. His book is about human beings and not factors in the production process. He realized that woman's education and employment were important to her not just because they would make her economically independent but because women were suffering personal frustration as a result of their exclusion from rational pursuits. He recognized that woman was not just sexually misused by men but that she had sexual needs; that she was not merely a bundle of maternal instincts or a class-conscious fighter, but yearned to be a "complete and useful member of society." He therefore did not dismiss the campaign of a handful of women for the right to study and enter the professions as an issue which could not concern working-class women. He thought it important both as a matter of principle and because it would prove that women are as capable as men.

"

The woman of future society is socially and economically independent; she is no longer subject to even a vestige of dominion and exploitation; she is free, the peer of man, mistress of her lot. Her education is the same as that of man, with such exceptions as the difference of sex and sexual function demand. . . . She chooses her occupation on such field as corresponds with her wishes, inclinations and natural abilities, and she works under conditions identical with man's. Even if engaged as a practical working-woman on some field or other, at other times of the day she may be educator, teacher or nurse, at yet others she may exercise herself in art, or cultivate some branch of science, and at yet others may be filling some administrative function. . . . In the choice of love, she is, like man, free and unhampered. She woos or is wooed, and closes the bond from no considerations other than her own inclinations. This bond is a private contract, celebrated without the intervention of any functionary. . . . *The satisfaction of the sexual instinct is as much a private concern as the satisfaction of any other natural instinct.*[6]

"

Engels's vision of a society in which housework would become a public industry would be realized by the application of new technology to domestic chores. Central heating, electric stoves, hot running water, and elevators were already beginning to revolutionize the households of the rich. It was only a matter of time until they would be available on a mass scale, and from there it was only a step to central kitchens and laundries. Who would want to do his own cooking and washing then? Social life would become increasingly public; domesticity would be confined to what was absolutely necessary. Theaters, parks, lectures, concerts, sports grounds would replace the individual's four walls.

In future society, Bebel said, there will be no property to bequeath other than household equipment and personal belongings; and bourgeois marriage, the result of bourgeois property relations, will be "devoid of foundation" and will collapse.

"Woman is, accordingly, free, and her children, where she has any, do not impair her freedom: they can only fill all the fuller the cup of her enjoyments and her pleasure in life. Nurses, teachers, female friends, the rising female generation — all these are ready at hand to help the mother when she needs help."

Here, in order to demonstrate the inevitability of this future, he had to call on that circular movement in the evolution of human society, ending on a higher plane, which seemed so reasonable to Bachofen, Morgan, and Engels.

"

Human society has traversed, in the course of thousands of years, all the various phases of development, to arrive in the end where it started from, communistic property and complete equality and fraternity, but no longer among congeners alone, but among the whole human race. . . . What bourgeois society has vainly striven for . . . Socialism will accomplish. . . .

Now woman again fills the active role that once was hers in primitive society. She does not become the mistress, she is equal of man.

"The end of social development resembles the beginning of human existence. The original equality returns. The mother web of existence starts and rounds up the cycle of human affairs"—thus writes Bachofen.[7]

"

The tone of personal identification with women's problems; the impressive collection of facts and statistics on everything from marriage, divorce, infanticide, and suicide to grain yields and vessel tonnage; and the promise of a bright future "approaching in giant strides" combined to make Bebel's work the handbook for several generations of socialists and Communists before and after the First World War. A Czech Communist historian, recalling his own youth, writes in the preface to a new edition published in Prague in 1962:

"

We remember the time when young workers brought it as a gift to their loved ones, and when socialist workers read it to their wives to awaken interest in their activities and win those closest to them for work in the movement. We experienced the passionate debates on questions of love, on the relations between men and women, girls and boys, in the revolutionary communist youth movement between the two world wars. We can truthfully say that Bebel's book gained not only thousands and thousands of women for socialism, but men as well, and strongly influenced the education of a whole generation.[8]

"

Clara Zetkin, who became interested in socialism just about the time Bebel's book was first published, wrote of it later: "As dynamite shatters the hardest rocks, so its ideas pulverized the old prejudices which blocked women's path to the battle-ground of the proletariat and to their complete liberation. They stimulated the self-confidence, the desire for self-realization, the efforts on behalf of justice, the class consciousness of oppressed and intimidated women." [9] This pioneering work, she said, closed the first period of the revolutionary women's movement, the period of search and clarification.

It fell to her to give the movement organizational form, and she thought it essential to keep it free from contamination by middle-class female illusions. For her the critical passage in Bebel's book occurred in the very first pages, where he took issue with those who believed that the "woman question" could be solved simply by giving women access to education, jobs, and civil rights within the existing social order. These measures, he said, will not abolish "the wage slavery under which the working women deeply pine" or the "sex slavery which is intimately con-nected with our property and industrial systems." The goal is "the removal of all impediments that make man dependent upon man; and, consequently, one sex upon the other." The Social-Democratic party is the only one which has placed full equality for women on its program, and it has done so "not for agitational reasons, but out of necessity, out of principle. *There can be no emancipation of humanity without the social inde-pendence and equality of the sexes.*" (The italics are Bebel's.)

The "female bourgeois" active in the women's movement did not understand the necessity for radical change, he wrote. "Influenced by their privileged social standing, they see in the more far-reaching working-women's movement dangers, not in-frequently abhorrent aims, which they feel constrained to ignore, eventually even to resist." The clash between the capitalists and the working class "turns up likewise on the surface of the Woman's Movement; and it finds its corresponding expression in the aims and tactics of those engaged in it." [10]

Nevertheless, Bebel thought, "the hostile sisters" have much more in common than the men of the two opposing classes and "can, although marching separately, strike jointly." Clara Zetkin was made of sterner stuff, and one of her consistent concerns was to prevent this kind of collaboration over the class fence, which in her opinion only dissipated the strength of working-class women. It was not just the wavering and timid campaigns of middle-class feminists and suffragettes — charity collections and elevating lectures, sometimes "decorated with the flower of interest" in the plight of working women — which drew her fire. It was not only their failure to realize that votes and the right to higher education alone could not change the condition of working women — who needed bread and jobs — which aroused her antagonism. These women represented to her a danger which must be defeated so that the proletariat could triumph, because they attempted to convince women that their aims could be realized by a battle between the sexes within the social order rather than a battle between the classes to change it. As she saw it, they "put bourgeois class interest above the equality of women. The terrorist tactics of self-sacrificing anarchistic suffragettes in the United States and England did emphasize the class character of the movement for woman's rights in the struggle for the vote, but did nothing to change this." [11]

Zetkin began her international career at the founding congress of the Second International in Paris in 1889 where she spoke with the backing of the German delegation. She drew applause for her condemnation of the feminist movement as a counterrevolutionary force with which there could be no compromise, and for her appeal to the parties and trade unions to recruit proletarian women into the ranks of working-class fighters. The congress clapped, but took no decision which would bind its members to action — an attitude typical of the Second International, she later wrote. It refused to take the initiative, she complained, in creating conditions to make the fight of working women for emancipation part of the class struggle and a moving force for social revolution, preferring to leave this task to the socialist women themselves. This refusal did not weaken her ideological commitment, however. There began the day-to-day struggle to persuade poor and semiliterate working women, after a long day at the machines, to leave their cookstoves and sit down to read a leaflet or a pamphlet, to support strikes, to take to the streets to demand cheaper bread. Following the example of the Social-Democratic women of Germany, socialist women in other countries tried to direct their sisters away from what they regarded as the ideological confusion and social reformism of the various feminist trends and to weld them into a militant, expressly socialist movement, directed not against men but against capitalism.

One of the first issues touching women specifically, around which debate raged in the Second International, was the question of protective legislation. Marx and Engels had strongly favored the Ten Hours Bill in England in the 1840s and consistently pressed for a ban on night work and other special protection for women who were "twice exploited." The feminist movement seemed more radical, with its resistance to legislating the physical differences between men and women. Sometimes this was, as the socialists charged, a vulgarization of the concept of equality, a misguided way of showing that women were as capable as men. More often, as in England, the feminist women's movement opposed such legislation quite logically as discriminatory because it weakened women's bargaining position. To socialists and trade unionists who were in constant contact with exhausted mothers of small children who were working a ten- or eleven-hour day, however, this seemed at best a ridiculously romantic position; and the decision of the Second International at its congress in Zürich in 1893 reaffirmed the position Marx had helped to forge in 1866.

The struggle to establish women's suffrage as a right which should apply to all women, without property qualifications and as a necessary weapon in both men's and women's continuing struggle, lasted considerably longer. The Second International did not even actively support the right of women to vote until 1891. Many of its members were beginning to regard their growing strength as evidence that their goals could be won in the arena of parliamentary politics or through general strikes alone, and were, as the left wing (which received guidance from Engels until his death in 1895) charged, becoming tacticians rather than revolutionaries. In the Austro-Hungarian monarchy, for example, the great political struggle of the years 1903–1905 was for a reform of the voting system which was based on property and gave one-third of male citizens of voting age the right to vote for 83 percent of the seats in parliament, while disfranchising completely all women and all males under twenty-four years of age. In this battle, which was strongly influenced by the abortive 1905 Revolution in Russia and which ended in a one-day general strike in November of that year, the Social-Democrats had abandoned the fight for women's suffrage in order to obtain universal and equal voting rights for men. Unanimity on the need to make full suffrage for women a question of principle was finally achieved at the congress of the International held in Stuttgart in 1907, when the German Social-Democrats, led by Zetkin, successfully defended their position that the campaign for the vote should be conducted on socialist principles and with no tactical compromises.

The Stuttgart meeting was important for other reasons. After heated debate it adopted an amendment put forward by the revolutionary German leader, Rosa Luxemburg, and the almost unknown head of the Russian delegation, V. I. Lenin, to an antiwar resolution formulated by Bebel. The final document called upon the working class and its parliamentary representatives to use every possible means to prevent war, and in the event that hostilities should break out, to intervene to terminate them and to use the situation to overthrow class rule. It was the violation of this pledge seven years later, when a majority of Social-Democratic parties followed the lead of the German party (by then the strongest single group in the German Reichstag, with more than one hundred seats) and voted to support the war effort of their governments, that led to the split in the Second International and the eventual formation of the Communist movement.

The 1907 congress also put its weight behind the first International Conference of Socialist Women, held in Stuttgart at the same time, at which fifty delegates from Germany, Austria, the Czech provinces, Belgium, Britain, France, Finland, Italy, Norway, Russia, Switzerland, and the United States agreed to form a loosely organized international women's organization; elected Clara Zetkin as secretary; and voted the German women's newspaper which she edited their official organ. It was at Stuttgart, too, that Zetkin met Lenin, who was to remain her political mentor for the next twenty years.

The second conference of socialist women, held in Copenhagen in 1910 and again coinciding with a congress of the Second International, adopted Zetkin's proposal that March 8 be set aside every year as International Women's Day — a date chosen to mark the strike of 40,000 New York seamstresses protesting sweatshop conditions. It also resolved that women's greatest task at that moment was the fight against war. This, together with demands for the right to vote and for equality with men on the job, brought tens of thousands of working women into the streets on March 8 all over Europe in the following years. But none of this stopped the landslide vote for war. The bitterness of Zetkin, against the women who had supported the "war on war" and who now betrayed Social-Democracy, knew no bounds. While a minority attended a socialist women's antiwar conference in Switzerland in 1915, "the majority of organized Social-Democratic women sank under the leadership of the Second International to the position of defenders of the national 'fatherlands' of imperialist bourgeoisie," she later wrote.

"

They competed with the ladies of the bourgeoisie in their chauvinistic ideas and behavior. They disappointed and misled proletarian women with their mendacious assertions about the aims and character of the imperialistic power struggle, and pushed them out of economic and all other sectors of social life. Having learned nothing from the powerful world storm of the proletarian revolution in the empire of the Czar, Social-Democratic women remained by the side of the bourgeoisie in defense of its class rule against the attacks of the advancing revolutionary exploited. . . . They have given up their basic aim — the proletarian revolution — and have thus rendered themselves incapable also of representing the day-to-day demands of proletarian women.[12]

,,

The war split the socialist movement throughout the world and at the same time divided the struggle for women's equality between East and West. Those who followed Zetkin and Lenin into the Communist movement shared their contempt for "well-disciplined female Social-Democrats," "pious Christian women," "daughters of privy councilors," "ladylike English pacifists and ardent French suffragettes." This attitude was to grow into a generalized disregard for that part of the history of the woman's rights movement not directly connected with the fight for socialism. It continues today in the lack of interest shown in the socialist countries for the women's liberation movement in the West.

The Bolshevik party of Russia came to power in November 1917. In some of the other countries of central and eastern Europe the left-wing socialist parties or their splinters continued their struggle against the war; and in the defeated countries — Germany and the Austro-Hungarian Empire — succeeded either in establishing short-lived socialist regimes (Hungary and Germany), or in rallying substantial working-class support for the Russian example, expressed in strikes and demonstrations.

Following the split in the Social-Democratic movement, Clara Zetkin had joined the *Spartakusbund,* that fraction of German Social-Democracy, represented by Karl Liebknecht and Rosa Luxemburg, which opposed the war. A week after Liebknecht and Luxemburg were assassinated on their way to jail during the suppression of the revolution in Berlin in January 1919, eight Marxist parties of central and eastern Europe issued a call for a world congress to establish a Third International. This founding congress of the Communist International, subsequently known as the Comintern, was held in March 1919

under the leadership of Lenin. Among the resolutions unani-
mously adopted was one put forward by Russian women
delegates, declaring that the dictatorship of the proletariat could
be realized and maintained only with the active participation of
working-class women. The second meeting of the Comintern a
year later took the first steps toward the formation of an international communist women's movement, not simply with
the blessing of the Comintern, as had been the case with its
predecessor in the Second International, but under its direct
leadership. In 1921 the second women's conference adopted a
program drawn up at Lenin's request under the direction of
Clara Zetkin, by now a member of the Central Committee of
the recently formed Communist party of Germany. As Marx and
Engels went far beyond the thinking of most of the membership
of the First International on the subject of women's position,
and as Bebel spoke for the passionate few and not the indifferent
many in the Second International, so Lenin found few people
in the Third International who were prepared to deal with this
subject. "Our Second International Congress unfortunately did
not come up to expectations in discussing the question of
women," he told Zetkin. "It posed the question but did not get
around to taking a definite stand." A committee appointed to
draw up a resolution, theses, and directives, was dragging its
feet, he told her, and he asked her help.[13]

These directives, as finally accepted, put forward the by-
now-familiar position that there can be no emancipation of
women without revolutionary class struggle, and no successful
revolution without women's participation. Legal and social reforms of themselves, it was stated, cannot liberate women; but
they should be fought for because they mitigate daily suffering
and because the fight for them educates the workers for further
political struggle. In line with Lenin's suggestion, the conference agreed that there was no place in the Communist movement
for a separate women's organization, since women joined communist parties and trade unions as equals with men. On the
other hand, because of the relative backwardness of women,
special working groups should be formed to arouse and educate
them. This represented a rejection of the more "radical" view

that in view of women's equality, political work should be carried on without differentiation.

From 1924 on, Clara Zetkin headed the International Women's Secretariat of the Comintern in Moscow, where she also served on the presidium of the executive committee of the Comintern. She remained a Communist deputy in the German Reichstag, and as its senior member she made a dramatic return to Germany in 1932 at the age of 75 — in spite of threats on her life — to open the next-to-last meeting of the Reichstag in the Weimar Republic a year before Hitler's seizure of power.

As far as the position of the Comintern on women was concerned, the program proposed in 1924 and eventually ratified by all national parties, included the following paragraph:

"

Complete equality between men and women before the law and in social life: a radical reform of marriage and family laws; recognition of maternity as a social function; protection of mothers and infants. Initiation of social care and upbringing of infants and children (crèches, kindergarten, children's homes, etc.). The establishment of institutions that will gradually relieve the burden of household drudgery (public kitchens and laundries) and systematic cultural struggle against the ideology and traditions of female bondage.

"

It also contains provisions calling for "prohibition, as a rule, of night work and employment in harmful trades for all females," as well as social insurance of all kinds and free medical care.[14] The Soviet state had begun to put these principles into practice immediately after the revolution, and in 1920, in a period of civil war and famine, Lenin was already impatient with the authorities for failing to provide more nurseries and more public kitchens and expecting women to wait until the budget permitted. Although at the time of the Revolution only 13 percent of Soviet women could read and write, Lenin repeatedly urged that more women be involved in administration and politics.

This was the moment when the Marxist program for women's emancipation was to be transformed from a compact set of propositions, of great agitational importance in the struggle for power, to hundreds of small decisions which were expected to create not just new relations between men and machines, but new relations among men, women, and children in their most private and intimate day-by-day and minute-by-minute contacts. No blueprint had been worked out. The principles established by Marx and Engels and elaborated on by Lenin covered a plan of action for women's economic liberation, and to that degree only were an expression of the ferment which had been going on in women's minds and hearts for the past century. It included no proposal for liberating women from the bondage of their own mentality, or from that of men's. The discussions which had taken place around Bebel's book had been abstract; now they had to be concrete. The Marxist parties, in common with other political parties, had never concerned themselves with the psychology of sex or the biosexual differences between men and women (except to recognize their existence in protective legislation and aid to mothers), and they had never taken cognizance of the drives that motivate individuals in their personal relationships. Yet, unlike other political parties, the first Communist party to come to power did not intend to sanctify the status quo with legislation and leave questions of personal hardship to the individual and his church. It proposed to settle relationships between people in a way consistent with principles of socialism. No one really knew how this was to be done.

It is clear from the conversations with Lenin which Clara Zetkin recorded, and from his correspondence on "free love" with Innessa Armand, a member of the Central Committee of the Soviet Communist party, that Lenin viewed the preoccupation with sex problems and forms of marriage by many women in the Soviet Union and in Germany, Austria, and other countries, as bourgeois deviations, or at best deplorable distractions from much more important questions. The right to divorce and to abortion, an end to the humiliating concept of illegitimacy — these were basic demands which he supported as helping to break the power of property relations over women. But, "I ask you," he said to Zetkin in 1920, "is this the time to keep working women busy for months at a stretch with such questions as how to love or be loved, how to woo or be wooed?" The discussions which were taking place were un-Marxist, he told her, because in them sex and marriage were not treated as part of the principal social problem, but on the contrary the principal social problem was regarded as subordinate to the sex problem. No one qualified was presently available to lead discussions of sex and marriage from the point of view of historical materialism, and "nowadays all the thoughts of Communist women, of working women, should be centered on the proletarian revolution, which will lay the foundation, among other things, for the necessary revision of material and sexual relations."

He described a widely read pamphlet by a Viennese Communist as rot, adding: "The workers read what is right in it long ago in Bebel. Only not in the tedious, cut-and-dried form found in the pamphlet, but in the form of gripping agitation that strikes out at bourgeois society." He evidently hoped for a "proletarian" revolution in sexual relations and marriage, which would do away with the "decay, putrescence and filth" of bourgeois marriage with its "license for the husband and bondage for the wife" and its hypocritical morality, and which would replace them with the purifying individual sexual love which Engels praised, accompanied by self-discipline and a sense of responsibility. "Nothing could be falser than to preach monastic self-denial and the sanctity of the filthy bourgeois morals to young people," he told Zetkin. "The coercion of bourgeois marriage and bourgeois legislation on the family enhance the evil and aggravate the conflicts." On the other hand, "promiscuity in sexual matters is bourgeois. It is a sign of degeneration." The "glass-of-water theory," according to which the satisfaction of sexual desire was as trivial an act as drinking a glass of water was "completely un-Marxist and . . . anti-social." Zetkin valiantly defended women's interests in these matters, pointing out that the war had intensified the many problems and conflicts already existing in sexual relations which caused suffering to women of all classes. New relations between people were appearing, and enlightenment about sex and the family was needed to help women cast off their old prejudices. Lenin failed to be convinced that these discussions were being held in a truly Marxist spirit. In the end, Zetkin agreed with him and begged him to write something on the problem, to which he replied: "Later, not now. Now all our time and strength must be concentrated on other things. There are bigger and more difficult jobs to do." Lenin's views have been quoted to discourage this kind of speculation among Communists and to encourage the sublimation of sex ever since.[15]

At the time this conversation took place, such an attitude could be easily defended. The civil war, the war of foreign intervention, was ending. Factories were not operating, mines were full of water, transport was disorganized, the drop in production was catastrophic, bread was scarce. Peasants rioted against the grain quotas, strikes broke out in Petrograd, the sailors in the Baltic base at Kronstadt rose in rebellion a few months later. Early in 1921 the New Economic Policy was introduced, a frank retreat toward state capitalism and a concession to the peasants, though it was powerless to halt the famine caused by a second year of drought in the Volga basin. Twenty-five million people in eastern Russia were starving. Families abandoned their dead by the roadside as they fled the region in search of food.

These were not favorable conditions for experiments in sexual revolution and in the complete abolition of the family as the stronghold of convention and reactionary ideology, or for the introduction of communal living. The state was simply not equipped to take over the functions of the family. No matter how convincing the arguments of its proponents, the attempt to do away overnight with all the accepted restrictions on individual behavior in a country of still-feudal relationships, unable to mobilize the necessary material resources, inevitably brought many distortions which had nothing to do with liberating women. Living in communes during a shortage of housing, heat, food, and clothing could not lighten women's household tasks, and it put the maximum strain on relationships between people. The new loose sexual ties were harder to adapt to for most women, brought up in patriarchal religious homes, than for men. Even the new laws favoring easy divorce and easy abortion tended to favor men in a situation where women were bound by ignorance and convention. The peasant who had now been forbidden by law to beat his wife could instead marry a husky young girl in the spring and abandon her in the autumn when the harvest was over. And why worry about getting her pregnant when she could always get an abortion? So she could and did, sometimes ten or twelve times.

Changes in the law in the mid-thirties which strengthened the family, making it more difficult to get a divorce (although by no means as difficult as in capitalist countries) and outlawing abortion except for medical reasons, were accompanied by discussions organized on a national scale and were presented as measures to correct these abuses. At the same time they represented the state's admission that it had a stake in more stable personal relationships and in the reproduction of the population. However, the new morality went so far in the other direction that it represented a setback even for the more conservative view represented by Lenin. The glorification of the "socialist family" and of motherhood was directed not just against chaos; it was part of a larger drive against all types of experimentation — whether in personal relationships, in education, or the arts — and against all innovations in social and even scientific theory which seemed to "serve the interests of the bourgeoisie." The mid-thirties put an end to "the right to be wrong," so important for progress in any theoretical field. Marx, Engels, and Lenin became "classics," presented as though they stood almost alone in their time, above the stream of contemporary thought, contributing ideas which were completely free from the bourgeois influences which had surrounded their birth, and timeless in their application. There were no problems which their writings could not answer, but at the same time the application of their works to new problems was reserved to a select few, and primarily to Stalin. Writings by the classics which did not support the current interpretation were suppressed or "reinterpreted."

This period represented an end to creative Marxist thinking on the "woman question" everywhere, since the Soviet Union was recognized as the ideological leader of the communist movement and none of the splinter Marxist parties concerned themselves seriously with the subject. Nonetheless, the impact of the ideas already given currency was sufficient to

maintain Soviet preeminence in this field. The Soviet Constitution of 1936, adopted the same year the family code was
amended, contained guarantees which no other country had
written into its highest law: the right to work, the right to
health, the right to education, equal rights for women in the
family and on the job, the protection of mothers and children.
In 1936, budget appropriations for maternity homes, nurseries,
and kindergartens were more than doubled. The regulations
strengthening the family did not appear to most Communists
outside the Soviet Union as a betrayal of a brave new world. On
the contrary, the publicity surrounding the "abolition of the
family," presented as the forcible breaking up of homes and the
collectivization of women — new proof of "bolshevik terror" —
had made the task of recruiting new adherents to communism
in capitalistic countries more difficult. The great experiment
had been something of an embarrassment, and in those days of
simplistic statistics, the fact that the Soviet birthrate and rate
of natural population increase remained high, while the plum-
meting birthrate was causing official alarm in many European
countries, seemed proof that socialism had brought about a
rebirth of family life.[16]

The twenties and thirties provided women in Europe with
enough issues of their own: political upheavals and the worst
economic crisis the world had ever seen. Price rises, wage cuts,
unemployment, lockouts, evictions, violations of the eight-hour-
day law, the plight of women farm-laborers, the deterioration of
children's health, people living on the starvation level, the profits of industrialists, the growing threat of fascism — with these
grievances, International Women's Day demonstrations became
increasingly militant and were often banned by the police. Germany had eight million unemployed at the time Hitler came to
power in 1933. In that year there were more than one million
unemployed in Czechoslovakia in a population of fourteen million; in the years 1930–34 the infant mortality rate averaged 128
per 1,000 live births. In 1935 women filled Prague's largest hall on
Women's Day shouting "We want work! We want bread!"
Communist women members of parliament proposed legislation protecting the health and jobs of pregnant workers. In 1938,

on the last Czechoslovak Women's Day before Hitler put an end to such nonsense, women carried red flags to anti-Fascist meetings. The year 1939 began with the dismissal of married women from their jobs in public services.

Many women all over Europe celebrated succeeding Women's Days in concentration camps or as Resistance fighters or in exile. But even for those who did not, and for those who escaped forced labor and who did not suffer the loss of husband, children, parents, brothers, and sisters, the war brought about a complete change in their values and their view of the world. Millions were radicalized by it and expected the postwar world to bring about a totally new way of life.

CHAPTER FOUR

CZECHOSLOVAKIA'S FIRST SOCIALIST YEARS

A great deal can be told about a country's image of itself from the great men it honors. Czechoslovakia's gallery of heroes begins with Charles IV, king of Bohemia and emperor of the Holy Roman Empire, who is remembered for putting Prague on the map as an important center of medieval Europe, and especially for founding in Prague in 1348 one of Europe's first universities, modeled after the University of Paris. The greatest star in the galaxy is, of course, John Huss, the religious and social reformer who was ordered burned at the stake by the Council of Constance in 1415 for refusing to recant, a century before Luther pinned his theses on the church door at Wittenberg. His ideas, which included not only reform of Church practices but social equality and justice, swept through Europe. "We are all Hussites," said Luther.[1]

The struggle between the Czech Hussites and the Catholic powers, represented by the Pope and the Habsburg monarchy, continued for another two hundred years until the forcible absorption of Bohemia and Moravia into the Austro-Hungarian Empire, following Czech defeat in one of the early battles of the Thirty Years' War in 1620.

Another bright star in the Czech firmament, Jan Amos Komenský, a Hussite bishop known as Comenius and considered to be the founder of modern universal democratic education, was forced into exile after this conflict along with many others who refused to give up their beliefs. He introduced his ideas for educational reform while in Poland, Hungary, Sweden, and England before dying in Holland. Finally, the man responsible for the creation of modern Czechoslovakia as a democratic republic when the Austro-Hungarian monarchy collapsed in 1918, and admired by many Czechoslovak Communists as Huss is admired by most Czechoslovak Catholics, was T. G. Masaryk, an elderly professor of philosophy.

People who choose such men to erect statues to in their public squares along with writers, artists, and musicians, and whose only famous general, one-eyed Jan Žižka, fought in the Hussite wars some five hundred years ago, have obviously spent a good deal of their history thinking about social justice and do not have much in the way of aggrandizement to boast about. They admire education and the arts, are fond of philosophical discussion, and insist on believing that it can settle differences of opinion. Their detractors find Czechs too stolid, too hard to arouse, too prone to talk instead of act, and too ready to feel sorry for themselves afterwards. Nevertheless, the values represented by the men they admire, which have been defeated time and time again only to rise in a new guise, have been invoked as the source of national consciousness in every period of modern history. This was true in the movement for national reawakening in the nineteenth century; in the twenty years of the pre-Munich First Republic; and again in socialist Czechoslovakia, where these names (except for the still-controversial figure of Masaryk) are the foundation of every schoolchild's reader. Highly humanistic ideals attracted many people to socialism, which they believed would be more capable of realizing them than the capitalism they had experienced. The effort to reconcile idealistic aims with the harsh measures of socialist rule and centralized decision-making provide the major conflict of the postwar period and are the background to this book.

In this dialectical struggle it is sometimes the indifference of bureaucracy (in Czechoslovakia's case, grafted onto healthy Austro-Hungarian roots) which comes to the fore: the forms to be filled out; the permissions requested and rubber stamps to be affixed; the long waits in anonymous corridors before one can change a job, exchange an apartment, take a trip, apply to a school. At other times it is the pleasure of being able to attend a good play or an excellent concert for next to nothing. A platitudinous press is balanced by exquisite children's books. The angry frustration of people who were not allowed to study or travel because their parents used to be in business, or went to church, or didn't belong to the Communist party, or were not members of the working class, coincided with the satisfaction of other people whose children's nursery school spent a month in the country. When one had to bribe a plumber to fix a tap during his working hours, with materials stolen from his employer, one recalled, perhaps, that infantile paralysis had been completely wiped out in one year, making Czechoslovakia the first country to rid itself of this disease.

There were years in which cantatas were written to Stalin and years in which they were written to the Warsaw ghetto, years in which Franz Kafka was banned and years in which he was issued in handsome new editions, years in which jazz and blue jeans were out-of-bounds and years in which they were approved by the official youth union. Although these shifts obviously reflected existing differences of opinion, there was at any one time only one correct point of view, because the Communist party is held to synthesize all views into the answer which represents the best interests of society. This, in the model of socialism which the countries of Eastern Europe have adopted, precludes all but officially sanctioned experiments, organizations, debates, and frames of reference. All creative thinking must take this reality into consideration.

No two socialist countries are just alike, and their differences are as important as their similarities. In fact it was their differences which most surprised the enterprising visitor who successfully met the complicated entry requirements. This was in the days before the travel leaflets for mass tourism made of Prague, Budapest, and Warsaw exciting gems of historical architecture and filled the modern Black Sea coast hotels of Rumania and Bulgaria with West German holiday-makers.

Visitors soon after the war saw a life open to various interpretations. People walked purposefully through the streets, shopped, went home to their individual dwellings, attended theaters, ate in restaurants, rode buses and streetcars to work. They walked in the woods on Sundays, trimmed Christmas trees, put candles on family graves on All Souls' Day. To visitors antagonistic to socialism they looked glum and shabby, the shops seemed drab; to socialism's advocates they were warmly and sensibly clad and were seen in animated conversation with their friends; the shops looked better than last year. The factories, which now belonged to the workers, resembled the old red-brick smoke-stained structures of the industrial revolution which may still be seen in England and other capitalist countries. Sometimes red streamers outside the factory gates greeted a Communist party congress or hailed the fight for peace. Collective farms could be recognized by the fact that small strips of land had been combined into huge fields, but the farmers lived in cottages grouped according to feudal patterns. The visible signs of collective work — the larger barns in which the pooled livestock of the farm members was now housed, and the collections of farm machinery, usually parked in the muddy courtyard which had once belonged to one of the more affluent landowners — seemed less like the agriculture of the future than do most large-scale farming enterprises in Britain or the United States. New housing looked like new housing, and new schools looked like new schools. Sometimes nursery schools or pioneer camps could be visited. University students were reported to be helping to build a railway, and mining apprentices were housed in a castle which had once belonged to the nobility.

But what the citizens of these countries seemed most anxious to show their visitors was, as in any country, the landmarks which documented their specific historical struggle for nationhood and cultural and social development.

Those visitors who stayed long enough, or came back a second or third time, eventually came to understand that the introduction of socialism was first of all a titanic upheaval in relationships and in the organization of society, whose multifaceted aspects could only dimly be perceived on the surface of life by the outsider. The transfer of a single cow to a coopera-

tive cowbarn could signify the eagerness of its owner to engage
in collective farming or the culmination of a bitter struggle in
which a whole community was involved; just as a May Day
demonstration could represent spontaneous enthusiasm or compulsory attendance or a combination of the two, and the un-
initiated viewer could never safely draw conclusions.

While all the socialist countries of Eastern Europe
adopted the Soviet model, each of them had to justify its individual components in terms of that country's own traditions
and aspirations and introduce them in the form permitted or
required by its own economic and cultural level. Where this
was impossible, the attempt had to be abandoned: Poland had
to give up its collectivization program and most of its land is
still cultivated by private farmers; it has also had to give the
Catholic Church a strong voice in national affairs. The German
Democratic Republic until recently left a not insignificant portion of its economy in private hands, and allowed doctors a private practice. Czechoslovakia reduced its term of compulsory
schooling to the Soviet level and had to raise it again. What is
acceptable modern art in Poland is anathema in Bulgaria. Rumania has an independent foreign policy.

Where the model was not adapted to fit, it creaked and
still creaks today. Accumulated grievances built up into explo-
sions, as in East Berlin in June 1952, the Poznan riots of 1956
and the demonstrations of the winter of 1970 in Poland, the
bloody "Hungarian Events" of 1956, and the peaceful "Prague
Spring" of 1968. The history of the past twenty-five years in
Eastern Europe is from one point of view the history of the
attempt to fit the Soviet model to six very different countries
of Eastern Europe (Yugoslavia took a different route following
the split between Tito and Stalin), and the way this process
of adjustment takes place will obviously determine their history for a very long time to come. From this continuing interaction arises the striking differences and striking similarities
between socialist practices in the six countries.

Socialism did not come to the countries of Eastern Europe, as it did in Russia, as the result of revolutionary struggles
against an entrenched government. It was brought to them at

the end of the Second World War by the Soviet Army, whose troops in most cases (Czechoslovakia was the exception) remained on their soil. Bulgaria and Rumania were previously feudal monarchies, while Hungary and Poland had been semifascist states. Bulgaria, Rumania, and Hungary had, moreover, fought on the side of Nazi Germany. To insure the existence of governments in these countries which would not again pose a threat to Soviet security, the Soviet Union gave its support to coalitions of anti-Fascist forces in which small but tightly knit Communist parties, whose leaders were trusted by Moscow, were destined to play the leading role. The German Democratic Republic was simply created in 1949 out of the Soviet zone of Allied-occupied Germany.

Among these feudal and semifascist countries, Czechoslovakia was unique. It had been a parliamentary democracy before the war, maintaining good relations with the Soviet Union, and already had a strong body of socialist sentiment which had built up over the preceding century when the Czech lands were still part of the Austro-Hungarian Empire and Slovakia belonged directly to Hungary. As the industrial base for the Empire, the Czechs had accounted for more than half its industrial proletariat as early as 1910, and had contributed 60 percent of the more than one million Social-Democratic votes polled in the first elections after the introduction of general male suffrage in 1907. Nowhere, said Lenin, had the sympathy with the 1905 Revolution in Russia been so great as in the lands ruled by the Habsburg monarchy. During the First World War there had been mass desertions of Czech troops from the German-Austrian to the Russian side, and some of these soldiers stayed on to fight in the Russian Revolution of 1917. The Revolution itself had given enormous impetus to the movement for national independence within the disintegrating Austro-Hungarian Empire which drew many workers and intellectuals to the socialist movement. In 1921, the Communist party of the recently established Czechoslovak Republic was the third largest party in the Communist International. In the economic crisis year of 1925 it polled almost one million votes and won forty-one seats in parliament, to become the second largest party in the Republic. Its members gained prestige in the 1930s as the most militant opponents of the fascist separatist movement of the German minority led by Henlein — Hitler's fifth column within Czechoslovakia — and many distinguished themselves during the war as Resistance fighters, either in Nazi-occupied Czechoslovakia or in Allied armies.

After the war the Czechoslovak situation remained unique not only in the size of its Communist party but in the fact that its government-in-exile in London, headed by President Beneš, was recognized by all liberation groups and was on friendly terms with the Soviet Union. Even before the liberation of Czechoslovakia, a twenty-year postwar treaty of friendship and mutual aid had been signed between the two countries in Moscow in the presence of Beneš; and Beneš had called for the formation of national committees, representing the revolutionary underground, to take power in the liberated territory as the Red Army advanced. The first postwar government program, proclaimed at Košice, Slovakia, when the liberation of the country had only begun, committed the country to gradual socialization. It had been worked out by Communist party leaders in exile in Moscow, but it was subscribed to by all the political parties which had come through the war without taint of collaboration with Hitler. In this grouping headed by Beneš, the Communist party had a large plurality and the Communist leader, Klement Gottwald, was given the post of premier. As was originally the case in Poland as well, there was to be a democratic transition to socialism in which the need for a dictatorship of the proletariat was said to be obviated by the fact that domestic counterrevolution was already discredited. By February 1948, however, an impasse had been reached concerning the legislation to implement the Košice Program, and political tension had reached fever pitch. The Communist party was able to take advantage of a parliamentary crisis, brought about by the resignation of nine conservative ministers, to come to power without a shot being fired and without the presence of foreign troops. In the new government formed after the "February Events," Gottwald retained the post of premier, and following new elections in June of that year became president.

In the original postwar program, the small tradesman was to be protected, and small farmers were not to be urged into collectivization, their attachment to the land which had recently been distributed being regarded as an important factor in winning their support. These principles were specifically stated in a speech to the National Assembly by Premier Gottwald just after the "February Events" in 1948. All this changed, however, after the Cominform expelled Tito's Yugoslavia in the summer of 1948, and Stalin formulated his thesis on the sharpening of the class struggle after the victory of socialism. The new policy was made clear: each country's traditions and particular economic and cultural level must of course be taken into consideration, but there was to be no specific Czechoslovakian or Polish or any other road to socialism. The new socialist countries were to walk in the footsteps of the Soviet Union.

January 1949 in Prague was cold and gray as it always is in most of Central Europe, but wartime neglect of its gray stone buildings, the lack of coal for heating, the almost complete absence of traffic in the streets, the obvious shortages of food and clothing and the amenities of life, made the cold more penetrating and the leaden skies more depressing. Yet there were signs everywhere of preparations for a great industrial effort which was to bring the "happy tomorrow" that now became, and was to remain, the central theme of all government and party promises and exhortations. The symbol of the first Five-Year Plan, which was launched officially on January 1, 1949, appeared on the ramparts of Prague Castle where it could be seen from the embankment on the other side of the Vltava River: a mammoth gear wheel outlined in electric lights with a number five and a hammer and sickle in the center, contrasting strangely with the medieval panorama — one of the most beautiful urban views in the world. The incongruity evidently struck the originators of this advertising stunt, because it quickly disappeared from the Castle walls. The symbol, however, and the reality for which it stood — the first Five-Year Plan — soon dominated the life of every man, woman, and child.

Czechoslovakia had been saved the physical destruction visited by Hitler on Poland and the Soviet Union, but the

Nazi occupiers plundered its resources. The Two-Year Plan for the restoration and reconstruction of wartime damage to the economy was intended to raise production in general 10 percent, and output in some key branches 50 percent over the prewar level, and to restore the living standard to where it had been before the war. While the main industrial goals had been reached by the end of 1948, achievements in agriculture and in the food and building industries had fallen considerably short of expectations. This was due in part to the catastrophic failure of the grain harvest and of livestock production caused by a severe drought in 1947.

The goals of the Five-Year Plan were ambitious. Total industrial production was to be increased by the end of 1953 by 57 percent. It was a plan for "development and conversion" which was to lay the foundations for rebuilding the country on a new basis, making it more self-sufficient and less dependent on capitalist markets. It would, of course, require the widest possible mobilization of labor. Said Premier Antonín Zápotocký: "We shall not be able to realize fully our plans for the building of a new society nor to insure decent living standards to all members of the population until we have convinced everyone of the necessity of work, and have compelled those who do not want to be convinced to fulfill their duties. . . . This is no punishment, no force nor terror, but the free democratic right of a state which guarantees the *right* to work, to demand unconditionally the fulfillment of the *duty* to work from each and every citizen." [2]

This meant in practice that every able-bodied person of working age who was not either a student or a housewife had to be able to show that he or she was employed. Ambitious as these plans were, they were not considered hard-driving enough. It was announced that work was going ahead so fast that sights could be raised. In 1951 the overall goal for production increase in industry was raised from 57 percent to 98 percent, with an even greater speedup in the tempo of growth in heavy industry. Heavy industry output would reach 230 percent of the 1948 level in 1953, and Czechoslovakia would become sixth in the world in production of steel.

Today, when industrial growth shows signs of going out of fashion as the chief indicator of the quality of life, and smoking factory chimneys mean pollution rather than progress, it is difficult to imagine that these figures possessed a dramatic power to move. For people who had just emerged from six years of Nazi occupation, who remembered prewar poverty and unemployment, or who had worked as agricultural labor on the estates of big landowners, the idea of rapidly expanding industry operated not for profit but to provide better housing, schools, paid holidays, health, pensions for everyone was the stuff from which dreams are fashioned. There were plenty of people who had the talent and imagination to give these ideas shape in words and pictures. If the means used to realize the dreams seemed stern and rough, it was enough for Communist leaders to recall the strength of American imperialism and its determination, made public in the Truman Doctrine, to quarantine the Soviet Union and the socialist countries and to intervene in the internal affairs of any country for its own good.[3] The class struggle, Stalin taught, and people were constantly reminded, intensified with the victory of the working class: reaction was strong, its tentacles reached everywhere.

The need for manpower was intense. In 1945 the industrial work force was only 80 percent of prewar figures. The Two-Year Plan had called for the direction of 270,000 additional workers into industry, about 90,000 into building, and about 230,000 into agriculture and forestry — a total of almost 600,000 new workers out of a population of twelve million. This effort called for the absorption of all persons capable of work who had not up to now been productively employed, including as many women as possible.

At the end of 1948 employment of women was already high. Women accounted for 38 percent of all workers. This was achieved not only by compulsory employment during the Nazi occupation but by the prevailing peasant character of agriculture. Of 2,100,000 women working in 1948, 1,200,000 — or more than half — were on farms. Or to put it another way, there were four women in agriculture for every three working somewhere else. The increase in women's employment began simultaneously with a shift from the country to the cities. By 1955 women made up 42.6 percent of the labor force, by 1965, 45 percent. However, figures for the latter year show that, while the total number of working women had increased by 800,000 (or 38 percent) since 1948 to reach 2,900,000, the number in agriculture had dropped to 625,000. The total increase in the employment of women outside agriculture was therefore almost 1,400,000, or about 150 percent.

The growth of women's employment is, of course, a worldwide phenomenon, especially since World War II. By 1960, 27 percent of the world's female population over fifteen was at work, and women made up one-third of the world's work force, according to the International Labor Office in Geneva. Yet while the United States and Canada fitted this statistical description almost exactly, as did also the countries of northwestern Europe (that is, excluding Spain, Greece, Italy, and Portugal) — the countries of Eastern Europe (Albania, Bulgaria, the German Democratic Republic, Hungary, Poland, Rumania, Czechoslovakia, and Yugoslavia) had found jobs for an average of 40 percent of their women, who supplied 42 percent of their countries' labor power. In the Soviet Union, women made up 53 percent of the civilian labor force including collective farmers.

Several factors are recognized to have influenced this trend in women's employment in addition to the need for workers, and their impact has obviously been stronger in some countries than in others. Among these influences were the high wartime employment of women, the expansion of education, and a change in ideas about what constitutes the necessities of life. Although many countries suffered a postwar labor shortage, it was particularly acute in the Soviet Union, where an official estimate put the population loss at twenty million, leaving a sex ratio of 73 men to 100 women in the fifteen to forty-nine age group in 1950.

In Germany after the war the number of unmarried women of childbearing age was double that of available men. While that part of Germany later to be known as the German Democratic Republic gained some population by the transfer of ethnic Germans from the border regions of Czechoslovakia, Poland, and the Soviet Union under the Potsdam Agreement in 1945, it lost steadily through migration to West Germany until the erection of the Berlin Wall in 1961. The citizens of German origin expelled by Czechoslovakia amounted to 2½ million, or 15 percent of her population. Poland's population loss through wartime deaths, border changes, and population transfers came to seven million, or 22 percent. In addition, all these countries embarked on ambitious industrialization programs at a time when their agriculture was still at a relatively backward level, employing a much larger proportion of the work force than did the more advanced industrial countries. As men were the first to be drawn off to the cities, women took their place on the farms, where, in most cases, they accounted for and still account for more than half of all workers.[4] In Poland in 1960, for example, women made up 44 percent of the total labor force and nearly 55 percent of workers in agriculture; while in Denmark and Sweden women accounted for 30 percent of all manpower and only 9 percent of workers engaged in agriculture. The only countries which could compete with the figures of the Soviet bloc were West Germany — where women made up 36.4 percent of the labor force and 54.1 percent of agricultural labor — and Austria and Japan — where women accounted for 40 percent of total manpower and 53 percent of agricultural workers.

There are, of course, other ways of expressing the employment of women which show a great deal about the need and/or desire of women to work and their particular country's need for them: by the percentage of the female labor force which comprises married women (or women with children, or women in the childbearing age groups); or by the percentage of all married women (or women with children, etc.) in the country who are employed. Most interesting for the purpose of this book is the growth in employment of married women, and especially those in the age group most likely to plan children or to have small children already. In almost all industrialized countries today about 55 percent of employed women are married. In Czechoslovakia in 1963, 68 percent of all working women were married; 55 percent of all women with children under fourteen were employed; and 53.2 percent of all women with two children, and 45.8 percent of all women with three children, were employed. By 1969 women made up 47.2 percent of the labor force, and well over 80 percent of all women of productive age (fifteen to fifty-four) were employed, so that women had actually ceased to be a source of new manpower. Czechoslovakia now stands third in the world, after the Soviet Union and the German Democratic Republic, in the percentage of all women employed.

The need for manpower thus coincided with the introduction into official life of the theoretical concepts that only socialism could carry out the full emancipation of women, and that only economic independence and the incorporation of women into productive work could achieve this end. It has been argued that, in view of manpower needs in the socialist countries, a large degree of opportunism was involved in the inducements offered to women to leave the home, and that these countries made a virtue of necessity. Certainly there is truth in this, as discussions regarding the "overemployment" of women in Czechoslovakia in the 1960s showed. Nevertheless, it is also a matter of fact that, with the exception of the Scandinavian countries, none of the Western capitalist countries accompanied the rapid entry of women into employment with comprehensive social and political legislation designed to give them equal rights; all the socialist countries did so, basing their programs for the most part on those measures already tested in the Soviet Union.

Although many firms in West Germany, Britain, France, and elsewhere introduced attractions for women and adjusted working hours for their convenience, legislation lagged far behind the realities of the situation. A series of archaic laws continued to underline women's inferior position. In the mid-sixties a British father still had the right to determine a child's religion and education without consulting his wife. A British woman automatically took the legal domicile of her husband until 1973. In West Germany the wife was obliged by law to run the household, and the husband had the exclusive right to decide family matters where there was disagreement. A bill to amend the family code was not introduced until 1973. The Gaullists made much in the 1965 elections of the fact that the Fifth Republic had allowed French married women to open a bank account without their husbands' agreement, although the law still specified that the husband was the head of the family. Most curious, perhaps, was the position of women in Italy. Although the constitution gave her "equal rights," the legal code permitted a husband to correct his wife by beating her, to read her correspondence, to refuse to permit her to go to the cinema. Everything she earned and any inheritance she might receive belonged to him. In Milan in 1966 a man was granted a separation from his wife (divorce not being permitted) because she demanded of him that he help with the housework, an activity which he thought did not become his status as a college graduate. Equal pay for equal work did not become law in Britain until 1970, and at this writing Britain has not adopted an antidiscrimination bill. In the United States the antidiscrimination amendment to the Constitution, approved by Congress, has not yet been ratified by two-thirds of the states.

By contrast, 1948 in Czechoslovakia saw the beginning of a deluge of social legislation designed to wipe out once and for all the accumulation of traditions, ancient codes, and rulings of the Habsburg monarchy, and the palliative efforts of twenty years of the First Republic, and to replace them by modern laws. The eighteenth-century Enlightenment had endowed man, in the name of his Creator, with "certain unalienable rights" — as has been recorded for all time in the United States Declaration of Independence — among them "Life, Liberty, and the Pursuit of Happiness." The nineteenth-century socialist labor movements spelled out their demands much more specifically: bread, jobs, security, health. Without them the pursuit of happiness seemed as insubstantial as the pursuit of a beautiful butterfly. The new rights were formulated in the Soviet Constitution of 1936, and they found their way into the government statements and constitutions of the new socialist states immediately after the Second World War.

In Czechoslovakia as early as 1945 the government had declared in its Košice Program:

"

The Government will make every effort to ensure that all men and women able to work shall have the opportunity to work and to receive pay according to the work done. Working hours, wages, and other conditions of work will be safeguarded by collective agreements and protected by law. The principles of equal pay for equal work will be followed for women and young people.

The Government will see to it that all working people have security in the event of unemployment, illness, disability and old age. . . . Care for mothers and children will be a primary concern of social welfare. The costs of social insurance of all types will be met from the resources of the state budget.[5]

"

This promise was implemented in the Constitution of May 1948, which guaranteed all citizens the right to work and all working people the right to "fair remuneration for work done" and to leisure. Everyone was declared entitled to health and to social security; women, to special care during pregnancy and maternity; and young people, to conditions conducive to their physical and mental development — these rights to be secured by "national insurance laws as well as by the public health and social welfare services."

The equality of women was made part of the fundamental law of the land in Chapter I, Section 1 ("Men and women shall hold equal rights in the family and in the community and shall have equal access to education, and to all professions, offices and honors") and in Section 27 (4) ("Men and women shall be entitled to equal remuneration for equal work under the same conditions"). The family was also singled out for protection: "The institution of marriage, the family and motherhood are under the protection of the state." [6]

Earlier in 1948, after the "February Events" had broken the legislative logjam, the National Insurance Act — demanded by the trade unions and pledged by the government immediately after the war — had been passed. Czechoslovakia had had a relatively advanced prewar social insurance system, but its critics charged that it was chaotically and unfairly administered. The new act provided for a system of uniform sickness benefits and pensions for old age and disability averaging about 50 percent of wages. It included an eighteen-week maternity leave at 100 percent of wages. Medical care and drugs were free to all insured persons and their dependent relatives. Self-employed persons could contribute toward their own insurance, and in 1950 the provisions of the act were extended to some farmers.

It is not necessary here to trace all the changes that were subsequently made in the social security system, which now also provides coverage for all cooperative farmers, or 95 percent of the farm population. Basically, the system is very similar to those in force in other socialist countries, but it has developed at its own rate and is certainly one of the most all-inclusive and generous in the world. A break with insurance traditions eliminated payment by employees of premiums for either sickness insurance or pension benefits, although the size of these benefits is, of course, based on earnings. Security in old age thus became a right which the working population owed to those of its members who had done their job, and not "insurance" paid for by the individual. This was regarded as an important difference in principle, even though it may be argued that under socialism it makes little difference which pocket pays out. Retirement age was set at sixty in the case of men and fifty-five in the case of women in the original Social Security Act; this was modified in 1962 to provide differing retirement ages for women, ranging from fifty-four to fifty-seven, depending on whether they had raised three or more children, two, one, or none. These are the lowest retirement ages in the world, so low in fact that new provisions were later required to encourage pensioners to continue to work beyond the retirement age.

Sickness benefits are paid for the first three days of illness at 50–70 percent of net wages depending on length of employment, and thereafter at 60–90 percent of wages for a period of up to one year. Maternity benefits are now paid for twenty-six weeks at 90 percent of net wages (only Sweden does as well as this). In addition, the law provides for single grants on the birth of each child, grants for funeral expenses paid to survivors, orphans' pensions, widows' and widowers' pensions, and family allowances. These monthly allowances are paid to all families beginning with the birth of the first child, and increase in size with each successive child. They have been adjusted upward many times to encourage larger families, and payment of the largest allowances for the second, third, and fourth child emphasizes that the ideal family is considered to be one with no less than two and no more than four children.[7]

This legislation is unusually comprehensive and generous, even for the socialist countries. It should be pointed out, however, that most European countries now provide for some form of government-subsidized maternity leave with job security, and family allowances, and that some give single grants on the birth of a child and other forms of aid to families with children. Only in the United States has this been considered a waste of money.[8]

The first country to introduce a system of family allowances was Belgium, at the beginning of the 1930s; it was followed by France. A number of other countries followed suit between the wars, but most schemes originated after 1949 when the International Social Security Association adopted a resolution in favor of the extension of such systems to all countries. Some countries pay these allowances to all families regardless of the source of their income. In the mid–1960s these were Australia, Canada, Finland, New Zealand, Sweden (to all children), Great Britain, Ireland, Iceland (beginning with the second child), and the Soviet Union (beginning with the fourth child). Others pay allowances only to workers and employees, in most cases beginning with the first child. These countries include Belgium, France, the Netherlands, Switzerland, Austria, Italy, Luxemburg, Chile, Portugal, Spain, Israel, Cambodia, and the other socialist countries of Eastern Europe — with the exception of Czechoslovakia which, since 1964, has paid allowances to members of agricultural cooperatives as well.

These allowances represent, in Czechoslovak social policy, "not merely the solidarity . . . of society with the parents of small children, but active social policy on the part of socialist society in fulfilling one of the major tasks of its own extended reproduction. It is not philanthropy but fulfillment of the obligations . . . set forth in the Constitution." [9]

Institutions actually administering health care were separated from the insurance scheme and combined in a unified health service under the supervision of the Ministry of Health. Thus the foundations were laid for the network of clinics, hospitals, and sanatoriums which today dispense preventive health care and medical aid free of charge to 97 percent of the population. This care — in addition to outpatient and hospital treatment of all kinds, including dentistry — covers mental illness, rehabilitation, spectacles, prostheses, and drugs. Since 1951, all pre- and post-natal care has been given free of charge whether the expectant mother was covered by health insurance or not.

Many other non-cash advantages were introduced which made the benefits of socialism seem even more concrete and immediate. A worker's family which still remembered unemployment, an empty larder, the desperation of illness, and furniture in the street found itself in low-cost government-subsidized housing, with guaranteed jobs, insured against all contingencies, enjoying paid vacations provided by law, and looking forward to the possibility of sending the children to college. If all this could be accomplished within a few short years, the future could certainly be said to belong to socialism.

Free cultural facilities — workers' clubs sponsored by the trade unions — were established near plants and gave rise to amateur theater and music and dance groups of all kinds, their activities financed from plant profits. Tickets for professional theaters and for concerts and opera were within the means of the average family, and out-of-town audiences were bused to performances by their factory or farm. All these benefits in kind encouraged collective life and seemed to be harbingers of the day when the state would absorb many of the family's economic and social functions.

The new Family Law, which went into effect on January 1, 1950, was almost identical with the Polish Family Rights Act and took its inspiration from the Soviet example. As Dr. Alexej Čepička, the Minister of Justice, pointed out when introducing the bill to parliament, "The example of the Soviet family as expressed in the provisions of Soviet family legislation has been a great source of instruction in our legislative work." The burden of the minister's remarks was an impassioned defense of the bill against attacks made on it by the Catholic hierarchy and the Vatican. There was no sentiment even among intellectuals at this time, as there had been in the Soviet Union after the Revolution, for the "abolition of the family." It seemed clear that the emphasis on collective life would tend to undermine the family's importance, and in any case Communists had accepted the Soviet view of the family as the basic unit of society. Many people, of course, had no family left to abolish. Nevertheless, horror stories of the prewar decades were now revived. "In vain are all the attempts of reaction to frighten especially countrywomen with horrific tales that the new family legislation means the socialization of women and the expropriation of children. . . . The socialist order could not be built without happy marriages and a strong and happy family life," Minister Čepička assured the National Assembly.[10]

The Family Law itself, a brief and simply phrased document, read to many people like a model of common sense. One of the objections of Catholic opponents was that it required that marriage be legalized in a civil ceremony at a local registry office, only then to be followed by a church wedding if desired. More important than this, from the point of view of the parties to the ceremony, it declared that husband and wife have the same rights and duties; that all important family matters shall be decided by mutual agreement and, in case of dispute, settled by a court; and that all property except for personal belongings, inheritances, or gifts, shall be joint property. It made both parties responsible for the support of the family in a significant provision which read: "It is the duty of both the spouses to satisfy the needs of the family founded by their marriage to the limit of their capacity and in proportion to their earnings and means. The providing of means for the support of the family may be offset in part or wholly by personal care of the children and of the joint household." Likewise, "both parents have an equal duty to provide for the education and maintenance of

CHAPTER FIVE

THE AWAKENING

At first the promises of socialism seemed on the verge of fulfillment. Although at the beginning everything was in short supply, the food stores displayed chiefly garlic and vinegar, and a lemon or a bar of soap was a gift beyond price, what there was was rationed, and everyone was assured of his minimum of milk, meat, fats, sugar, shoes, and basic clothing at low prices. Additional supplies of necessities and a good many "luxuries" like tea, coffee, chocolate, and cocoa were available on the free market at prices which seemed astronomical, but were intended to siphon off black-market earnings and the excess purchasing power of miners and other privileged industrial workers. Prices did not rise as they were doing, according to press reports, in the West; on the contrary, the prices of rationed articles remained stable, and those of free-market goods dropped sharply over the next years. Day-to-day existence was hard, but the difficulties were still a challenge. A kind of euphoria gripped Communists and their supporters, for whom all the changes introduced were the products of historical necessity and held the promise of a just future. "Our eyes were blazing; we hardly had time to catch our breath. Most of us were spared the existential scepticism that plagued our generation of peers in the West. We felt that we knew how to solve human problems. We stepped from the darkness of Nazism straight into the sunny realm of freedom, friendship, and happiness — in short, so-

their child. Personal care of a child may partially or wholly offset the contribution to its maintenance and education." The law specified that neither spouse required the consent of the other to take a job or change his or her place of employment.

All these provisions represented threats to the patriarchal concept of the family as viewed by the Church, as did the paragraph permitting the parties to retain their existing surnames or to take either one for their joint surname. Even more controversial was the simple statement that in case of a "profound and permanent rift" either husband or wife could apply to the court for divorce; this was to be followed by an equal division of their jointly acquired property, with due regard paid to whether the property had actually been acquired jointly and "to whether either of the spouses had personal care of the children and the joint household."

The only obstacle to divorce sanctioned by the law was the interests of the underage children; the marriage could not be dissolved if the court decided that divorce would be detrimental to them, and divorce could not be granted until the rights and duties of both parents with respect to the child and its property had been determined for the post-divorce period. A number of provisions related to the rights of the "innocent" party, a concept which was totally abandoned when the law was amended some years later. Only the future maintenance of the child was provided for; a maintenance allowance could be awarded exceptionally to a spouse who was "not of himself (herself) able to maintain himself (herself)." The rights of children were the same whether they were born in wedlock or out of it, and paternity was defined in considerable detail, so that illegitimacy as a legal category ceased to exist.

Again assuring the clergy and the "countrywomen," the minister stressed that conditions for successful marriage would now be much better than they had been in the past, and that "the community will therefore admit the dissolution of marriage only in exceptional cases where for grave reasons a profound rift has arisen in virtue of which the marriage is unable to fulfill its basic mission." He recalled, however, that there was a "legacy" of unhappy marriages and unions which had ceased to exist except for the legal bond; these included especially those entered into during the German occupation to prevent one of the partners being sent to Germany as forced labor, as well as marriages "ruined . . . by capitalist conditions and capitalist morality."

A fourth legislative area in which the interests of women and working mothers received support was education. The establishment of a nine-year unified school system up to the legal school-leaving age of 15, with various educational avenues open after that (some of them leading to a university or technical college), was a goal for which many educators with advanced ideas had been working before the war. Private schools had been few in the prewar Republic, and public schools were on a high level, so that public opinion was prepared for this kind of a democratic solution. All school fees and charges were abolished, including those for universities, and a system of night schools and extramural studies was established to make it possible for people who were already working to complete their education. One of the results was a rapid increase in the number of women seeking higher education, as we have seen in Chapter One. While in 1955 every third girl went to work at 15 directly from the last year of compulsory school, nine out of ten girls were going on to receive further education or training in 1961.

At the other end of the educational ladder were the nurseries for children from six months to three years and the nursery schools for children from three to six. These were regarded not simply as aids for working mothers but as institutions which would be beneficial to the children, giving them the advantages of collective life and a democratic upbringing, and providing many opportunities for play and mental stimulation which they could not get while tied to mother's apron strings at home. Nursery schools were already accepted institutions for the children of needy working mothers in the nineteenth century in Bohemia and Moravia, and in 1936 there had been some 2,500 nurseries and nursery schools with a total enrollment of 104,000. After the war the network was rebuilt and expanded. In 1950 alone 14,000 places were added

in nurseries and 50,000 in nursery schools
of the year there were more than 23,000 c
and 256,000 between three and six, receivii
1967 the figures had grown to 67,000 and
schools accommodated about 10 percent and
respective age groups.

So, in the space of a few years, and with
apparent dissent, a complete social foundation
tended to give birth to a new way of life and to a
woman was moved into place. It borrowed mu
Soviet Union, but it also incorporated many of
which radical planners in Czechoslovakia had had l
the Second World War. Few people stopped to cor
completeness and luxury of this structure with the im
tions that surrounded them in daily life. The proble
volved in obtaining food, clothing, housing, fuel, in gett
work and home again, occupied too much time and er
The day-to-day political events were much more dramatic,
their impact more immediate. One Western observer v
studied the economic transition of Czechoslovakia at that tir
commented:

"

Looking back upon the various services in kind provided . . .
one is struck by the discrepancy all along the line between the level
attained by workers in that part of their consumption which had to
come out of wages, and the high level built into the services in kind.
The whole unmistakably suggested a building for the future. The idea
seemed to be that while wages in cash would have to wait upon increases in production, income in kind must lay a pattern for the future
that would not have to be done over again because of poor quality.[11]

"

their child. Personal care of a child may partially or wholly offset the contribution to its maintenance and education." The law specified that neither spouse required the consent of the other to take a job or change his or her place of employment.

All these provisions represented threats to the patriarchal concept of the family as viewed by the Church, as did the paragraph permitting the parties to retain their existing surnames or to take either one for their joint surname. Even more controversial was the simple statement that in case of a "profound and permanent rift" either husband or wife could apply to the court for divorce; this was to be followed by an equal division of their jointly acquired property, with due regard paid to whether the property had actually been acquired jointly and "to whether either of the spouses had personal care of the children and the joint household."

The only obstacle to divorce sanctioned by the law was the interests of the underage children; the marriage could not be dissolved if the court decided that divorce would be detrimental to them, and divorce could not be granted until the rights and duties of both parents with respect to the child and its property had been determined for the post-divorce period. A number of provisions related to the rights of the "innocent" party, a concept which was totally abandoned when the law was amended some years later. Only the future maintenance of the child was provided for; a maintenance allowance could be awarded exceptionally to a spouse who was "not of himself (herself) able to maintain himself (herself)." The rights of children were the same whether they were born in wedlock or out of it, and paternity was defined in considerable detail, so that illegitimacy as a legal category ceased to exist.

Again assuring the clergy and the "countrywomen," the minister stressed that conditions for successful marriage would now be much better than they had been in the past, and that "the community will therefore admit the dissolution of marriage only in exceptional cases where for grave reasons a profound rift has arisen in virtue of which the marriage is unable to fulfill its basic mission." He recalled, however, that there was a "legacy" of unhappy marriages and unions which had ceased to exist except for the legal bond; these included especially those entered into during the German occupation to prevent one of the partners being sent to Germany as forced labor, as well as marriages "ruined . . . by capitalist conditions and capitalist morality."

A fourth legislative area in which the interests of women and working mothers received support was education. The establishment of a nine-year unified school system up to the legal school-leaving age of 15, with various educational avenues open after that (some of them leading to a university or technical college), was a goal for which many educators with advanced ideas had been working before the war. Private schools had been few in the prewar Republic, and public schools were on a high level, so that public opinion was prepared for this kind of a democratic solution. All school fees and charges were abolished, including those for universities, and a system of night schools and extramural studies was established to make it possible for people who were already working to complete their education. One of the results was a rapid increase in the number of women seeking higher education, as we have seen in Chapter One. While in 1955 every third girl went to work at 15 directly from the last year of compulsory school, nine out of ten girls were going on to receive further education or training in 1961.

At the other end of the educational ladder were the nurseries for children from six months to three years and the nursery schools for children from three to six. These were regarded not simply as aids for working mothers but as institutions which would be beneficial to the children, giving them the advantages of collective life and a democratic upbringing, and providing many opportunities for play and mental stimulation which they could not get while tied to mother's apron strings at home. Nursery schools were already accepted institutions for the children of needy working mothers in the nineteenth century in Bohemia and Moravia, and in 1936 there had been some 2,500 nurseries and nursery schools with a total enrollment of 104,000. After the war the network was rebuilt and expanded. In 1950 alone 14,000 places were added in nurseries and 50,000 in nursery schools, so that by the end of the year there were more than 23,000 children under three, and 256,000 between three and six, receiving all-day care. By 1967 the figures had grown to 67,000 and 356,000, and these schools accommodated about 10 percent and 55 percent of the respective age groups.

So, in the space of a few years, and with a minimum of apparent dissent, a complete social foundation which was intended to give birth to a new way of life and to a new man and woman was moved into place. It borrowed much from the Soviet Union, but it also incorporated many of the dreams which radical planners in Czechoslovakia had had long before the Second World War. Few people stopped to contrast the completeness and luxury of this structure with the improvisations that surrounded them in daily life. The problems involved in obtaining food, clothing, housing, fuel, in getting to work and home again, occupied too much time and energy. The day-to-day political events were much more dramatic, and their impact more immediate. One Western observer who studied the economic transition of Czechoslovakia at that time commented:

"

Looking back upon the various services in kind provided . . . one is struck by the discrepancy all along the line between the level attained by workers in that part of their consumption which had to come out of wages, and the high level built into the services in kind. The whole unmistakably suggested a building for the future. The idea seemed to be that while wages in cash would have to wait upon increases in production, income in kind must lay a pattern for the future that would not have to be done over again because of poor quality.[11]

"

THE AWAKENING

A t first the promises of socialism seemed on the verge of fulfillment. Although at the beginning everything was in short supply, the food stores displayed chiefly garlic and vinegar, and a lemon or a bar of soap was a gift beyond price, what there was was rationed, and everyone was assured of his minimum of milk, meat, fats, sugar, shoes, and basic clothing at low prices. Additional supplies of necessities and a good many "luxuries" like tea, coffee, chocolate, and cocoa were available on the free market at prices which seemed astronomical, but were intended to siphon off black-market earnings and the excess purchasing power of miners and other privileged industrial workers. Prices did not rise as they were doing, according to press reports, in the West; on the contrary, the prices of rationed articles remained stable, and those of free-market goods dropped sharply over the next years. Day-to-day existence was hard, but the difficulties were still a challenge. A kind of euphoria gripped Communists and their supporters, for whom all the changes introduced were the products of historical necessity and held the promise of a just future. "Our eyes were blazing; we hardly had time to catch our breath. Most of us were spared the existential scepticism that plagued our generation of peers in the West. We felt that we knew how to solve human problems. We stepped from the darkness of Nazism straight into the sunny realm of freedom, friendship, and happiness — in short, socialism. We considered anyone who failed to understand this as a reactionary bourgeois — everything was clear and simple." This is the way one well-known journalist, now fifty, describes his generation, looking back now, half a lifetime later.

The future lay with heavy industry, destined to solve the country's problems. Now it was understandably turning out coal and steel; later, the press explained, it would produce farm machinery, cars, and refrigerators. "I am a miner, who is more?" This slogan appeared on recruiting posters all over the country, the grimy but proud visage of a miner fresh from the coal face, in his characteristic helmet, calling other young men to the mines. In recognition of their arduous job and their importance to the economy, miners not only received the highest pay, but had the longest holidays and the best recreation facilities, and were eligible for pension at an earlier age than other workers.

Steel workers were almost on a par with miners, and the steel industry accepted women. In 1951 the United Steel Works in Kladno issued a call for women to become welders, lathe operators, crane operators, and engine drivers, with the promise of three times the pay they had been earning as dressmakers or office workers after a few weeks of training. Newspapers reported human interest stories about women who took jobs at the furnace, a position previously open only to men, and were earning as much as the best of them. The United Steel Works was offering more reluctant housewives part-time jobs, and advertised that it had opened three nurseries and two nursery schools for the children of working women. It had also established three school lunchrooms and a laundry, and planned a service open from 6 A.M. to 10 P.M. where women could leave their shopping bags and lists on their way to work and pick up their purchases on the way home.

Of course most women went into light industry, but there they began to be discovered in executive positions which previously had been reserved for men. At the Orion chocolate factory in Prague a woman who had been employed in the plant since 1923 became plant manager, on the suggestion of her fellow workers, at the age of forty-two. She told an inquiring reporter: "I was one of nine children. We lived eleven in one room. Our clothes were passed down from one to another. If we got a sausage it was a great treat. Now I can buy what I want, eat as much as I want. I have my own one-room apartment with all modern conveniences. Last summer I spent my vacation in Rumania on the Black Sea in the former summer palace of King Carol." The fact that she had become an executive made her unusual, but as far as the holiday was concerned hers was not a unique case.

A municipally operated enterprise with the poetic name of the Liberated Household was established and promised to lighten the tasks of working women. It offered a laundry service which included collection at the factory or office, if necessary, and promised to do mending. It was also ready to provide housecleaning services, either on a regular basis or for special jobs like polishing floors or washing windows. When it opened a fully mechanized laundry, the largest in Czechoslovakia, it declared war on torn shirts, lost buttons, and white sheets stained by red socks. It even advertised a special laundry marker which used an ink visible only under a special light, and it boasted that its machines could handle 1,500 pounds of wash every two hours. The management pointed out that it employed 98 percent women, who were working in clean, well-lighted halls supplied with lockers, showers, a canteen, and music while they worked. Each of them, it was said, liberated eighty other women from washtub drudgery, which was easy to believe, since at that time all washing was done by hand.

A chain of shops began to offer prepared dishes and cuts of meat ready to cook, which caused something of a sensation in the days when poultry was still sold as nature made it, except for the feathers. Shopping hours were adjusted everywhere, by agreement between the Ministry of Trade and the Union of Retail Trade Workers, so that dairies were open from six to six, and other food stores from seven to seven; in every neighborhood there were some shops open through the lunch hour.

These were years in which successes were emphasized and problems swept under the carpet. International Women's Day was celebrated every year on March 8 as a substitute for the capitalist Mother's Day, with little ceremonies in plants and offices where women were thanked for their part in building the economy and were treated to sandwiches and coffee, while "best workers" received books or other small gifts. An inevitable accompaniment to this day was speeches and editorials which reviewed the long struggle for women's rights. The privileges which socialist women now enjoyed were contrasted with the difficulties of women in capitalist lands, where equal pay for equal work was not guaranteed by law, where nursery schools were a rarity, and where medical care was a luxury; special emphasis was placed on the plight of women and their children in the colonial and semicolonial countries. The self-satisfied tone of these pronouncements was tiresome, the posters of smiling farm women with a child on one arm and a sheaf of wheat on the other were naïve, but one could not argue with the facts: 50,000 new places in nursery schools in 1950; 83,000 women added to the industrial force in the same year; 24,000 women already working advanced to better jobs. In 1951 the number of primary-school children receiving hot lunches doubled, 63 of 368 members of the National Assembly were women . . .

The year 1953 was a kind of watershed. A currency reform coincided with the abolition of rationing and officially marked the end of the postwar economic emergency. In September the government passed a series of sweeping measures aimed at speeding up work on the Five-Year Plan, including the production of consumer goods. A large part of the government decree was devoted to improving the quantity and quality of consumer goods and services and the production of many items which had not been adequately supplied, including household articles, tools, and farm implements. More meat, bakery products, soap, cosmetics, and better supplies of milk were promised. Synthetic fabrics would be introduced, home washing-machines and refrigerators, more and better and cleaner shops and restaurants. To advance the improvement of services to the consumer, a Ministry of Local Economy was established to sponsor the setting up of municipally operated small plants using local raw materials and scrap from large factories to meet local needs.

They were to see that every residential neighborhood, and especially new housing projects and farm villages, had their laundries, dry-cleaning establishments, shoe-repair services, hairdressers, photographic studios, dressmakers and tailors, building repair and maintenance services, and so on. Even independent plumbers, electricians, and other craftsmen, where they still existed, were to receive encouragement in the form of better access to materials and lower taxes.

Best of all, perhaps, extensive and continuous marketing research would be instituted to find out what people wanted and thus see to it that changing demands were met.

The year 1953 was also the year in which Stalin died, his police chief, Beria, was arrested, and the "doctors' plot" in the Soviet Union was admitted to have been a frame-up. These events heralded the beginning of sober realization that there were many things below the surface of a planned society that had not been planned and that needed explaining. Khrushchev's famous "secret speech" to the Twentieth Congress of the Communist party of the Soviet Union in 1956, in which he revealed some of the excesses of Stalinism, was presented to Czechoslovaks in a very diluted form, but this was enough to spark a wave of agonizing reappraisal in which every individual began to reevaluate his own experiences and to consider everything he had heard, seen, or been told in a new light. Although only a fraction of this feeling came to the surface and could be expressed in public life, the rest remained not far below and was sifted and analyzed year after year, as persons of every persuasion — those dedicated to socialism, those for whom socialism was simply the status quo, those for whom it meant a career, those who opposed it, and those who had known nothing else — tried to come to terms with their new knowledge, with the whole amorphous body of anonymous public activity labeled "cult of the personality," to which all mistakes could now be officially ascribed.

The Soviet writer Ilya Ehrenburg called his novel written in this period *The Thaw,* evoking a picture of the melting of ice and the running of rivers that precedes spring. The first signs of thaw were the admissions of error, and this implied the possibility of criticism, of humor and satire. The first targets were the nameless little people — petty bureaucrats, narrow-minded cooperative-farm chairmen, small officials who handed down pronouncements on art, science, and international affairs in pseudo-Marxist lingo. And then there were the municipal services: the laundries which took a month to return the wash and kept the buttons, the plumbers who took six weeks to answer a call while the customer stood with his finger in the leak, the shops that sold skis only in summer and bathing suits only in winter, elevators marked Out of Order and buildings carrying the warning Falling Plaster — all were fair game for the satire which began to blossom in the press and on the stage and screen.

In spite of promises and decrees, and in spite of this "municipal humor" (so called because no one higher than a local plant director or local government official could be criticized), day-to-day conditions remained very difficult. Coal shortages inevitably occurred during the worst periods of winter frost, and burst pipes often added absence of running water to the discomfort of cold rooms. Gas and electricity supplies were frequently disrupted during peak cooking hours. Food shortages and faulty distribution made shopping a major problem. Working women left the house early and returned late, but the customer who was not on hand when the vegetables were delivered could not count on having any. Stores were the small, crowded shops which had served the prewar generation, and pressure on them was increased by the closing of the outdoor markets at which small farmers had previously sold their produce. Queues of shoppers waiting for such ordinary necessities as potatoes and onions stretched out into the street. There was hardly a staple which did not at one time or another mysteriously disappear from the market for a protracted period, due to complicated chains of circumstances which were eventually reported in the press to have been corrected, but always seemed to re-form somewhere else. The convenience foods which had made such a brave start were hard to find and expensive; their producers also complained of lack of raw materials and manpower.

Women were, of course, expected to play a part in correcting the problems which plagued them, but not through the Union of Czechoslovak Women. This organization had been formed after the war and had worked through community branches, which, it was said, drew their membership primarily from among urban housewives (although working women were indirectly affiliated through trade unions). In 1952 this organization had agreed that it had served its purpose and had been dissolved, except for a kind of front office, a "roof organization," known as the Czechoslovak Women's Committee. This one-hundred-member body, elected by a national conference of women, continued to represent Czechoslovakia at international women's meetings, to play host to foreign delegations, to publish two women's magazines in Czech and Slovak, and to call conferences from time to time.

There were several reasons given for disbanding the Union. One was that the socialist labor movement had historically identified the problems of women with those of the working class as a whole. As will be remembered, Lenin had expressed himself to Clara Zetkin in 1920 as being opposed to special organizations for women. "We derive our organizational ideas from our ideological conceptions. We want no separate organizations of communist women! She who is a communist belongs as a member to the Party, just as he who is a Communist," he told her.[1] No such women's union existed in the Soviet Union, and in Czechoslovakia it was considered to be a vestige of the immediate postwar period of compromise. Besides, the major conditions for women's liberation having been met, it was said that the "woman question" as such no longer existed. Women had equal status in the home, the community, and at work; they had equal access to education and to public honors. Women now served as trade union executives and were elected to national committees, the local government councils at town, district, and regional levels; they could use their positions to protect women's gains and to bring about improvements. However, since Lenin had recognized that the party needed working groups or committees whose duty it was to bring the masses of women workers into contact with the party, women's committees were to be attached directly to municipal, district, and regional councils, and were to be elected by the women of the community from a list of capable women prepared by the local council. These women's committees, it was argued, would be close to the community and would be able to play a much more direct role in solving women's problems. They would succeed in involving many more women in activity, and their recommendations would go straight to the appropriate council to be acted upon.

Among their responsibilities was assuring that more services for women were organized, that shopping hours suited women's needs, that the rights of the consumer were looked after, that after-school care for children was satisfactory. They were also to persuade women to take a more active part in public life and to combat the remnants of old ideas about the inferiority of women. At the same time, one of the major tasks given them was the recruiting of women workers for agriculture and industry. In the villages they helped to persuade women of the advantages of cooperative farming; to mobilize women to help bring in the sugar beet and potato crops on time; to recommend the most capable women for training as agronomists or tractor-drivers, or for placement in other skilled jobs.

When women took part, as they often did, in peace meetings to protest the war in Korea, the danger of nuclear warfare, or the remilitarization of West Germany, they appealed to their fellow women to "strengthen the camp of peace and socialism by helping to build their country through their own work."

Within six months 10,000 such committees had been set up in approximately 80 percent of all Czechoslovak communities. Though they had many tasks, they had no authority and nothing to say about how funds were spent. Their recommendations were appreciated but rarely acted upon because pressing industrial tasks specified by the national economic plan had first priority, and after that local industries had urgent financial and manpower needs; municipal services got the leavings, and voluntary brigades who were ready to improve their neighborhoods could not be supplied with the basic do-it-yourself materials. In the towns, particularly, the women became discouraged with the results of their efforts.

The difficulties encountered by women in industry were one of the points on the agenda of the Fourth Trade Union Congress in 1959. The economic plan required an additional 420,000 to 480,000 workers by 1975, of whom 200,000 would be housewives and the rest new school graduates — including, of course, girls. Bedřich Kozelka, secretary of the Central Council of Trade Unions, and Marie Trojanová, secretary of the Prague Council, reported at length on the problems these women faced to two hundred women delegates called together by the Women's Committee.

One of the points raised by the Trade Union Congress, he told them, was that most women were unskilled or semiskilled, while only a fraction were highly skilled. More than 60 percent of women in industry were in the three lowest of the eight wage categories applied in industry on a national scale, while only 8 percent of men workers were to be found there. So while women received equal pay for equal work, they were not actually doing equal work and earned on the average one-third less than men.

The solution which had been suggested at the congress was more factory schools for raising workers' qualifications, with courses arranged at hours convenient for housewives. Unions were to "insist" that such schools be made a point in every annual collective agreement signed with management. Regional trade union councils together with managements of larger plants were to examine possibilities for the establishment of training schemes for women before they took up employment.

Mrs. Trojanová pointed to another aspect of the difficulty: the relatively small number of girls who were specializing in technical subjects, either at the vocational schools or at the college level — one out of six students in the first case and one out of seven in the second. "Why?" she asked. "Are girls less capable in these subjects?" The parents are the problem, she concluded. Somehow their old-fashioned ideas should be corrected so that they would encourage their daughters to seek a more unconventional future.

Some of the things that the trade union bodies at the plant level, which negotiated directly with management, were to "insist upon" were mechanization of minor operations and organizational changes so that women would not have to lift heavy weights or stand when they could just as well sit. Because old plants had been built almost exclusively for men, and new ones without special regard for the needs of women, local trade union bodies were to "see to it" that at least minimum facilities in old plants, and maximum conveniences in new ones, were written into collective agreements for 1960 or for the third Five-Year Plan (1961–65). They were also "finally" to solve the question of what to do about the small child who is kept home from school with a minor illness, and thus reduce the absenteeism of employed mothers — one cause of employer prejudice against women workers. It was suggested that local Red Cross branches seek out older women who would like occasional employment and who would be under contract to the plant to act as baby-sitters. Finally, the unions must not let management find excuses for not offering women part-time work where desirable — a six-hour shift beginning at 8 A.M., for example, so that mothers would have time to get their children off to school. Arrangements should also be made so that women would not have to work night shifts or overtime. Women themselves should take an active part in bringing about these improvements through the women's committees and the trade unions, and should come up with concrete proposals. "Fine words," said Marie Trojanová, "won't build one nursery school, won't improve the works canteen, won't raise the qualifications of our women." [2]

Undoubtedly one of the most important catalysts in bringing the developing conflict between the rights of women and the possibilities for exercising them into the open for national debate was the passage in December 1957 of a law legalizing abortion. The impact of this legislation will be discussed in more detail later, but here it should be pointed out that this was not an individual action by Czechoslovakia (although it was presented strictly in terms of Czechoslovak needs), but part of a general action by all the socialist countries. In 1955, the Soviet Union restored to women the right (which had been withdrawn in 1936) to decide for themselves whether they wanted to be mothers. This was followed in 1956 by the promulgation of laws — some more permissive than others — allowing abortion on social as well as medical grounds in Bulgaria, Poland, Hungary, and Rumania, and finally in Czechoslovakia in 1957. The German Democratic Republic, which had modified its liberal legislation of 1947 in 1950, did not introduce any changes at this time.

The major reason given for this step was to control widespread illegal abortion practices. Czechoslovakia had introduced abortion for medical and eugenic reasons in 1952, but the number of illegal abortions performed annually was estimated to be 100,000. Discussion in the press of the impending legislation resulted almost immediately in a more liberal interpretation of medical indications: there were 7,300 legal abortions performed in 1957 — more than double the number carried out in the previous year — while the number of "other" abortions (hospital admissions for "spontaneous" abortions) remained at about 30,000. In 1958, the first year of the new law, the number of legal abortions rose to 61,400, while the number of "other" dropped by only 3,000. From that year on, the number of legal abortions climbed steadily to 94,300 in 1961, and the total number of known abortions in that year was 110,000. Obviously the law was doing more than legalizing abortions which would have been induced illegally anyway, since the birthrate dropped rapidly, from 20.3 per one thousand inhabitants in 1955 to 15.9 in 1960 — a loss of about 140,000 births for the five-year period. This decrease would be felt in the labor force in the early 1970s and would be projected into the future, of course, in the form of fewer potential parents.

Clearly a strong reluctance to reproduce had developed in the population, which was quite out of keeping with the Marxist assumption that security and prospects for an even better future would engender a desire for children in the kind of people who, in the past, had not wanted them because they felt they would not be able to provide for them. Young couples had been infected with a kind of consumerism obviously imported from the West, it was said. They wanted nylon sweaters and transistor radios and cars and summer cottages and trips abroad, and they put these materialistic desires ahead of having children. When we were young, we were happy when we could take a bicycle trip to the country on Sunday; this was the tone of numerous remonstrative articles and speeches which began to be read and heard in the early 1960s.

Official concern had begun to be apparent. A new Constitution was promulgated on July 11, 1960, the Constitution of 1948 having become "obsolete in the best sense of the word: its purpose had been fulfilled." [3] Among other changes incorporated into the new document was the introduction of an article reading: "The equal status of women in the family, at work, and in public life shall be secured by special adjustment of working conditions and special health care during pregnancy and maternity, as well as by the development of facilities and services which will enable women fully to participate in the life of society." As a Czech specialist in family law has pointed out, this passage emphasizes that the declaration of women's equality is not enough, that it is necessary also to establish the principle of implementation of women's right to equality by state authorities. It gave women, in addition to the constitutional right to work on an equal basis with men, the right to the conditions which would make this possible.

None of these changes in attitude would have been possible if it had not been for the gradual rehabilitation of the social sciences — particularly sociology, demography, and psychology — following the Twentieth Congress of the Soviet Communist party in 1956, which made it possible to examine in a more objective fashion the extent to which life had deviated from the blueprints.[4] According to the simple economic determinism which had prevailed, social problems had their roots in private property and in the dog-eat-dog social relationships born of capitalism.

They would automatically be solved when socialism was ushered in. When cheating, stealing, prejudices, discrimination, selfishness, and individualism did not disappear, this was attributed to remnants of capitalism in men's thinking or to the ideological penetration of the West — "cosmopolitanism," as it was called. Since figures were not made public, no one actually knew how widespread crime, mental illness, prostitution, and other signs of social malaise were; and the particular cases of divorce or suicide known to any individual could be dismissed as exceptions. When in 1957 government statistics began to be published, research institutes sprang up to investigate conditions and opinions in every field, and journalists enthusiastically conducted polls and surveys and invited experts to participate in round tables. While acceptance of the socialist order was one of the rules of debate, and criticism was never to be directed at individual ministers or leaders, it was possible within this framework to make good the lack of facts and to attempt an interpretation. One of the most important agencies contributing specifically to the clarification of women's problems was the State Population Commission, appointed in 1958 as an advisory body to the government; its main task was to investigate why the birthrate was dropping and to recommend measures that would reverse this undesirable trend. The Commission's tiny paid staff, together with a group of demographers, economists, doctors, educators, and statisticians whose cooperation was enlisted — and with the help of existing research organizations — carried out investigations which led to sometimes surprising conclusions; these concerned such matters as the living conditions of families with several children, the problems of young married couples, housing, services, and many related subjects. The group began to publish its findings in 1961 and to popularize them in the press and on radio and TV. One survey made at this time showed that a woman with two children typically spent 9 hours a day in work and travel; 5 to 5½ hours in shopping and housework; a maximum of 1½ hours on her children; and 1 hour and 40 minutes on herself, including any reading, self-education, or sport she might indulge in. After that she dropped into bed for 6 hours of sleep. Her husband had 4 more hours of free time per day than she did. Where was she to find time for "raising her qualifications," for keeping up with developments in her field, or for taking an active part in public affairs?

Among other early findings by the State Population Com-

mission in a study of 1,886 young urban couples who applied
for marriage licenses at the end of 1963 were these: that 25 percent of the women were already pregnant, that almost 60
percent of all the engaged pairs planned to live temporarily
with one or the other set of parents, and that another 20 percent would have to live apart for the time being. Most of the
couples had no savings, and the vast majority believed that
they would eventually get state apartments. They did not seem
to be aware that state housing was sufficient only to replace
dwellings that had to be demolished and to relieve cases of
urgent need involving families living in substandard dwellings.
The housing shortage alone would be enough to discourage
families from having more than one child, the Commission
concluded, for even couples who had the money to buy into a
cooperative or purchase a house had to face a wait of many
years before they could move in.

But still another upheaval was in store for conventional
socialist thinking. While respect for the family was emphasized
and the rights and responsibilities of the family were stressed
in the Constitution and in family law, it was axiomatic for
postwar socialist society that man prospers in a collective under
all circumstances because it educates him to look outward
toward society and to use his abilities for society's benefit, correcting tendencies to egoism and selfishness associated with
capitalist individualism. Thus the child, and even the infant,
could only benefit from being educated in the spirit of the new
society from his earliest years and in the company of his peers
— learning to give and take and work with others. Psychological
problems were interpreted in the light of the teachings of the
Russian physiologist and experimental psychologist I. P. Pavlov
(1849–1936) concerning the role of the central nervous system
in mediating the individual's response to new experience. This
theory was applied with the same one-sided, oversimplified
fervor in the socialist countries that characterized the use of
Freud's teachings in the United States at this time. The physical, the palpable, the material were real and primary; the brain
was simply highly organized matter; and the subconscious could
not exist. Badly conditioned reflexes could be reconditioned by

the proper training and the proper environment. Other schools of psychology had been demoted by Stalin to the status of bourgeois pseudosciences and could not be discussed. No official cognizance could be taken of the findings of Bowles and others, or of World Health Organization reports, concerning the effect on small children of prolonged hospitalization or institutional life, and their need for emotional security through firm ties in the earliest months of life with the mother or other nurturing person. Nor was much weight given to the possibility that not all children start life with the same chances, because this could all be made good by environment. Nevertheless, a number of pediatricians, child psychologists, and directors of children's homes had drawn their own conclusions from Czechoslovak conditions and were familiar with work done elsewhere. While they were not ready to extend their findings to include condemnation of nurseries and nursery schools, in the new atmosphere of questioning and search they began to call for a reevaluation of the importance of family life — with emphasis on the importance of the mother to the child — and for a reexamination of the policy of encouraging institutional care. They pointed out that collective life had its advantages, certainly, but as an adjunct to, not as a substitute for, family life. The nursery should be planned for the benefit of the child, not for the convenience of the adults, they said. Further, one could not leave every child under the age of three in a nursery for eight or more hours a day without anticipating some emotional or physical reaction. This conclusion represented a complete reversal of what the public and the pediatricians had been asked to believe until then and, together with the discovery that many young couples were not having children, eroded optimism concerning women's emancipation.

The results of the second Five-Year Plan were heralded as a success. Industrial production had increased by 66 percent between 1956 and 1960, or 12 percent more than had been planned. The average wage had risen, and real purchasing power had been improved by four price cuts; the average calorie intake had surpassed the recommended level of 3,000 daily. While at the beginning of the Plan years one vacuum cleaner served 30 people; one semiautomatic washing machine, 10; one refrigerator, 108; and one TV set, 139 people; by 1960 there was a vacuum cleaner for every 14 people, a washing machine for every 6, a refrigerator for every 30 people, and a TV set in every fifth family. The number of doctors and dentists had increased from one per 718 to one per 571 inhabitants, and 97 percent of the population was receiving free medical care. Yet the third Five-Year Plan began badly. Economic failures in 1961 and 1962 revealed such far-reaching and unexpected weaknesses in the whole system of planning and management that the entire plan was scrapped. Annual planning was continued, however, while economic reforms were worked out which were put into practice beginning in 1966.

The stage was set for a critical appraisal of women's position, going much deeper than the alternating complaints and reassurances that had characterized the end of the 1950s. Just when the American woman was starting to look around her and discover that her next-door neighbor felt as frustrated and unfulfilled as she did, the Czechoslovak woman was beginning to realize that the woman next door felt as overworked and exhausted as she did. Her day was never-ending, she had somehow lost track of her children, she spent as much time on her household as she ever had, she had too many responsibilities to try for a better job — and most of them went to men anyway. A pretty blond young journalist, obviously pregnant and serving on a panel of experts at an "open forum on marriage and the family" held in Prague in 1963, received a round of applause from an audience of eight hundred when she said, "There is an unresolved conflict between the need of a mother to express herself in a job and the need of a child for its mother." A woman spokesman for the Ministry of Health remarked on this same occasion: "If there are more neurotic women than men it is not because they have won equality but because they have *not yet* won equality. So far they have only an equal right to work."

Typical of the kind of discussion held for the benefit of professionals was a seminar on the position of women in socialist society in Brno in April 1965, sponsored jointly by the So-

ciety for the Dissemination of Political and Scientific Knowledge (popularly known as the Society with the Long Name),
the Czechoslovak Women's Committee, and the State Population Commission. More than a dozen experts, most of them
from research institutions with statistics at their disposal and
the majority — but not all — of them women, pointed to the
disparity between the declarations of principles and intentions
and the reality. One of the chief speakers, Libuše Háková, a
sociologist and instructor at the College of Marxism-Leninism,
commented:

"

The substitution of the ideal model for the concrete state of
affairs, so typical for the period of the "cult of the personality," has
not only been reflected in the theoretical approach to the "woman
question" but has had a marked effect on practice. For many years
theory was silently based on the assumption that — in conformity with
generally known statements by the classics of Marxism — the basic
liberation of woman had been achieved by the victory of the socialist
revolution, and that legislative action guaranteeing woman equal right
in economic, political and family spheres was sufficient to confirm
that emancipation. Eyes were closed to conflicting practice which
offered a much less ideal picture. . . . The mental and often physical
exertion required of a woman who wants to excel in her occupation
and keep step with her male colleagues discourages many other
women who, in addition, appraise the material and spiritual rewards
for this effort very realistically. . . . Even if the abolition of private
ownership of the means of production and other revolutionary changes
in our society have undermined the roots of the subordinate position
of women in the family, other circumstances — primarily the level of
the forces of production under socialism — have resulted in the fact
that the contemporary family is heavily branded by the previous
period and that within it there are combined, in an extremely in-
harmonious fashion, the old features of the typical petty bourgeois
family and new aspects.

"

Jiří Prokopec of the State Population Commission added:

"

I have been thinking about what we, contemporary men in this
second half of the twentieth century are asking of women and I have
concluded that our demands are considerable. We want them first of

all to be good wives, good lovers, to take exemplary care of the magic of the domestic hearth, and to devote no less care to the children and to the family. Besides this primary requirement, we want a much higher level of intellectual understanding between them and ourselves than formerly, and we want women together with us men to help attain that burgeoning living standard whose ladder is ever steeper and whose requirements are increasing, that is, to share in the economic security of the family.

It seems to me that in the race to keep up with the constantly increasing tempo of civilization we have for a time lost sight of why we are doing all this, that the price we are paying is sometimes extremely high. The tremendous expansion of women's employment is something we have to only a very small degree succeeded in harmonizing with the goal towards which we are aiming, a happy and balanced life for the individual and for society.

,,

And finally a spokesman for the Central Committee of the Communist party:

``

Our education — by which I mean Party education and educational programs in mass organizations — owes a tremendous debt to the woman question. We still have many officials in the villages and factories who have an almost feudal attitude toward their own wives. . . . I think it would be quite difficult for the newly established Sociological Institute to begin by trying to solve the woman question in all its complexity. . . . It is necessary for us all to see to it that sociology, economy, philosophy, and all scientific disciplines contribute their part, because women are an organic part of our society and because the economic, scientific, and emotional sides of their development are closely bound to that of men.[5]

,,

Even though all women's problems might be closely tied to those of men and were basically part of the general human condition, it no longer seemed likely that individual manifestations of these problems in factories or communities would receive attention — no matter how many surveys and studies might be made — without a woman's organization to push for it. In 1962 the Communist party at its Twelfth Congress had still announced with characteristic assurance:

"

We will continue to raise the living standard of families with children and a low per capita income by placing an increasing burden for the expense of the education and care of children on society. This is also connected with the growth of the employment of women. It is assumed that the capacity of nurseries and nursery schools will grow so that it will be possible to accommodate 70–75 percent of children between three and five years of age, and so that by 1970 about 85 percent of the children of employed mothers will eat in school. . . . The extension and improvement of services must, among other things, help to free women from the most arduous household work. This includes the development of those services which insure the maintenance of dwellings, and necessary repairs to the equipment of a modern household. . . .[6]

"

In 1963, the women's committees attached to local councils in towns had been dissolved, although they remained at the district and regional level and in the farm villages and the smallest communities. Again the reason given was that there was no separate "woman's question" and there were enough other organizations through which women could express themselves. Yet less than a year later came the first admission that this was not true. The Czechoslovak Women's Committee, that head without a body, responded to a "decision on ideological work" by the Central Committee of the Communist Party by holding a two-day discussion at which it decided (in the words of a brief news item which appeared in one of the morning papers in January 1964) "to put an end to the incorrect ideas on the woman question dating from the period of the cult of the personality" and to "solve the problems of women in connection with the economic, cultural, and moral problems of society." To this end it agreed to set up commissions of experts who were to concern themselves with the problems of women in industry, in the family and society, and in agriculture, and, with the aid of these commissions and the magazines which it published, to conduct research and plan campaigns on the two problems which it considered most urgent: women's qualifications and their participation in public life. Finally, in 1965, one of the "theses" put forward for public discussion in preparation for the Thirteenth Party Congress in 1966 was the proposition that a "firmer organizational basis" was necessary to coordinate the women's movement if the activity of women in economic, political, and cultural life was to be intensified, and that the previous way of doing things "did not correspond to present tasks." Or as the more plain-speaking women who took part in district meetings put it, the women's committees were chiefly concerned with helping national committees to fulfill their economic assignments, and much less concerned with the specific problems of women. In fact, these committees had not changed their way of working since they were established more than a decade ago, and "weren't making any progress."

Complaints poured forth at these meetings: about women's double shift; about the low level of all services and their practical nonexistence in farm villages, where life was described as lagging farther and farther behind city existence. Although women made up more than half of farm workers, new cooperative buildings lacked the most primitive hygienic facilities; farm life was without attraction for young people; alcoholism was a growing problem. In one district where 6,400 women were employed in crop and livestock production, only 120 were found to be serving in the administration of farms. In another, not a single woman chairman of a farm cooperative could be located. The factories? Yes, they hired women, but again the most necessary social and cultural facilities were lacking. Working hours weren't suitable: most women had to be at work at 6 A.M.; children had to be awakened at dawn and taken to nursery school. Yet other women did not want to change the hours because they had to be home in time to shop, cook, and do the housework. Women pointed out that they were employed for heavy work in jobs which were so badly paid that no man would do them. If men had to clean railway cars the work would have been mechanized long ago; as it was, women were still doing the job with buckets and rags. The fact that 80 percent of employees of retail shops were women meant that women were daily shifting hundreds of pounds of weight in the form of crates and boxes not designed for their smaller stature. Longer shopping hours introduced as a convenience to women were a burden to the predominantly female personnel behind the counter. "They talk about unhealthy feminization of certain branches as though it were our fault," these women complained. "Are we stopping men from working in the school system, the health services, in retail trade, or on farms?" One irate delegate set the mood for organizational change when she snapped, "The men have had plenty of time and opportunity to help us solve our problems — we can't wait any more."

The Party Congress of 1966 came and went. It ushered in a new Five-Year Plan and a new system of economic planning and management described by Premier Jozef Lenart, a member of the party presidium, as combining central planning and market relations, and permitting more individual initiative and responsibility with corresponding financial rewards. In the autumn of 1966 the Women's Committee announced its intention of establishing a Czechoslovak Union of Women, whose activity would be directed toward a "fundamentally socialist conception of the solution of the woman question." The chairman of the Women's Committee, Helena Leflerová, referring to the job that had been done recruiting women for industry and agriculture in the past, told a press conference preceding the refounding of the Union in July, 1967: "We fulfilled our tasks too well. The problems have grown up right over our heads." And later, at the founding congress, she added: "Practice proved to be quite different from our theoretical conceptions. . . . Our aim is to contribute to solving the conflict between the rights which socialist society offers women and the limited possibility of realizing them." The new Union, which planned to work as a mass organization without formal membership or dues, said that it wanted to "create a progressive climate of opinion" regarding women's desire to be active outside the home, and to fight the tendency to solve problems by sending women back to the kitchen by undertaking:

1. To press for part-time work for women where desirable, and to fight both the tendency to give lower-paid jobs to women and outright violations of the law guaranteeing equal pay for equal work

2. To investigate pay levels in those fields where the employment of women is highest

3. To pay special attention to raising women's qualifica-

tions and to organize short-term courses for women who have had to interrupt employment

4. To investigate why more women do not hold top jobs and positions in public life

When one looks back at the discussions that filled the pages of the newspapers, magazines, and learned journals; inspired round tables and open forums; provided meat for radio and TV programs; and enlivened coffee breaks and family give-and-takes in the late 1960s; they group themselves around five general themes:

1. The general desirability of women's employment on a mass scale. Do women really want to work? Does it really give them a feeling of emancipation and equality? Is it really economically effective to employ so many women? Wouldn't it be better to retire less skilled women to the home and reduce the expenses connected with child care, absences due to maternity leave and children's illness, and the provision of services that would take housework out of the home?

2. The apparent conflict between woman's reproductive and maternal functions and her employment, expressed in a falling birthrate which represented a serious threat to the future of the labor force.

3. The particular situation of mothers with very young children. Are nurseries the answer for the child under three? Who should get preference for the limited places: qualified women who can contribute more to society, or families with several children where the mother's employment is essential to maintain a minimum living standard?

4. Equal rights on the job. All types of employment are theoretically open to women, but in practice women are not found in them. In spite of the increasing number of university-educated or otherwise trained women, they continue to occupy a minority of well-paid and prestigious posts and are found by and large in the traditional poorly paid women's occupations — and there usually in the lowest wage categories; in public life they are found in the minor jobs that require industriousness behind the scenes.

5. Free time. What can be done to relieve women's drudg-

ery, and what is to be expected of the family in a socialist society?

Czechoslovakia's experience in dealing with these questions is described in the following chapters, and in Chapter One.

CHAPTER SIX

WHY WOMEN WORK—AND SHOULD THEY?

W hy do women work? The very fact that the question could be asked was significant. It was as though society had said, "Let's forget those Marxist principles to which we have all been paying lip service for twenty years and find out what really makes things tick." It also implied recognition that women did not have the same status on the labor market as men, since no one thought of asking men why they worked. Women have two obligations, or a choice, depending on how you look at it.

The reason for asking the question, of course, depended upon who asked it. Was it to find out how far Marx's dictum — which links woman's freedom directly to her economic independence and her participation in productive work as opposed to unproductive housework — had penetrated the consciousness of women and their husbands? Was the questioner looking for ways of reducing women's "double shift," or was the question an expression of concern about the most economical use of manpower? In every case it was important to separate the real motivation of individual flesh-and-blood women from the theoretical motivation which had been imputed to them, or to find out to what extent the two coincided.

All Czechoslovak research conducted on this theme, most of it done as a part of larger studies of women's and family problems, revealed that when questioned the overwhelming majority of women replied that they worked out of "financial necessity" or at least "to improve the family financial situation." This was the answer given either as the chief reason or as a major reason for working by 80 percent of respondents in a survey of "The Married Woman in the Family and on the Job," the results of which were published in 1963. In another study conducted in 1965 of 1,971 women who took jobs in industry in 1963 and 1964 — either for the first time in their lives or after an interval of at least two years — 68 percent said that they had done so out of financial necessity, another 10.5 percent wanted to raise the family living standard, still another 3.4 percent were saving toward a particular short-term goal. Only 1.1 percent gave as the reason for going to work an urge for personal financial independence, and only 6.9 percent said they preferred working to staying at home. These women were for the most part unskilled or semiskilled workers. More than 80 percent had received an education only up to the legal school-leaving age of fifteen. These figures are not very different from those obtained in similar surveys in Western countries. For example, a study of women administrative workers published in France in 1965 showed that 92.5 percent worked for "financial reasons," while 51 percent said their pay was "essential." Another Czechoslovak investigation, in which young couples living in rural areas took part in an extensive and continuing survey carried out by the State Population Commission in 1967–68, revealed that 78 percent of the women — all of them under thirty and married only a few years — would stay at home until their children were three years old if their husbands wished it, and provided the family income was sufficient, even if they liked their jobs. When their husbands were questioned, three-quarters of them said they would prefer that their wives did not work. A small number, less than 15 percent, thought it right that women should have a profession or an occupation of their own outside the family. The answer given depended very much on whether the husband had been to college, had completed secondary school, or had had only an elementary school education, this last group being by far the most conservative.

The term "financial necessity" obviously requires closer definition, since it can be used to mean the basic necessities of life — minimum food, shelter, and clothing — or a certain standard considered acceptable by the community. This point did not escape the investigators in the first survey mentioned. "Financial reasons were given," one of them wrote, "by women with several children only slightly more frequently than women with one child, and by women in the lower income brackets only slightly more often than those in the higher. The expression 'financial situation' was thus understood completely subjectively, almost without regard to actual income per person. It can therefore be said that the main reason for the employment of women is not economic necessity in a substantial number of families." [1] This suggested that a good many women did find satisfaction in their work outside the home, but who were they?

Another approach was used in a later, very detailed and representative, study carried out for the Trade Union Research Institute, involving nearly 1,200 employed women in the Liberec area, a district of northern Bohemia characterized by light industry and high employment of women. Slightly more than one-third of the women questioned were factory workers; another 40 percent were administrative workers; and the rest worked in the health service, as salesgirls, or in other relatively qualified jobs. The authors phrased their questions more exactly, and as a result discovered that for 12 percent of the sample the job was a financial necessity because the woman was the sole breadwinner, and for another 38 percent it was a necessity because "we couldn't get along on my husband's pay." Thus, about one-half of the women questioned were under actual economic pressure. One-fourth gave reasons like "to give the children a better life" or "saving up for new furniture." Only 12.5 percent of those questioned said they liked their work and would not want to stay at home.

To check their results, the investigators asked, "Would you stay at home if you could?" They received yes replies in 33 percent of the answers; 35 percent replied no; the others were undecided or did not answer — revealing that in actual fact the number of women who got satisfaction from working was larger than it at first appeared. One-half had to work for financial reasons, but only one-third would definitely stay home if the financial reasons were not present. When the answers were broken down by occupation the results were even more revealing. Asked to check the reasons why they worked, the women chose "I like my job and would not want to stay home" by the following percentages: 56 percent of women doctors, 26 percent of nurses and other health personnel, 20 percent of salesgirls and administrative workers, and only a little over 5 percent of workers. Asked to say whether they would stay home if they could, 80 percent of doctors said they definitely would not, the rest being undecided; 43 percent of workers said they would stay home, while more than one-quarter said they would not.

These and other similar results suggest how unclear women's reasons for working sometimes are, even to themselves; how many factors enter into each woman's decision to work and her feelings about her job; and how far from the truth sweeping generalizations can be. When the replies in this survey were broken down by age, marital status, and number of children this was even more apparent. Thus a thirty-year-old doctor with two preschool children was determined to work and to maintain her place in her chosen profession, while her counterpart standing on her feet all day supervising spinning machines on the factory floor had her mind on family concerns and would rather be at home. Yet this same routine job for an unmarried nineteen-year-old was an introduction to the adult world, a source of social contacts, and a means of independence from her family. For a fifty-two-year-old grandmother returning to work after raising her own family it was escape from an empty house, a way of earning treats for her grandchildren or of helping her children establish themselves without being tied to their households. Could the same criteria of emancipation be applied to all these women? Obviously not.

Certainly the economic factor was the major reason for a woman to work, if not always the only one, in all cases where she — single, divorced, or widowed — was the sole support of a family or even simply had to support herself; there are no inherited incomes, no wise investments, and no alimony under socialism, and social security benefits for widows and orphans provide a thin cushion. The woman's job was a necessity in the case of young married couples saving up for a cooperative apartment or for furniture, often with the first child already on the way. Families with two children faced a hard decision. This was the point where it became financially difficult for the woman to stay at home, yet the burden of her dual role was often too much for her. In families with three or more children, employment of women dropped in spite of the economic squeeze involved in trying to make ends meet on a single pay envelope.

The fact that this particular generalization about families with two or more children could be made was the result of the process of wage leveling — a process far more intensely felt in Czechoslovakia than in any of the other socialist countries — that had been under way since 1945.[2] This was not a consequence of an intentional policy intended to make all men equal, but the effect of several conflicting policies governing the distribution of the national wealth at a time when this wealth was severely limited. It had been a natural postwar step to raise first the earnings of the lowest paid; next to reward the working class which had given its support to revolutionary changes; then, because of an economic policy favoring heavy industry, to give premiums for brawn rather than brain. But because there was full employment and the national cake was small, this policy of distribution could not help but be at the expense of the highly skilled workers and the intellectuals. Thus, the average monthly wage of a lathe operator in industry in 1965 was 2,422 crowns; of a general practitioner in the health service, 2,243 crowns; of a machinist, 2,010 crowns; of a secondary-school teacher with a university education, 1,907 crowns; and of a pick-and-shovel worker, 1,757 crowns. More than 80 percent of employed persons were in the 1,000–2,500 crowns bracket, the average monthly earning being about 1,500 crowns. From this it can be seen that a family's standard of living was directly related to the number of dependent children and the number of working members it had. A per capita income of 400–600 crowns monthly meant that the family diet fell below recommended levels, not only in terms of proteins, calcium, iron, and vitamin C, but in actual calorie intake, according to a

study made of more than 3,500 families whose budgets were
regularly followed for the official cost-of-living index. In 1965
more than half of all Czechoslovak families with three dependent children were in this next-to-lowest per capita income
category.

Reports of huge amounts of unrealized buying power
lying in the banks waiting for unavailable consumer durables
also had to be reinterpreted, because savings in relation to
total income were stagnating at this time, and almost half the
annual growth in savings went into the accounts of less than
15 percent of families. The majority of families with several
children did not have savings to tide the family over for a
few years while mother stayed at home.

Two problems met head on. One involved the difficulties
which a family with two or more children faced (a) if the
mother worked and (b) if she didn't. The other lay in the economic imbalances which had recently become obvious and
whose solution, everyone agreed, required not only changes in
structure (more emphasis on light industry and housing, less
on industries which needed large amounts of imported raw
materials), and not only more flexible and sensitive planning.
A major factor for a country "on the threshold of the scientific
and technological revolution" — the phrase of the day — must
be more efficient use of manpower, higher productivity. With
the aid of mechanization and automation, fewer people would
produce more. And if workers were to work more efficiently,
sad experience had already shown, they must be paid for their
efficiency and their skill. Who wanted to be a foreman and to
bear the slings and arrows of outraged workers unless there
was some financial satisfaction in it? Why study for four years
at a technical high school when one could earn just as good
money, and perhaps better, straight from elementary school
after a few months of training? Funds had to be found for fairer
pay differentials.

There was one obvious solution, and even a plant manager with cast-iron Marxist-Leninist principles could hardly re-
strain himself from voicing it. If we are to produce more with
fewer people, the unskilled workers at the bottom of the pay

scale — these troublesome women with their sick children and their maternity leaves and their shopping and their shorter hours and complaints about washrooms will be the first to go. "Many people in management make no secret of the fact that, in connection with the introduction of the new economic system, 'the blow will fall,' where necessary, on the women first," wrote one Slovak journalist, pointing out that this would be a violation of the Constitution which gave the right to work to all alike.[3] Justification for the point of view of the men who were going to be responsible for producing more at less cost could be found in such incontrovertible statements as that of a member of the presidium of the Communist party, who told a meeting of women that while it was true that the rapid growth in employment had contributed a great deal to the increase in production and the improvement of the standard of living, at the same time the extensive rather than intensive use of manpower had achieved this growth at the expense of new technology. Expressions like "overemployment" and "social employment" began to be used, and were put by some to be as high as 20 percent of the labor force. Would it not be more practical to pay higher wages to men so that at least unqualified women could stay at home with their children? There were women as well as men who considered this the simplest way to solve things and were ready to welcome such a solution.[4]

A sophisticated version of this argument was presented by a young economist in the cultural weekly *Literarni noviny* on the occasion of International Women's Day, 1965. Taking note of the fact that women's work load was greater by one-third to one-half than that of men, and that women in the same social group and in the same employment had half as much free time as men, he invoked the "natural division of labor in the family" which, he said, was obviously not abolished by socialism, "at least for as long as the family continues to exist as the basic biological and economic unit of society." According to this natural division, "the man devotes himself more intensively to his work, and perhaps to public activity or self-improvement connected with his job or his function, while the woman concentrates on the children and the household." He did not think it rational to correct the balance by redistributing the tasks in the family because of "the desire of the woman for motherhood and her need to create a favorable family atmosphere for the raising of children"; while the fact that usually the man is better qualified and has a better job makes his income vital to the family budget. At the same time, his need for self-realization in public life is much more intense than that of the woman.

He did not see why woman's work in the household should receive less social recognition than man's work in production, nor why public activity should be the measure of her emancipation. "I see no problem," he wrote, "in the fact that women devote . . . more work to the household and children than men; I see the problem in the fact that care for the household and children is, as a result of shortcomings in transport, supplies, housing and services, too demanding on time, tiring, and unnecessarily difficult. If the division of labor itself, which is unfavorable to women, cannot immediately be changed, we can at least lighten their burden and make it more agreeable by giving priority to those branches of industry, trade, and the services most closely connected with domestic work and child care" — as long as economic necessity, in the given conditions, requires that she be tied to the household.[5]

He and others with similar views were given a dressing down by a woman editor (who happened to be in charge of a publishing house specializing in political literature) in the Communist party daily, Rudé právo. It was interesting, she wrote, that when it came to women there were plenty of advisers around to lecture them in the old bourgeois spirit. When the divorce rate rises they are called upon to strengthen the family; why only the women? When the number of abortions increases, it's the women who are condemned; and few stop to consider that her decision incorporates that of a man. As for woman's "burden" and the "natural division of labor" in the family, they seem natural to an older generation who married in that spirit; while for their daughters — the women for whom the new legislation was passed and the nurseries established — the traditions died slowly and created conflict situations. As for the girls now going to work, marrying, and having children, "try telling them that they must pay for their maternal instinct by taking on their back all the domestic work!" They are more likely to answer by limiting the number of children, and in fact are doing so.

"Socialism is not an ideology of hypocrisy," she wrote. "When we promulgate more just laws, don't we do so in order to create a more just family life?" Women's lag in qualifications is a temporary affair, much less marked in the younger generation. "What kind of managers would we be if we gave women skills but expected that sooner or later they would return to the home?" The division of labor in the home has changed, she said, because society needed the work of qualified women as well as men; the patriarchal tradition had to give way to economic progress. "If we are in favor of equal rights for women, let us enforce them. If there are unpaid debts in the realm of understanding the new roles of men and women, it is primarily due to us, ideological workers, because we have devoted little effort to helping clarify the revolutionary process which affects us all." [6]

There she obviously put her finger on the crux of the matter. She was echoed a few months later by one of the best-informed writers on women's problems, Libuše Háková, in another cultural weekly, *Kulturní tvorba*. "The present discussion of the woman's question differs from all other discussions," she wrote.

"

While in arguments about science and ideology, economics, esthetics, and so on, theoretical solutions have been examined and participants have tried to cleanse them of foreign ballast and arrive at the most precise Marxist conception possible, in the debate about women's problems theory is rarely mentioned. Obviously the Marxist approach to the woman question is supposed to be taken for granted. Experience, and the reaction to published articles suggest, however, that it would not be harmful occasionally to recall these old truths (in so far, of course, as we accept them as truths).

"

The entry of women into industry had been an inevitable result of the industrial revolution, she recalled, and even though their work at that time was highly unattractive (as it

often still is today), Marx and Engels saw it as a basic and un-
avoidable condition for women's emancipation. It has often
been necessary to defend this stand, she said, and the revolutionary workers' movement always did so. She added:

"

It is paradoxical that after twenty years of building socialism
one must recall this experience to head off tendencies to solve the
conflicts of employed women by not employing them unless they are
able to solve their own problems; and where we have to employ them,
by pretending that we don't know anything about their problems or
that nothing can be done about them.

It can be expected that now everyone who ever wrote anything
about women, and all those whose job it is to "take care of" employed
women will fly out of their chairs, crying indignantly "We never said
anything like that!" Of course not, in that bald form, but so far the
idea (born somewhere in the Ministry of Finance) that in the present
difficult economic situation nurseries are a luxury, and that it would
pay if women with small children stayed at home so that it would not
be necessary to build more, has not yet disappeared in thin air.[7]

"

Suggestions of this kind, which were offered under the
heading of economy from "not insignificant quarters" (as
spokesmen for the State Population Commission claimed in a
reply to the anti-nurseries argument), were based on figures
purporting to show that the earnings of women in the lower
income categories did not cover the cost of providing nursery
care for their children (toward which these mothers contributed
only 10 percent); when there was another child or two in the
family requiring nursery-school care or school lunches, the
value of their employment was even more questionable. It was
proposed that places in existing nurseries be reserved for "social cases," where the mother's pay was an absolute necessity
or, alternatively, for highly qualified women whose contribution to society was greater, who paid higher nursery fees, and
who could not afford to drop behind in their professions by
staying home. The effect of these opinions soon became manifest in a lag in fulfillment of the plan for new nurseries and a
lack of interest on the part of national committees in pressing
for new facilities. The ever-alert permanent staff of the State
Population Commission was the first to rush into the lists with

an analysis, published in an economic weekly read by all managers, and described by the editors as the first successful attempt to throw light on the problem from an economic point of view. They rejected the idea that each individual mother must pay her way at every stage of her employed life. Their statistics showed that even if all of the country's 300,000 working mothers with a child under three had their children in nurseries, instead of the 60,000 who were then actually being served by nurseries, society would still profit from their work. They also produced figures to show that if the state were to build nurseries with 185,000 places instead of the planned 25,000 in the next five years, the value produced by women with infants and toddlers would pay off the investment in less than four years.[8]

Other economists agreed. Even if the cost of nurseries reduces the economic contribution of working mothers to a minimum, the idea of closing them must be rejected because of the anti-baby mood it would produce, said one. The bookkeeping approach toward working mothers caused another participant in the argument to comment that "one is forced to conclude that the wealth created by women over the years is so great that the delay in building facilities for children and the lag in services . . . is, from a purely economic point of view, an injury which society has inflicted on working women."[9] The manpower savings which may result from improved technology should obviously be used under socialism not to reduce employment but to reduce working time for those already employed and for those who will be employed in the future, he said. Others observed that the majority of women were employed in light industry, the food industry, and electrical engineering — traditional women's industries characterized by mass production, "hard norms" (that is, high production quotas), low prices, and low wages — while in the industries where most of the workers were men, prices and wages were high and norms were much softer as a result of the preference shown to heavy industry for two decades. If an attempt were made to replace these women by men, what man would take these "women's jobs," calling for such high intensity of labor for so little money?

The argument which had appeared most important to the

experts of the State Population Commission seemed to interest the economists the least: that is, the equality of women, which depended on women being able to occupy the same place in the production process as men. If women with small children stayed home until the youngest was three, it would mean, in the case of a mother of two children, an interval of about five years in which she would be eliminated from employment — a serious handicap in view of the rapid progress of technology. Members of the Women's Committee intervened to point out that nurseries and other services are not just for the benefit of "the woman" but serve the whole family.

Having lifted the lid off Pandora's box it was not easy to get it back on, and the voices continued on both sides. One of the longest and most heated exchanges took place in the pages of the Communist party daily, *Rudé právo,* and lasted throughout the last three months of 1966, fired by an emotional letter from a woman in a farming village of 376 houses (as she wrote) which was published under the heading "What Have You Got Against Us?" "At the present time an employed woman is almost afraid to read the newspapers or listen to the radio or TV. It's not her life that's at stake but her peace of mind," she complained.

The letters poured in:

"

Let some of those women in the factories come out and help us women on the farm bring in the crops. I'm 62 . . .

"Don't Wash at Home! We'll Wash for You! We Use Tix!" The results are awful. . . .

What can we expect from the upbringing of children who from the age of ten are left to play in the street unsupervised?

It's true that everyone has a right to work, but why do women work who don't need the money and just work to relieve their boredom?

I believe that if there really is an economic reform there will be work for both men and women who really want to work, who are interested in their work, and who are prepared to improve their skills, and that unqualified labor will be used to relieve them of their routine duties instead of representing "overemployment" in some office. Perhaps then, too, we'll live to see equal pay for equal work.

We can't go on increasing outlays for nurseries, after-school care, and nursery schools indefinitely. These social advantages are used by many families which could get along without them. . . . Today women themselves are calling for the defeminization of some fields — schools, for example — because they themselves would benefit from this; and feminization and the overemployment of women are concepts that are very close to each other.

Probably women will be reserved primarily for typical occupations.

The movement for the emancipation of women was and is a just one. I think that it should be realized slightly differently. Not by blindly imitating men, but by allowing for what is specific to women. And give women the assurance that housework is just as important as other work which is paid for.

In 1964 we were sent a teacher, the mother of one — now two. Shortly thereafter, in September, she was absent two days because of her child's illness. In October, another two days; from November to December, twenty-four days; in January, for difficulties connected with pregnancy, twenty days. In one school semester she worked fifty-three days and was home forty-eight.

I recall the attitude toward nonworking women eighteen years ago. I had three children — at that time ten, five, and one year old. I was at home and was afraid to tell anyone that I was trying to get along on my husband's pay. Some women who were working at the time were my harshest judges. Either I was lazy, or a poor backward creature imprisoned by four walls, a slave, and I don't know what else. It's true that I sacrificed myself for my family, and I don't know why I should regret it.

If things go on like this, and if any kind of measures are taken against the employment of women instead of society's creating favorable conditions for their work, socialism will lose all its attraction for me personally, and I will be intensely sorry that two of my three children are girls.

,,

The Women's Committee sent two of its experts into the fray to try to give the discussion a concrete direction. "The idea of a differentiated approach to employed women according to age, number of children, and qualifications is gaining favor, but what is lacking is a firm economic foundation for it; that is, it is not based on any detailed information regarding probable economic changes. Apparently the problem of employed women falls outside the concern of our political economy," wrote Libuše Háková.

Senta Radvanová added: "I personally think that the situation would be ideal if a woman could decide at certain times in her life, without having to worry about what would happen to her family, between care of her household and children and her job. At the present time her choice is limited economically (the average four-member family depends on two salaries) and by fear of losing her qualifications, her chances for a better job, and so on." [10]

Noting that they had published dozens of letters and had received many more, the editors of Rudé právo brought the discussion to a close with a lengthy interview with the deputy head of the State Planning Commission in which several other manpower experts participated. It was published with the title "No New Policy," and its message was full employment. There would be a shortage of labor in the future as there had been in the past, and woman power would be needed as it was all over the industrialized world. Overemployment in particular instances, and the closing of economically unprofitable enterprises, were not questions which touched only women. Solutions lay in policies designed to protect the interests of workers while they were being retrained or relocated. The restructuring of industry would actually be favorable to women because there were to be new jobs in the service industries. Promises were made: the number of places in nurseries would be increased to 100,000 and in nursery schools, to almost 400,000 by 1970; the number of new apartments, by 460,000. Other problems — like public transportation, shopping facilities, and better supplies of consumer goods — would be solved gradually when the economy had been put on a sound basis. A complex series of measures constituting a new social policy for the improvement of the position of families with small children was in the works, readers were assured.

How different everything would look, a member of the State Planning Commission told an interviewer, if only all the laws and regulations which existed for the benefit of employed women were actually enforced. How differently all of us, not just women, would live if all the services — which it was believed until recently would take housework out of the home — really functioned, if time were not lost in transportation and everywhere else, if women with children could really take advantage of their legal right to a shorter working day.

"

To think that there will be a mass exodus and a return to the home is an illusion, however, and a dangerous one. It leads to comfortable passivity regarding the preparation of conditions not just for the present but for the future, and . . . these conditions include not only nurseries but the entire technological level of the workplace, the mechanization and automation of auxiliary jobs, equipment which takes into account basic scientific knowledge concerning the specificity of women. We go on designing new plants which we know will be operated by women for a male workforce. . . .

Even the best-intentioned one sided generalizations, usually the result of experience with single individuals or groups which is automatically stretched to cover all women, are more likely to do more harm than good and to cloud the situation. More information, more objective analyses, greater differentiation in whatever measures are taken — this is what we need.[11]

"

The new approach to women's employment, which took into account that at various times in their lives women have different reasons for working or not working, met with general approval. It was a victory over the old, mechanical application of Marxist theory, and a recognition that having children was more than just a matter of producing them and putting them into a nursery. It pleased those who had argued that women's specificity, both biologically and culturally determined, was real, and it gave some status to work in the home. It seemed plain to everyone that only a flexible policy which could take into account each woman's unique set of circumstances could succeed in ameliorating the situation in which society now found itself.

The first concrete measure was the lengthening of paid maternity leave to twenty-six weeks (thirty-five weeks for unmarried, divorced, or widowed mothers), with another optional half year of unpaid leave without loss of job tenure. This was later extended to a year and a half. Another measure which took effect in January 1971, offers five hundred crowns monthly to all mothers of two children (regardless of previous employment) who stay at home as long as at least one of the children is still under two years of age. At the same time, single grants on the birth of each child were increased to two thousand crowns (the equivalent of the average monthly wage). Substantially increased monthly family allowances for the third and fourth child make it easier for young families to get along on one pay if the mother wants to stay at home or if, in fact, she cannot find a place in a nursery. (It was recognized that even if the goal of 100,000 places were reached by 1970 — and actually there were only 66,000 places by that date, as it turned out — they would not accommodate more than 18 percent of the children in that age group whose mothers were employed.) Another step, in 1973, provided loans under favorable conditions, including a write-off for each child born, to young married couples.

What would have happened if the economy had become so efficient as to make possible the elimination of overemployment or hidden unemployment will never be known, since "no marked advance in the intensification of the economy occurred because of the complicated political situation in recent years," as Senta Radvanová laconically put it.[12] Women's employment actually increased by 370,000 between 1965 and 1970.

Several things are striking about this phase of the discussion. Some participants were shocked that the supposedly firm structure of Marxist principles gave way so quickly to expediency when exposed to pressure — not only in the ranks of "ordinary husbands" but at a level of management and policy making where a maximum of political maturity might have been expected. There was just as much reason to be surprised that in view of the political, economic, and ideological inadequacies which were freely admitted in the 1960s to be the result of mistakes made in the period of the "cult of the personality," so many people could still be found who were prepared to defend the classical Marxist concept of women's emancipation and declare it workable if properly applied. One thing that does emerge is that, of all the many aspects of Marxism-Leninism which made up the curriculum in many types of Communist party schooling and which were introduced into education generally, one that was consistently neglected was the role of women in the society of the future. The woman question could be disposed of simply by describing the laws that had been passed and the facilities "we have given them." It escaped notice that "what we have given women" was not a generous gift, as implied, but simply what men had already been enjoying for decades and in some cases centuries, and therefore women's due. The controversy which finally broke out never got down to basic principles; those most sincerely engaged in it were also responsible for working out quick, financially practical ways of relieving immediate distress. Generous as these were and much as they were welcomed, the steps taken were basically population measures, designed to make it easier for a young woman to stay at home. No parallel measures were introduced to strengthen her position on the labor market or to make it easier for her to go to work if she preferred. Woman's value as a potential employee dropped, and acceptance of her dual role — half worker, half mother — was strengthened.

Some of the conditions which precipitated the discussion were specific to Czechoslovakia: the extreme leveling of wages, for example, and the threat of manpower cuts. More of them were characteristic of Eastern European socialism in general, judging from the very similar airings of women's grievances which took place in the other socialist countries during the same decade.

Poland was a country which had studied women's problems consistently, not having allowed its prewar gains in sociology to lapse even during the days when the subject was officially taboo. Magdalena Sokolowska is a recognized expert on women's employment. During a visit to Czechoslovakia in 1965 she remarked: "As long as women worked in factories and in the fields it didn't bother anyone very much. As soon as they started to learn skills and to ask for the same money for the same work, men began to worry about their health, their nerves, to claim that employment doesn't agree with them, and that they are neglecting the family." She castigated Polish law which allowed only the mother, not the father, to stay home with a sick child, and scoffed at men who "help" in the household. They should, in her opinion, "share" the household. To her, the stream of women into employment could no more be turned back than the waters of the Vistula, which flows through Poland. The real problem was to "break down the psychological and biological barriers preventing women from holding leading position." [13]

Hungary, with what was then the lowest birthrate in the world (13 per 1,000 inhabitants in 1964–65), was the first country to pay mothers a housewives' allowance to stay home and thus was the first to formally recognize work in the household as productive of social values (although the amount paid was a purely arbitrary one, dependent on the availability of funds). Beginning in 1967, a working woman was entitled to stay at home, following the expiration of paid maternity leave, until her child was three years old; and to receive a monthly payment of six hundred forints, which was about enough to cover the child's basic expenses. Women who took advantage of this grant did not lose their right to their job or its equivalent, and of course continued to receive the usual family allowance as well. The position of Hungarian women prompted a special decision by the central committee of the Hungarian Socialist Workers' party in February 1970, which called attention to conditions similar to those prevailing in Czechoslovakia: women's lower wages, their overwork, insufficient facilities for children, and inadequate services. After three years' experience, the Hungarians pointed out that since 180,000 women had taken advantage of the housewives' allowance, factories were neglecting their duty to build nurseries and nursery schools for their employees.

In the Soviet Union, in a round-table discussion reported in a Soviet weekly in 1968 and headed "Should Women Work?," the moderator started the conversation going by noting that, of ten women questioned at random, eight had said they could not imagine life without their jobs. Seven of the ten husbands, however, had sighed, "Oh, if only she would stay at home." V. L.

Bilshai, a lawyer with many years of experience working with women, who was at the time writing her doctorate on "The Woman Question in the Theory of Scientific Communism," held out for the classic solution proposed by Engels. The state should take over the care of the household and help with the care of the children. The idea that men and women should divide the housework evenly violated her sense of the specificity of men and women. Man as a friend, counselor, and partner, yes; as a dressmaker and washerwoman, no.

A woman demographer commented that in the early days it had obviously been necessary to involve women in industry on a mass scale, but that it was no longer essential; and that while the economy could obviously not get along without women, to have almost half of all women in production was too much. "It is not yet clear," she said, "whether it is more advantageous for the state to build more nurseries or to free young mothers from production for a few years." [14] We should stop looking at a woman worker just like a man worker, declared the only man present, an economist from the Office of Economic Planning. The day off for housework, allowed working women once a month in the German Democratic Republic, appealed to the participants.

Moscow demographers devoted a special session to women's employment in February 1969. They pointed out that according to official cost-of-living figures it was impossible for four people to live on one salary. The difficulties of combining work and housekeeping were such, however, that of 70,000 women surveyed in twenty-two Ukrainian factories, all who had children had taken a three-month unpaid leave after their four-month maternity leave, and 70 percent stayed home for at least a year. Only 0.3 percent of these women had three or more children. The demographers looked with approval at the Hungarian idea of a housewives' allowance.

The German Democratic Republic has taken note of the special problems of women somewhat later than the other socialist countries, although its record for the employment of women is second only to that of the Soviet Union, and 57 percent of its women with three children are working. As early as

1965, however, officials noted a tendency of women to leave employment between the ages of twenty-five and thirty-five, a situation which a country with a severe shortage of male manpower could ill afford. In 1969, the Institute for Social Hygiene at Magdeburg began a continuing examination of 2,500 women to find out why women fell ill more often than men and left their jobs more frequently. As might have been expected, they found signs of overstrain due to the conflict between job and household. Of the women questioned, 55 percent said they slept only six or seven hours a night, half had little or no free time — figures which correspond to those found in investigations of working women in most industrialized countries.

In Bulgaria, the Tenth Congress of the Communist party in March 1972 took notice of women's excessive burden, of problems connected with housekeeping and nurseries, and of the dropping birthrate, and it promised to quadruple the sum to be spent on building nurseries in the next Five-Year Plan. The chairman of the Bulgarian Women's Committee had already appealed to a meeting of the executive committee of the Council for Mutual Economic Assistance (COMECON) of the Eastern European socialist countries in Moscow earlier in the year, asking that the appropriate commissions find ways of improving conditions for working women in the member countries. The executive committee publicly acknowledged this request, which was another way of admitting that all the socialist countries, regardless of differences in economic development, are facing the same basic dilemma. They need women's productive power, and they need their reproductive power; but without much more effective measures than they have been able to take to date, one cannot be had without sacrificing some of the other.

While the 1950s were devoted to recruiting women as quickly as possible, the 1960s were characterized by the startled recognition that women were having significantly fewer babies. For a long time it had been believed in the socialist countries that employment of women was not a factor which influenced population growth, that the reason working women had so few children was that the small size of their families (whether planned that way or otherwise) was what made it possible for them to work, while women with several children had to stay at home. It turned out that this was not the case at all, that the reason working women had fewer children was simply because they were working. The employed mother postponed her second child, often indefinitely, and almost never had a third. It was the woman who stayed at home who insured the population growth.

Why had this realization been so long in coming?

CHAPTER SEVEN

THE UNDERPOPULATION CRISIS

Woman's "biological role," her function as the giver of life, has always been the one stubbornly changeless, limiting, and determining factor in her personal and public life, and today it still appears as the final insurmountable barrier to equality between the sexes. The problem now is not the demands which pregnancy and childbirth put upon a woman who produces perhaps two, or at most three, children in a lifetime, but the fact that only woman can do it. Obviously, if this function were shared by men the wheels of progress would long ago have adjusted their rhythm to the menstrual cycle and all the other biological cycles that make women undependable" employees — and also, no doubt, to the demands of tiny infants and ill children.

The founders of Marxism did not consider this biological difference in itself as a factor making for inequality. Engels noted, it is true, that the first division of labor was that between man and woman for the reproduction of the species. He went further, in his preface to the first edition of *The Origin of the Family,* declaring that the production which was the decisive factor in history was of a two-fold character: one, the production of the means of subsistence; the other, the production of human beings themselves; and that these two — the development of labor on the one hand and of the family on the other — determined the social institutions under which men of a particular historical epoch lived. In his view, the more limited the production of material wealth, as in primitive society, the more the social order was determined by "ties of sex"—that is, the production of human beings; in other words, the form of the family. Conversely, as the productivity of labor increased, the importance of relationships in material production outweighed those in the family and, in fact, determined them.[1] As we have seen, he argued that this eventually placed women in an inferior position, but this was not because of her biological specificity; it was due to private property, which had made her natural role into a handicap.

Marx and Engels believed that woman's fear of conception, as well as her problems when she did conceive, would be resolved under socialism since society would take care of the children. Obviously, they never considered how this would be carried out in detail, nor did they give any consideration to the drawbacks which childbirth and nursing might be to the woman who presumably would want to work under socialism, as opposed to the woman who had to work under capitalism. The women they were concerned with were ciphers in the production process; it was their misery they wanted to cure. Bebel, on the other hand, foresaw that "the higher, freer position which all women will then occupy" would make them disinclined to "spend the best years of their own lives in pregnancy, or with a child at their breasts." He thought that in spite of the solicitude which socialism would show for mothers, the "increase of population will proceed slower than in bourgeois society." [2] Where women decided to have children, society, including female relatives and friends, would see to it that they were not a burden. Lenin, the first to be faced with a real-life situation, recognized woman's right to control the number of her children, but he did not visualize a situation in which woman would suffer from divided loyalties to her home and her job; this was probably because the women he was interested in at the moment were the poor peasants who were toiling in the fields or beginning to take up unskilled jobs in the new industries. To be free, it was only necessary for women to do productive work instead of house-work, which is, he said, "the most unproductive, the most savage, and the most arduous work a woman can do." She did not have to be considered a worker on a par with a man. "We are not, of course, speaking of making women the equal of men as far as productivity of labour, the quality of labour, the length of the working day, labour conditions, etc., are concerned," he explained.[3]

None of these early Marxists gave any weight to the fact that socialism — a change from private to social ownership of the plants and the machinery — would not alter the reality that the working world into which women stepped from the kitchen had been arranged and structured by men for their own convenience, and that any inability to adapt to these arrangements on the part of women would be regarded as a female shortcoming. The struggle had been between capitalists and workers, not between men and women. The idea of a conflict under socialism between men's and women's interests would have seemed absurd. Nor were they aware of the complexity of the parent-child relationship, and the far-reaching consequences of this for the mother, the family, the woman's place of work, and ultimately, the economy. All personal relationships appeared to them so distorted by capitalism that it seemed obvious that once capitalist conditions were eliminated, personal problems would be solved by rational behavior and common sense. The possibility that these factors might have a serious influence on population growth could never have occurred to them. Socialism would create ideal conditions for mothers and children, so naturally families would want to have children.

These were the theoretical gaps and the premises which the postwar socialist societies inherited, at a time when "woman's right to control over her own body" was becoming an issue all over the world. The granting of easy access to abortion for women in the socialist countries (with the exception of Albania and China) in the mid-fifties seemed like an act of great foresight to women in other countries who were to suffer for at least another fifteen years under absurdly archaic anti-abortion legislation. They could not know, nor did the socialist countries themselves guess, that these governments were taking a step in the dark. The states that had believed they were making motherhood a blessing that could be combined with self-fulfillment in other spheres of life, found themselves at the beginning of the 1960s with staggering abortion rates and some of the lowest birthrates in the world — too low in some cases to insure the simple reproduction of the population. The result has been a prolonged tug-of-war, in which women's rights are emphasized on one side and population requirements on the other.

Czechoslovakia's new abortion law went into effect on January 1, 1958, and permitted abortion, under hospital conditions, in the first twelve weeks of pregnancy for women of advanced age or with a large number of children (later defined as three); for women whose husbands had died or become invalids; for divorced and unmarried women; for those having "other compelling social or economic reasons," and for women who had been raped. Self-induced abortion was no longer considered a crime. The woman requesting abortion was required to take her case to a commission consisting of the director of the district National Health Service, two other physicians, and a lay member — a woman "who commanded the respect of the community." A charge of between 200 and 500 crowns could be made when the operation was performed for other than medical reasons, rather high in view of the average industrial wage of 1,200 crowns monthly. An unfavorable decision could be appealed to a higher commission. The agreement of parents in the case of underage girls was not required, although a later provision empowered the commission to call them in for consultation.

The bill had been introduced by the Ministry of Health, as the chairman of the Health Committee of the National Assembly explained, following study of the experience of the Soviet Union and Hungary, in order to limit the number of illegal abortions. Study had shown, he said, that there was no simple relationship between abortion and population. "Population growth is dependent first of all on the economic situation, on health and social measures, on the moral maturity of the population, its political consciousness. . . . Normal women want children and the education of young people to parenthood, and the existence of economic and social conditions which make it possible to have children, lead to better results than regulations, prohibitions, and punishments. . . ." Previous regulations "which no longer correspond to the legal norms of a society in which woman is completely equal with man, are abrogated," he continued, adding that the new law was an expression of great confidence in women, and assuring them that "motherhood and parenthood must not be a difficulty in our socialist society but an honor and a joy." Czechoslovakia was not aiming for a large population, he declared, but "we do want to be sufficient in number and to know that the nation is being renewed in our children in undiminished strength." [4]

A little over a year later, however, the Ministry of Health complained that the large number of legal abortions performed during the law's first year constituted a serious problem, and it reminded physicians that the systematic education of the public, and of women especially, in the use of contraceptives was part of their job. National committees were urged to eliminate the causes that led women to ask for abortion, a process which the ministry believed would be accelerated by the measures which the government had already taken. Nevertheless, by 1961 the number of abortions had jumped to forty-three for every one hundred births, and the ministry entrusted the "interruption" commissions with new responsibilities. They were asked to help young people to overcome the barriers which stand in the way — "and which in some cases they invent" — of welcoming a child of their own. They were to give assistance in housing, social, and employment matters; but they also had an educational function "where young people consider a child an obstacle to a carefree life, where their interest in having an automobile and other luxuries takes precedence over concern for a happy family." At the begining of 1963, fees for abortions (which had been abolished in 1960 as discriminatory, since an application for abortion so often implied economic straits) were reintroduced, and the regulations were tightened to require a woman to go before a commission in the district in which she lived. Some women, it was said, had taken advantage of the fact that they could apply in any district to support their requests with "false statements which the commission could not verify."[5] The commissions were also instructed to be stricter in granting abortions in the case of first pregnancies.

These new rules, as well as the extension of maternity leave from eighteen to twenty-two weeks and the lowering of the retirement age for women with three or more children, helped to raise the number of live births and increase the birthrate in the next two years; but it also brought about an increase in illegal abortions. With a relaxation of the commission's interpretation of their guidelines, the downward trend in births began again, and by 1968 the annual number of abortions had reached the 100,000 mark. Together with 24,000 "hospitalized spontaneous abortions," they amounted to 57.7 for every 100 live births. In 1967 the birthrate, 15.1 per 1,000 inhabitants, was the lowest in fifty years, and the prospective replacement of the population was not assured.

New permissive abortion policies touched off similar trends in the other Eastern European countries. In the Soviet Union between 1960 and 1969 the birthrate plunged from 24.9 to 17.0 (compared to 17.7 in the United States in the latter year). Although no absolute figures for abortions in the Soviet Union are available, Henry David cites figures to suggest that in 1965 it had the highest rate in Eastern Europe, 2.5–3.0 abortions for every live birth, while according to a Soviet author, in Leningrad in 1967 four out of every five pregnancies ended in abortion.[6]

Hungary, which had a birthrate of 21.4 in 1955, recorded a drop to 12.9 in 1962, the lowest rate in Europe. The absolute number of abortions in Hungary in each year of the decade between 1958 and 1968 was almost twice the already-high Czechoslovak figure, although its population — ten million — is nearly one-third less. In 1969 its abortion rate, 136 legal induced abortions for every 100 live births, was three times Czechoslovakia's.

In Rumania, where abortions were performed almost on the assembly line after 1956, the birthrate dropped from 24.2 to 14.3 in a decade, and caused a complete reversal of policy; after 1966 abortions could be performed for medical reasons only, and the importation of contraceptives was stopped. Neighboring

Bulgaria changed its attitude several times: a permissive law introduced in 1956 was amended to allow abortions for medical reasons only in 1967, by which time Bulgaria was recording three abortions for every four pregnancies brought to term. Then, in 1970, it legalized abortion on demand.

Strongly Catholic Poland was not immune to the effects of legalized abortion. The birthrate dropped by 45 percent, from 29.1 to 16.3, between 1955 and 1967. The absolute number of abortions began to decline in 1962, however, possibly because of improved contraceptive practices, since Poland is the one Eastern European country with a history of active family planning. The German Democratic Republic had a birthrate of 13.0 in 1947 and 1948, and between 1950 and 1970 the government permitted only medical abortions. This strict attitude was accompanied by an improvement in the population picture, and in 1970, apparently believing the situation had stabilized, East Germany introduced abortion on demand. It now has one of the lowest birthrates in the world.

Of course, abortions do not cause an anti-reproduction mood; they merely expose it. These alarming statistics brought about studies of the relation between employment and childbearing, and the social measures aimed at encouraging births described in the preceding chapter. But the abortion habit itself had to be reckoned with. What the socialist countries had believed was simply a humane measure which would be used in emergencies had become the universal method of birth control. As such, it was a very unsatisfactory one.

From the point of view of the woman, particularly if she is a young unmarried girl, an abortion is always an unpleasant experience. Aside from this, abortion as a birth-control method puts all the responsibility for the future of the unborn child on the woman. She makes the application, she agrees to the operation, she pays the fee. If, as in Czechoslovakia, she must go before an interruption commission, she is the one who receives the lecture, is subjected to pressure to have the child, is reproached for getting herself "into trouble." As a leading gynecologist who was one of the authors of the Czechoslovak law himself admitted, its humanitarian purpose had not been realized. The interruption commissions, instead of helping eliminate the causes of abortions, had become "bodies which hand down sentences and determine fines in the form of fees for unwanted pregnancies. . . . The majority of women who have experienced one such discussion are mentally traumatized by it and often declare that if they have another unwanted pregnancy they would rather take the illegal way out." [7]

"Few members of the commission realize," wrote one mother of five to a weekly magazine, "what it means for a sensitive mother with human feelings to sit before them as in a pillory." Another described her feelings this way: "The operation itself caused me no special trouble, but every time I think of the commission (and especially one of the woman members) I'm filled with panic and I can't bring myself to sleep with my husband." [8] Other critics of the procedure pointed out that it encourages hypocrisy. Because it may speed up the hearing before the commission if the woman claims to have conceived out of wedlock, she and her husband fabricate a lover, and the commission, although suspecting the story to be an invention, must still accept it since it can hardly order an investigation. This type of birth control also encourages irresponsibility on the part of men; if it is entirely the woman's business whether she gives birth to the child or not, he often does not worry much about its conception.

The dissatisfaction of the population experts and of the medical profession with the legislation, which began to make itself heard within a few years of its passage, was not justified by moral arguments (for insofar as such objections existed within the Catholic church or elsewhere they were never expressed); but stemmed from the fact that the law was introduced without prior consultation with the appropriate experts and on the basis of assumptions for which there was no evidence. Thus, no preparations were made to counter its impact, either by giving support to young families to encourage them to have children if they wanted them, or by providing birth control education and supplies of contraceptives to those who did not. "We had certain objections and proposals when the law was drawn up," the chairman of the Czech Gynecological Society later told a reporter, "but the vice premier at that time, who was responsible for presenting the matter to the government, refused to receive us." [9]

Once it was passed, however, the actual implementation of the law — which turned out to be social rather than medical in content — fell to the doctors. They were expected not only to perform the abortions and give contraceptive advice, but also to sit on abortion commissions, take responsibility for their decisions, help solve the problems of applicants, and explain the potential dangers of abortion — all this in spite of the fact that in 80 percent of cases abortion was requested for nonmedical reasons. (In 1969, 29 percent of applicants already had three or more children, 14 percent were unmarried, and 10 percent gave housing problems as their reason. Only 20 percent of abortions were requested on medical grounds.) At a symposium sponsored in 1968 by the Gynecological Society and the State Population Commission to discuss possible changes in the law, the commissions were described as inexpert, impotent institutions which humiliated the women who came before them but were powerless to help them, and so, in the end, were forced to approve more than 90 percent of the applications.

The commissions suffered from a lack of nationally accepted criteria. One decision made by a district commission, read out at the symposium as an example, upheld a ruling refusing abortion to a mother of two who had argued that her husband was studying and that they were in debt for their cooperative apartment. "At the present time," the decision stated, "there is hardly a young couple which does not have either housing problems or is not in financial difficulties due to a cooperative flat, furnishing an apartment, etc. If we were to consider these temporary difficulties as sufficiently serious to permit abortion, there would be no need for a commission at all, since almost all applicants would have a right to abortion." [10]

Nevertheless, the medical profession did not want to see the commissions abolished. On the contrary, the gynecologists called for stricter regulations. Some argued that the procedure at least discouraged some women from asking for abortions, and that to put the whole responsibility on the woman's gynecologist might expose him to denunciations and persecution. Their

principal reason was the relatively high incidence of late complications which, they said, became apparent only when a woman
who had had one or more abortions decided to have a child or
actually became pregnant. The Czechoslovak death rate for the
operation was extremely low: 2.5 per 100,000 abortions (compared with 17 in Great Britain in the first year of the British
abortion law, 5.3 in New York City in 1970–71, and 8.2 in the
United States, according to a study made by Tietze and Lewit of
The Population Council covering the same period).

This is no doubt due to the fact that in Czechoslovakia, as
in the other socialist countries, abortion is permitted only in the
first trimester of pregnancy, except in unusual cases. (According
to Tietze and Lewit, the risk of complications is three to four
times as high in the second trimester.) However, the frequency
of complications following abortions performed on young wom-
en pregnant for the first time is greater than that occurring with
other women, Czechoslovak specialists claim. The result is often
sterility and vain regrets, and patients blame their physicians for
not warning them. An advisory group set up by the Ministry of
Health came to the conclusion that even with the most carefully
performed legal abortions there were early or late medical complications in 20 percent of cases. According to reports from
Hungary, 10 percent of women who had had at least one abortion gave birth to children weighing less than five pounds — that
is, did not carry their pregnancies to term. The incidence rose
to 18 percent among women who had had three or more abortions. The advisory committee called for amendment of the law
to rule out abortions in the case of all first pregnancies, and in
the case of second pregnancies where the woman was married.
It was necessary, they said, to prolong the interval between per-
missible abortions from six months to one year, and, in a
punitive mood, they suggested refusing abortion to women who
had already had one legal abortion and had been "properly
instructed in contraception."

The chief consulting gynecologist to the Ministry of
Health was in agreement with restricting abortion of first pregnancies in married women. He cited a review of five thousand
legal abortions in Czechoslovakia which showed that the inci-

dence of early complications of an inflammatory nature had dropped to 2.3 percent by late 1964 and of late complications, to 6.5 percent; but he agreed that the incidence was substantially higher in young women and those whose first pregnancy had been interrupted. The study showed, he said, that 17 percent of women visiting fertility clinics had legal abortions in their case histories, while 53 percent had had "spontaneous abortions" with inflammatory complications. He was reluctant to exclude unmarried women from the protection of the law, for fear of driving them to abort themselves. The suspicion that many cases of "spontaneous" abortion in hospital records were actually self-inflicted was supported, he said, by the fact that, whenever the commission adopted a stricter attitude, the number of recorded "spontaneous" abortions rose noticeably, but dropped again when the commissions relaxed their stance. Another reason for believing that a substantial number of young women pregnant for the first time were resorting to self-induced abortions was, he continued, the fact that more than 80 percent of all abortions recorded for these women were listed as "spontaneous," while less than 20 percent were "legally induced" abortions. In the case of women who had already had one child it was the other way around: only 27 percent of their known abortions fell into the "spontaneous" category.

Those concerned with the social aspects of abortion stood firm. Modification of the law would lead to clandestine abortions and suicides, they said. Only the creation of suitable conditions for young married couples, plus the widest possible distribution of contraceptive advice and materials would solve the abortion and population crises. "It is amazing," said a spokesman for the State Population Commission, "how prudish and embarrassed we are about the dissemination of contraception information. And I am not thinking so much of the embarrassment of individuals as of the prudery of the authorities and institutions concerned." [11]

The result of these debates between medical and social experts was agreement to postpone changes in abortion policy — except for improving the composition of the commissions — until instruction in contraception had been widely expanded,

the availability of suitable contraceptive methods had been assured, sex education had been introduced as a separate subject
in the schools, and an adequate network of marital and premarital counseling centers had been established.

There was a long way to go. At the time of this decision in
1969 only about 150,000 women, or 5 percent of the three million Czechoslovak women of childbearing age, were using oral
contraceptives or an intrauterine device. Of course, the habit of
resorting to abortion even when contraceptives are available is
not peculiar to Czechoslovakia or to Eastern Europe. In the
years 1948–58 Japan intentionally decreased its birthrate more
rapidly than any other country in history — 45 percent below
the prewar level — by introducing widespread instruction in
conventional methods of contraception (the pill was not yet
available), together with easy abortion. Authorities were able
to calculate, however, that only a very small percentage of the
decrease could have been due to contraceptive practices, since
each year the number of abortions exceeded the decrease in
births compared to the base year. Subsequently, Japan began an
active campaign to replace abortion by contraception, which
was apparently successful, because the number of abortions
thereafter decreased by 150,000 per year and the rate per 1,000
population was "down" to 8.6 by 1965. In Czechoslovakia in
1968 it was "up" to 6.9; it was 19.7 in Hungary, but only 1.4 in
Sweden, which has had easy abortion but also intensive family
planning for many years.

These examples illustrate one thing that family planners
already know: that it is not enough for couples to be aware that
contraceptive advice is available somewhere. Under circumstances where sex education and family planning are not
actively encouraged and contraceptives made available without
embarrassment, many people will take risks and rely on abortions to end an unwanted pregnancy. But the problem does not
end with "proper instruction in contraception," and all the
factors that cause women to end up on the surgical table are not
fully understood. Even when family planning is widespread and
contraceptives are easy to come by, there are some couples who
will not use them and will resort to abortion. According to a

study made in Hawaii during the first year of its law permitting abortion on demand, 1970–71, the investigators were surprised to find that abortion was by no means a last resort when contraception failed; in fact, 75 percent of women who utilized abortion were doing so because they had not been using contraception. Why? In another Hawaiian study the reason most frequently given by women who fell into this category was, "I didn't want sex to seem planned," although almost all of them had expected intercourse to take place. This was particularly true of young and single women.[12]

When the socialist countries introduced abortion, no family-planning groundwork had been laid; and although doctors were cautioned from the beginning to instruct their patients in birth control, in actual fact supplies of conventional contraceptives were limited, and advice was rarely offered. Undoubtedly several factors were involved, including the traditional conservatism of European countries and the influence of religion. Certainly an important role was played by the fact that for a long time the socialist countries had associated family planning with "neo-Malthusianism," which was understood to be a proposal to eliminate poverty by persuading the poor not to multiply. In the mid–1960s a Czech demographer, Helena Švarcová, still felt it necessary to point out that Lenin had not disapproved of family planning, and that

"

contraceptive techniques are in themselves only a means of controlling natality and nothing more. The principles of controlling natality, as well as the many means to that control, cannot be equated with the *social* basis of neo-Malthusianism. From this there follow essential and, in view of existing general opinions and prejudices, far-reaching conclusions for socialist population policy. Socialist policy cannot a priori reject the possibility of controlling natality, and need not be afraid to use the means to control it just because similar means are used in capitalist countries or recommended by bourgeois science.[13]

"

In 1962, when the International Planned Parenthood Federation held an international conference in Poland's capital city, Warsaw, the host country was the only one of the Eastern

THE UNDERPOPULATION CRISIS 151

European socialist countries which was a member of the organization, although the German Democratic Republic was to join the following year and Yugoslavia, in 1967. At that meeting the United States reported on its experience with two million users of oral contraceptives, and the British Family Planning Association announced that it had officially approved the pill for use in its clinics; but the Soviet delegation declared that Soviet health authorities categorically disapproved of any interference with woman's hormonal activity or modification of her menstrual cycle. At that time a spokesman for the Soviet Ministry of Health announced that work on a nonsteroid pill was in the experimental stage. This pill was never produced, but the Soviet Union has not modified its attitude, and in 1968 it announced that it would concentrate on mass production of the intra-uterine device. Poland was already experimenting with the pill, however, and in several other socialist countries intensive research was begun. Today only Rumania and Albania neither produce nor import IUDs or pills.

A Czechoslovak oral contraceptive was put on the market at the end of 1965. A year later, however, there were complaints that supplies were sufficient for only 100,000 of the three million potential customers, that only 15,000 women were using pessaries, and that only eighteen million sheaths were being produced annually. IUDs were also introduced at about this time but could be inserted in hospital outpatient departments only. Pills, of course, required a prescription, and in view of the possible side effects the Ministry of Health ruled that users were to be examined six times annually. At a quarter-hour per examination, it can be calculated that if only 100,000 women took the pill, these examinations would consume 150,000 doctor-hours annually — work for one hundred gynecologists. Since this additional manpower could not be provided, the overworked gynecologists in the health service were asked to add these examinations to their load. The fee charged for the pill and the service may have been enough to discourage some women; the additional small remuneration received by the gynecologists was obviously not sufficient to reconcile them to the extra work. In addition, many of these physicians were not personally convinced of the desirability of prescribing oral contraceptives for unmarried women, particularly young girls, and — being under pressure to encourage childbearing — often felt it necessary to try to persuade their patients to get married (if they were not) and to have babies. Understandably, many young women were shy about facing these reluctant practitioners, and even older women were embarrassed to bring the subject up themselves.

A shortage of the pill in 1969 (and not the last one), when manufacturers, discouraged by what they took to be the lack of interest, ceased to produce it and supplies ran out, set the campaign back again. Professor Jan Horský, director of the Institute for Mother and Child, a research hospital in Prague, described the quantity and quality of available contraceptives as unsatisfactory. "We have directives from the Ministry of Health," he said, "[to the effect] that every doctor is responsible for contraception, but there are no systematically directed clinics; they are not unified either methodologically or organizationally. There is a handful of premarital clinics. For this reason, the systematic propagation of and education for planned parenthood is not even possible. . . . Education in the schools on this subject is minimal or does not exist at all." [14]

Sex education in the schools consisted of a single lecture to fourteen-year-olds in the eighth year, usually given by the school doctor to boys and girls separately. Proposals by younger teachers for a more modern approach were generally quashed by middle-aged school directors. There was a woeful lack of suitable literature for children and young people, and even for parents, on this subject. At the same time, the number of school girls who became pregnant was increasing, and youngsters and their parents were regularly castigated in the press for their irresponsibility; sometimes the influence of the capitalist West, with its lax morals, was blamed. It was not until 1972 that the Ministry of Education announced that it was finally at work on a comprehensive new system of "education for parenthood," taking into consideration the recommendations of gynecologists that such education start in childhood.

Child psychologists and psychiatrists were among those who were opposed to any measures designed to bring pressure on a woman to have a child she did not want. "Most laymen and many doctors believe that once a woman has a child, the maternal instinct gets the upper hand. We are not convinced," one of them commented. "On the contrary, we believe that a child born as the result of an unwanted pregnancy is more likely than a wanted child to develop personality problems and physical complaints which make him a social liability." There was support for their opinion, for example, in the results of a long-term study carried out in Sweden, which had permitted abortions under approximately the same conditions as Czechoslovakia for several decades. In this study, 196 unwanted pregnancies were followed up. One-third ended in spontaneous or induced abortion, while 128 were brought to term, resulting in 134 infants. Four were stillborn, while 10 died before the age of three — an unusually high death rate. The progress of the remaining 120 children was followed until they were twenty-one years old, with disturbing findings: 60 percent had an insecure childhood, 28 percent required psychiatric care, 22 percent were registered with child welfare boards for delinquency, and 15 percent, for drunken misconduct.[15]

Nevertheless, the gynecologists were given the last word. Although the conditions which were to precede such a change had not been met, new regulations were issued in the middle of 1973 instructing the abortion commissions that only in exceptional cases were there to be abortions for other than medical reasons in the case of childless married women and those with one child. The rationale was the still-precarious population situation and the danger which abortion represents to women who have not yet completed their families. Because of what was termed the growing irresponsibility, especially of young people, toward sexual life, the abortion commissions were encouraged to invite the parents of unmarried boys and girls under eighteen whose relationship had resulted in an unwanted pregnancy to attend the hearing with their children.

The ambivalence with which the socialist countries now regard legalized abortion is underlined by the contrast between these new Czechoslovak rules and the present attitude of the neighboring German Democratic Republic, which, with an even more unfavorable population situation and a generally similar level of health services, has only recently legalized abortion on demand. Similarly, Bulgaria permits abortion on demand while neighboring Rumania, on approximately the same economic level, does not allow any kind of birth control. Except for Scandinavia, no other countries have had such long experience with large-scale interruptions of pregnancy as those of Eastern Europe, and consequently there is no material with which to compare the pessimistic long-term follow-up studies conducted in Czechoslovakia. Women sometimes suspect male gynecologists of viewing themselves as the Lord's surrogates in the process of creation, and of allowing this to color their attitude toward legalized abortion. If so, they have been encouraged in this view in Czechoslovakia by having a large share of responsibility for the implementation of population policy placed upon them. For the time being there is no evidence to dispute their figures, however, and there is no reason to believe that the conditions under which abortions are performed in Czechoslovakia are not just as good as they are in the United States or Great Britain. The early complication rates are certainly no higher than those found in the study conducted in the United States in 1970–71 by The Population Council. If a woman whose first pregnancy has been terminated by abortion is more than twice as likely to miscarry when she becomes pregnant again as a woman who has not had an abortion, as Czechoslovak gynecologists claim, this knowledge may dampen the general enthusiasm for abortion on demand, just as the original enthusiasm for the pill has subsided. Thus woman's "right to decide," which socialists had agreed ought to be her private concern, is never completely separated from medical considerations, although improved methods of contraception and abortion should gradually reduce this dependence on doctors' opinions.

The second set of pressures on potential mothers has come from the population experts. Every country has a population policy in the sense that, consciously or not, it influences one way or another the individual's decisions regarding family size. These, in turn, have far-reaching consequences for future labor power, population density, the armed forces, the structure of the population, and even prospects for national survival. Consequently, population policy has a direct bearing on women's rights. A nation should be actively concerned with population because, quite apart from the question of national extinction, the change in the population structure caused by a sudden decline in the birthrate creates extreme changes in demand — a sudden oversupply of schools and teachers, for example — as well as an increasingly larger proportion of aged people supported by an increasingly smaller percentage of productive adults, a situation which threatens to become a brake on economic and social progress. Alfred Sauvy, the French population expert, has pointed out that there is no population optimum which applies to all countries; an aging population, "where society is advancing to its own doom," must encourage births, while "a society suffering from exuberance" must curb its natural fertility.

The apparently obsessive concern of the socialist countries with their population figures is due to the fact that their birthrates dropped so suddenly and so rapidly from relatively high levels in the early 1950s to low rates in the mid–1960s; and continued to fall in spite of an increased number of women then entering the reproductive period of their lives — a result of the brief postwar baby boom which most of these countries experienced. In the majority of the socialist countries the annual rate of natural population increase (the difference between the live-birth rate and the death rate) is now well below the average for Europe and the United States of eight per one thousand inhabitants. The German Democratic Republic actually recorded a population loss in 1969 and 1970, and its growth rate stood at zero in 1971.

European countries may increase their population by adopting Asian orphans or encouraging immigration, as Sweden has done, but this creates long-term problems for the newly absorbed population, and, as far as world population is concerned, only siphons off a few drops from a rapidly swelling ocean in those countries where the population is exploding. Advanced technology may eliminate some manpower needs, but it does not solve problems of an unfavorable age structure, among which is a general loss of vitality and the initiative of youth. Moreover, it is an illusion to think that the mechanization and automation of all manual and unskilled work are just around the corner and that there is therefore no need to worry about manpower. The Western European countries have met their severe manpower shortages by attracting labor from poorer countries, thus creating new ghettos, new outbursts of racial tension, new political issues, and new education and housing problems. The employment of foreign workers from Yugoslavia, Turkey, Greece, and North Africa may bring some temporary economic relief to the countries of their origin, but it does not solve their basic problems. The unskilled jobs done by an estimated eight million *Gastarbeiter* ("guest workers") in the Common Market countries in 1973 are performed in the United States by blacks, Mexicans, and Puerto Ricans. A great unknown is what the effect of permissive abortion legislation will be on Western European population figures. Some of these countries may find it necessary to step up pro-childbirth policies to prevent national stagnation.

These are some of the complex ramifications of woman's personal decision to have or not to have children. Interest in protecting women's fertility and in maintaining a suitable population structure and a prospective labor force are not in themselves invasions of women's privacy; they become invasions of privacy when they take the form of restrictions on abortion which permit a commission to subject a woman to questioning, to subjective moral criticism of her sexual behaviour, and to exhortations to have more children. The alternative is positive family planning and prevention of unwanted pregnancies, together with conditions which make it possible for people who want to have children to do so without sharply reducing their standard of living, and without the mother's having to sacrifice all her interests outside the home. The socialist countries could have avoided an underpopulation crisis, or at least mitigated its most unpleasant consequences, if they had not been wedded from the beginning to the belief that socialism brings about an automatic increase in births; and if they had not made of the production of children a criterion of socialist and working-class morality, instead of recognizing it as a process influenced by a multiplicity of objective and subjective factors. Švarcová has attributed the failure to take notice earlier of what was going on under their noses to "a suspicious attitude toward facts and the study of long-term trends." Thus "it was possible for the opinion to be formed and strengthened that the new social order must be, and is, destined to show its superiority over capitalism in the field of population as elsewhere, that it will achieve a permanently greater rate of population increase than the capitalist countries. This extreme vulgarization was a considerable distortion of Marxism." [16]

This view of socialist population growth was adopted by the Soviet Union in the 1930s, where publication of official figures stopped at the same time, and it was taken over unquestioningly by the postwar socialist governments. Demographic studies, where they had existed (as in Czechoslovakia), were not officially resumed until 1957, and until then the pertinent statistical material was considered classified. Statisticians whose job it was to compile the government figures warned in the early 1950s that the birthrate had already started to fall after 1947, but that this fact had been obscured by the rapid postwar decline in the death rate and particularly in the infant mortality rate, which could not be expected to continue. Their warning was ignored, as was the experience of industrialized countries: that the shift of population to the cities brings about a permanent change in reproduction habits. The socialist countries' ability to see reality was obscured by their involvement in an ideological struggle which was sometimes described as Malthusianism vs. Marxism, but could more accurately have been called neo-Malthusianism vs. pseudo-Marxism. It is worth making a short excursion into history to understand how this situation which has had so direct an effect on the lives of women came about.

At the end of the eighteenth century, an Anglican clergyman by the name of Thomas Robert Malthus wrote his famous *Essay on the Principle of Population* as an indignant reply to William Goodwin and other thinkers influenced by the French Revolution, who saw the cause of poverty in private property. Population, wrote Malthus without benefit of statistics, grows in geometric progression, while the world's food increases in arithmetic progression. Absolute overpopulation is consequently a natural law, and poverty cannot be abolished by a change of government or a more equal distribution of property. He ruled out birth control, however, since expanding industry needed workers. Although his warning that population would outdistance resources eventually proved justified, his reasoning was unacceptable to many since he provided a theoretical justification for the idea that the conflicts and injustices of capitalism were natural and inevitable, however regrettable, and were not amenable to change because there were just too many people and too little to eat.

Writing fifty years later, Marx and Engels approached the problem from a very different position. To them, what distinguished man from the rest of the animal world was that he was not at nature's mercy, but could change nature through his ability to work and to produce new values. Engels's earliest economic essay criticizing bourgeois theories from a socialist point of view, *Outlines of a Critique of Political Economy*, written in 1843–44, pointed out that according to Malthus's doctrine even the first man was one too many, considering the level of agriculture at that time. He objected: "the productive power at mankind's disposal is immeasurable. The productivity of the soil can be increased *ad infinitum* by the application of capital, labour and science. . . . This immeasurable productive capacity, handled with consciousness and in the interest of all, would soon reduce to a minimum the labour falling to the share of mankind." [17] Much later, he acknowledged the abstract possibility that the number of people would one day be so large that its further growth would have to be limited, but he expected that if this happened it would occur when society was already communist and would know how to deal with the problem.

Marx had observed in his study of nineteenth-century capitalist growth that capital needs an increasing amount of labor to expand, but the tendency toward centralization in larger plants and the improved productivity of labor at intervals produces overemployment, and either workers are thrown out of jobs or no new ones are created. The result is an apparent "surplus population," until further expansion produces new employment opportunities which, however, never quite absorb the available labor. He formulated a population law quite different from that put forward by Malthus:

"

The labouring population produces, along with the accumulation of capital produced by it, the means by which itself is made relatively superfluous, is turned into a relative surplus population; and it does this to an always increasing extent. This is a law of population peculiar to the capitalist mode of production; and in fact every special historic mode of production has its own special law of population, historically valid within its limits alone. An abstract law of population exists for plants and animals only, and only in so far as man has not interfered with them.[18]

"

The value of Marx's observations for demographers, wrote Švarcová, is that it suggests looking for the dialetical relationship between the natural and social sides of reproduction, instead of regarding them as two parallel but independent processes. In this view, human population is seen as the unity of biological and social aspects which condition each other, the social aspects being the chief but not the only factor. This could be the key, she says, to discovering the objective factors which determine the development of population in concrete historical circumstances.

Instead, in the two decades from 1936 to 1956, Marx's law — which he deduced from nineteenth-century premonopoly capitalism, unmodified by labor or state intervention — was taken out of context and given the permanent validity of Boyle's Law of Gases. In its new interpretation, apparent population surpluses were due to capitalist exploitation. There could be no real overpopulation, and suggestions that the developing countries should restrict births could only be regarded as an attempt to evade a revolutionary solution to the crisis of imperialism and to use genocide to dominate the darker populations of the world.

At the same time, it was thought necessary to "discover" a population law for socialism, and this effort produced a series of formulations culminating in the one offered in a 1959 Soviet textbook of political economy, still in use in Czechoslovakia in the 1960s:

"

That capitalist population law according to which, parallel to the growth of social wealth, an increasingly large part of the working population becomes redundant, is forced out of production, and swells the ranks of the unemployed completely ceases to operate under socialism. [The socialist order guarantees full employment, a growing demand for workers, and their rational use.] This is the basis of the *socialist population law*. Full employment of all inhabitants capable of work and the continuous growth of the people's welfare leads under socialism to a reduction of the death and morbidity rates and to the rapid growth of the population.[19]

"

Even while this textbook was still in use, however, the authorities were acknowledging that socialism does not automatically bring population growth. They also came to appreciate that a pro-birth policy is not the only possible policy, that in certain conditions too rapid a population growth can be an obstacle to the development of the production forces, and that such a situation had arisen in the developing countries. Gradually they passed from a position of emphatic opposition to any action by the United Nations in support of family planning to cautious acceptance of the need for population control. In 1947 a Soviet delegate had declared to the United Nations Population Commission: "We consider any proposition formulated by this commission in favor of limiting marriage or birth in wedlock as barbarous. Over-population is only a fruit of capitalism. . . ."[20] A revision of opinion took place in the late sixties, and a leading Soviet demographer wrote in 1971, "It must be said that the effort to regulate the reproduction of the population as part of the solution to the problem of economic development is fully justified."[21]

East and West now share a belief in the need for population planning, although the socialist countries still accept the "doomsday" predictions of Western statisticians with considerable reservations.

If we adopt as one criterion of women's freedom the ability to limit their families or to have wanted children, it must be said that over the past quarter of a century socialist women have been subjected to a series of improvisations, conflicting demands, and changes in emphasis which have created an atmosphere of uncertainty. Early in 1968, a Czechoslovak population expert wrote:

"

The whole complex of frequently difficult-to-solve problems of young couples has culminated in an unfavorable population climate which already some years ago passed from the area of the purely material to the psychological sphere: for this reason almost two-thirds of young couples reject the idea of a third child under any circumstances; for this reason even families with satisfactory flats and sufficient income frequently have only one or two children. This may be an expression of selfishness (children do not occupy a foremost place in the hierarchy of life values today), but it may also be greater sense of responsibility (higher standards for the material welfare of children, their upbringing, education, etc.) .[22]

"

At the time he wrote this, half of Czechoslovak families had no dependent children, and less than 10 percent had three or more. In 1971 a survey of newlyweds showed that only 5.5 percent wanted three children. Not only shortages of housing, services, and nurseries and shortcomings in municipal transportation and shopping facilities, but other frustrations: intermittent shortages of maternity dresses, children's clothing, diapers, baby bottles, and nipples; the failure of buildings to provide parking spaces for carriages — all of these contributed to the impression that having a child was not a natural function but something out of the ordinary. Mothers of several children complained of the hostile stares and the comments of neighbors and strangers who obviously regarded a large family as a drain on public resources. "A woman's feeling that pregnancy is a socially unwelcome event is not infrequently produced by her place of work," wrote Radvanová.[23] Management thinks in terms of smoothly running production; a pregnant woman represents a hitch.

Apparently as a result of the complex of population measures described in the last chapter, Czechoslovakia has been able to reverse the downward trend, and has become the only country in Europe to achieve an increase in the birthrate four years in a row — from the low of 14.9 per 1,000 inhabitants in 1968 to 17.3 in 1972 (about the U.S. level). According to its statisticians, however, the battle is far from won, and it will not be able to maintain a birthrate which will prevent a prospective decline in the population unless it can persuade almost every second family to have three children. The government has made this a priority goal and has invested heavily in it.

Every measure has its side effects, however, and some of the possible consequences can be judged from the experience of Hungary, where the tendency to deemphasize nursery building has already been noted. Though in Czechoslovakia in 1973, almost 90 percent of the new mothers who were entitled to the housewives' allowance were staying home, in Hungary the allowance, which was introduced in 1967, was not having the desired effect; after a slight rise, the birthrate dropped once more. In 1972, 60 percent of Hungarian mothers who had taken advantage of the allowance decided to return to their jobs when their children were eighteen months old, that is, a year-and-a-half ahead of time. In a majority of cases the reason was financial: the rise in the cost of living had wiped out much of the value of the allowance.[24] Other disadvantages of the long stay at home which have been noted include the fact that the woman loses her length-of-service increment while she is away; also, that it is hard to find a "temporary" replacement for a three-year period, and thus enterprises are reluctant to hire for skilled jobs women who have not yet had their families. The allowance also has an effect on the division of household tasks. The husband is unwilling to share the housework when his wife is at home, and this in turn reduces the amount of free time she has for recreation, study, or other interests.

Woman's "natural role" thus remains a handicap. It will clearly require a great deal more study to arrive at a program which will synthesize woman's aspirations and society's needs in

a truly harmonious fashion. Practices which are one-sided —
that is, which are aimed at changing the attitudes and behavior
of women without at the same time altering those of men,
whether they are husbands, gynecologists, or plant managers —
can be expected to have one-sided results.

CHAPTER EIGHT

COLLECTIVE VS. FAMILY CARE

"

Our parachutes are the same as theirs, we jump from the same planes, we've got guts, and our performance isn't much different from the men's, but that's where emancipation ends. I'm married, I'm employed, and I have a daughter. And a granny. If I couldn't say: "Granny, keep an eye on her," my sporting career would be at an end.

"

So spoke a member of Czechoslovakia's women's national parachute-jumping team when she was asked for her views on women's emancipation in sports early in 1972.[1] Grannies, as household aids, are on the way out all over the world, however. According to a survey made in 1968 in eighty-one Czechoslovak day nurseries for children under three, in those cases where Granny was still alive she was not available to help with the children because, in 35 percent of instances, Granny was employed herself, and in 45 percent, she lived too far away. In only 15 percent was old age or illness the main reason.

Day-care centers are coming to be thought of as the only answer for trapped mothers, even in those countries — like the United States — where opposition, until recently, has been most violent. This is an East-West rapprochement of ideas which has taken more than half a century to achieve, if one considers that the Russian Communist party wrote into its program in 1917 a provision calling for the establishment of nurseries for infants and young children at all factories and other enterprises where women were employed, with half-hour recesses every three hours for nursing mothers. Collective care of small children is not a bolshevik idea, however, but can be traced back at least to Jan Amos Comenius, who in the mid–seventeenth century put forward in *Pampaedia,* the fourth book of his *General Treatise on the Improvement of Human Life,* a plan for nursery schools which corresponds closely to what is considered a good nursery school today, including visual aids and learning through play. Young children need the company of other children, he said, and one child can sharpen the brain of another better than anyone else. The first real nursery schools in Europe were formed in the early decades of the nineteenth century as philanthropic institutions, coincident with the employment of women and older children in industry, and in most Western European countries they have until recently preserved the character of social institutions for children whose mothers could not otherwise care for them.

The Second World War, which put so many women in men's jobs, saw the establishment of many day-care centers on an emergency basis, and while the number dropped again in the postwar years, the demand had been created and it grew. Places in publicly supported nurseries in Great Britain dropped from 30,000 in 1953 to 22,000 in 1961. In the industrial city of Birmingham in England, an area which in 1965 was seeking female labor, the eighty nurseries operated by the local authorities during the war had shrunk to twenty, with places for only 950 children. At the same time, private nurseries were springing up, many operating only part-time and serving children whose mothers thought it would benefit them, or who wanted more free time for themselves. France in 1962 had 702 nurseries with twenty-five thousand places and 785 nursery schools with space for thirty thousand children, and in line with its pro-birth policy planned to establish 200 nurseries annually thereafter, about half of what experts foresaw as the actual need. In Sweden, one of the countries most dependent on female labor and most active in promoting women's equality, the building of state-supported preschool institutions stagnated. In 1968, according to a government report, they had places for whole-day care of only twenty thousand preschool children, but since then funds have been appropriated for rapid expansion. In 1958 the United States Children's Bureau made a study of the child-care arrangements of American working women with children under twelve. They found that 57 percent were cared for by relatives; 21 percent, by nonrelatives; 8 percent were latchkey children; and only 2 percent were in day-care centers.

By contrast, in the Soviet Union, in spite of wartime setbacks, there were in 1962 1,750,000 places for nursery-age children (excluding seasonal nurseries in rural regions), and 3,750,000 children from three to six years old enrolled in kindergartens — three times the prewar level.[2] Yet if such institutions are to be regarded as the mainstay of the working mother, these staggering figures represented a very partial solution in a country where so many mothers are employed, since they accounted for only 12 percent and 20 percent, respectively, of the children in the appropriate age groups. The figures have since been replaced by still more staggering ones. By 1967, 7.2 million preschool children were receiving day care. Nevertheless, at a meeting of Moscow demographers in 1969 to discuss the effect of women's employment on population trends, this was described as far from adequate. The participants concluded that for some time to come a considerable number of mothers, especially those with several children, would have no alternative but to stay at home.

Czechoslovakia, in 1971, had 66,300 children under three years of age in day nurseries (representing 10 percent of the total age-group and 37 percent of children in this age-group whose mothers were working), and 377,600 children between three and six in nursery schools (50 percent of the age-group and 77 percent of the children of working mothers). The Five-Year Plan, which ends in 1975, contains a pledge to increase the number of places in nursery schools to accommodate 65 percent of all children of eligible age.

Even such a superficial survey as this one inevitably raises two questions. The first one is to what extent it is possible to meet the potential demand for day-care centers with government resources. The second is to what extent it is desirable to do so.

To deal with the second one first: The arguments which kept so many American women in their homes in the postwar years are well known, although perhaps not yet fully analyzed and understood; they were chiefly interpretations and popularizations of some of Freud's ideas which happened to fit the prevailing mores. In summary, it was bluntly stated that any woman who could not find fulfillment in her biologically ordained functions of motherhood and wifehood should have her head examined. Reluctance to entrust small children to care outside the home — and this was true not only in the United States but in Western Europe as well — also stemmed from the postwar findings of Rene Spitz (1945) and John Bowlby (1951) in their studies of "hospitalism" in children kept in hospitals or children's homes for extended periods. They concluded that it is disastrous to rear an infant away from its mother, and that this can cause severe pathology in later life. The United States Children's Bureau declared unequivocally, "Young children need individual attention from their parents and do not fare well in groups." [3] Many child psychologists, psychiatrists, educators, and social workers were reluctant to modify their views even when faced with what seemed to be incontrovertible evidence in Israeli kibbutzim which in the 1960s were already raising a second generation of children who had been separated from their mothers almost from birth.

Reviewing the report of one such group of fifty experts who attended a five-day "institute" on the subject in Israel in 1963, the psychoanalyst Bruno Bettelheim commented: "Here, at the meeting, clashing head on, were two views of what is the best way to raise children. By the end of the book, however, this reader was left with the feeling that while initially the visitors from abroad wanted on the whole to prove to the Kibbutz that its method of child-rearing is harmful to the child, they were reluctantly forced to conclude that things are not quite so bad as they expected." [4] In 1969, Dr. Bettelheim published his own observations about kibbutz education based on a seven-week study in *Children of the Dream*. He concluded that the kibbutz produces a healthy personality which — while somewhat different from the American ideal, placing less emphasis on personal identity, emotional intimacy, and individual achievement — is well adapted to kibbutz culture and society. He made the key observation that the child's peer group, which remains the same throughout his education, replaces its parents as the object of early, deep, and lasting attachment. These children, he said, seem to do better than many children raised in underprivileged American homes and better than quite a few brought up at home by middle-class parents. He felt, however, that there was little that could be applied immediately in a practical way to the United States. This is obvious, for the kibbutz is — or was at that time — a closed, essentially agricultural community, a highly cohesive society whose members have the same cultural background and status and share the same values and goals. The parents may be in contact with their children during the day, the children's group is not isolated from society but integrated into it, and the membership of the group remains stable from the cradle through adolescence. The kibbutzim grew up under certain historical conditions as a result of a shared philosophy; the situation could hardly be reproduced in any industrial society, although it might be in China or the other developing countries. At present the kibbutzim themselves are undergoing industrialization and have already modified some of their original practices.

The experience of the socialist countries is much more difficult to study because there are so many variables. One thing can be said definitely: nursery schools for children from three to six have become an accepted part of the educational system, regarded as a valuable preparation for school itself, and almost no one questions their worth for the majority of children. The same attitude can be found in Sweden, where the aim is to give all children of five and all underprivileged children of four the chance to attend. It is also gaining ground in other European countries. In 1972–73 more than half of three- and four-year-olds were receiving at least part-time state-financed preschool education in France, Belgium, Holland, and Italy. Great Britain is far behind this, but has set the goal of providing nursery schooling for all children of this age whose parents want it by 1983. On the other hand, as has been seen in previous chapters, there is a trend in a number of socialist countries (among them Czechoslovakia) away from the care of children under the age of two in collective institutions. Medical opinion, concepts of mental health, and problems of financing all play a part in this development, in addition to the population worries which have already been discussed.

The original socialist idea of placing infants and children in day-care centers was motivated by a concern for women's freedom. In a frequently quoted passage from *A Great Beginning*, a pamphlet published in 1919, Lenin calls for the liberation of women from the "unproductive, petty, nerve-racking, stultifying, and crushing drudgery" of work in the house.

"Do we in practice pay sufficient attention to the question which in theory every Communist considers indisputable?" he inquired. "Of course not. Do we take proper care of the *shoots* of communism which already exists in this sphere? Again the answer is *no*. Public catering establishments, nurseries, kindergartens — here we have examples of these shoots, here we have the simple, everyday means involving nothing pompous, grandiloquent or ceremonial, which can *really emancipate women*. . . ." [5] The great majority of the prewar nurseries in the Soviet Union were temporary establishments set up in the fields with no plant or equipment to speak of, to relieve farm women during the peak of the harvest season. Thus, according to the figures compiled by Dodge, of 4,868,600 children in all nurseries in 1932, 3,920,300 were in seasonal nurseries, while in 1940 the total was about the same, but the proportion of children in seasonal nurseries had increased. There were at most 800,000 children in permanent nurseries in the prewar Soviet Union, a figure which, while still impressive, was hardly enough to justify either the outraged cries often heard in the thirties that "Russia is nationalizing the children," or the optimistic reports that "in the Soviet Union every mother can put her child in a nursery." After the war, the proportion was reversed, and emphasis was put on expanding permanent facilities.

Between the wars, when child psychology enjoyed its first

period of rapid growth, major emphasis in child-study circles in the United States and Europe had been on the physical health and well-being of the child, and on implanting in it from the earliest weeks and months of life the habits society required. The child was a tablet of clay on which anything could be written; all that was needed was consistency and thoroughness. People whose memory goes back far enough will recall that mothers were counseled not to spoil their children; not to pick them up, cuddle them, or overstimulate them; to feed them by the clock; and not to give in to their whims — otherwise bad habits would be learned, and the damage might never be undone. Even moral qualities could be inculcated by correct habit-forming procedures. A good nursery could presumably follow these rules better than an unscientific mother.

This system of child-rearing owed its origins to various schools of behaviorist psychology, which was introduced in the United States by J. B. Watson before the First World War, and was the dominant — although, of course, not the only — influence in psychology in the between-the-wars period. (Behaviorism has since then been modified and refined in the United States by B. F. Skinner.) The founding father — although he considered himself a physiologist and not a psychologist — was the Russian scientist I. P. Pavlov, who, in his famous experiments with dogs, made the important discovery that there are two kinds of reflexes: unconditioned, with which the animal is born, and conditioned, which he develops in response to stimuli in his surroundings and which are mediated by the higher nervous centers of the brain. In very simplified terms, behaviorism made child training a matter of properly conditioned reactions — a job much more complex, of course, than conditioning a dog to salivate or a rat to press a lever, since in man other stimuli (like speech) modify the direct response to the original stimulus.

This explanation of behavior and the learning process was in a direct line with the materialist and positivist thinking of natural scientists of the nineteenth century, whose central concern since Darwin had been the adaptation of an organism to its environment. Pavlov's work made it possible to put psychology on a strictly material basis, amenable to concrete tests and demonstrations; it eliminated reliance on speculation about what went on in the conscious mind. Matter was, after all, the only thing that could be shown to exist, and thinking and feeling must be somehow reflected in it. This idea, together with Marxist determinism, which was to provide the key to understanding the environment that interacted with the human mind, was the basis for the new Soviet psychology. "Where Darwin showed how living organisms can adapt to their environment by changing slowly from one generation to the next, Pavlov showed how a living organism can adapt by changing rapidly during its own lifetime." [6]

Soviet psychology was destined to develop outside the mainstream of world thought for many years, and without the dialectical interplay and the stimulus which other theories, however unacceptable they might have been, would have provided. In this period the idea that all men can be made equal by the right environment was pushed to its furthest limits. If man could change rapidly in the course of his lifetime, surely he would change for the better in an environment free from exploitation and poverty. A compelling need was felt to show the immediate superiority of socialism, to provide proof that it is environment and not heredity that counts, and to demonstrate that socialist man could conquer environment more rapidly and more thoroughly than capitalist man had dreamed. The agronomist T. S. Lysenko provided the theory, claiming to show experimentally that changes brought about in an organism's lifetime were permanently fixed after one or two generations. He declared Darwin's theory of natural selection to be a bourgeois invention (pointing to the way the "survival of the fittest" was used to justify capitalist competition in the United States), and proclaimed the essence of true Darwinism to be the inheritance of acquired characteristics. (This, of course, is true Lamarckianism.) Unfortunately for Lysenko, geneticists had by this time shown quite conclusively (at least to Westerners) that inherited changes take place very slowly, through random variations in the combination of the genes and through unpredictable mutations. If the differences give their possessor a better chance to survive and multiply they are passed on in the same slow way to their offspring, and this constitutes "natural selection." The conflict between this theory of inheritance and Lysenko's caused its originators to be branded in the Soviet Union the "founders of modern reactionary genetics" — particularly Darwin's contemporary Gregor Mendel, who was the first to describe the laws governing heredity; the American scientist T. H. Morgan, who discovered the function of the chromosome; and the German biologist Leopold Weismann, who showed that genetic material was not affected by body changes. Lysenko ultimately succeeded in having the study of Mendelian genetics banned from the Soviet Union.[7]

Under the influence of Lysenko's ideas, the people of the Soviet Union had from the mid–1930s on been encouraged to believe that a few generations of socialism would lead to a genetic improvement in the physical and mental makeup of the population. This, of course, required not only the rooting out of bourgeois theory in science but the establishment of a purely socialist education. The educator whose ideas were believed to incorporate Marxist principles to the highest degree was the successful reformer of juvenile delinquents, A. S. Makarenko. His pedagogical system had been developed during the years 1920–28, when he directed the Gorky Colony for homeless children, an experience which he described in his book *The Road to Life* (and which was portrayed in the Soviet film classic of the same name by the director Nikolai Ekk in 1931). Makarenko later applied his theories in a similar colony, the Dzerzhinsky Commune. In his teaching and writing he stressed the individual approach to the child and the importance of the educator's personal influence. His central theme was the transforming effect of useful work and responsibility, and he combined respect for the child's personality with maximum demands and strict, although reasonable, discipline — "the discipline of combating and surmounting difficulties." In his colony important decisions were made by the young people themselves. He trusted them, he said, because he believed in their future and not in their past.

At the same time, he rejected out of hand all the experimental work in child study and in education which was taking place in capitalist countries at the time, and which had previously received considerable attention in the Soviet Union — the work of Gesell, Piaget, and Dewey; the Dalton Plan; any emphasis on heredity; any attempt to probe the child's personality by psychological testing. After his death in 1939 his writings were promoted to the status of a unique, all-inclusive science of pedagogy which dominated socialist education all through the fifties and into the sixties. One of his greatest contributions was considered to be his emphasis on the educational significance of the collective. In the introduction to a Soviet edition of Makarenko's *Book for Parents* Professor V. Kolbanovsky writes:

"

Collectivism is the buttress of the educational system of A. S. Makarenko. Anton Semyonovich's deep conviction regarding the powerful force of a well-organized collective and its ability to exercise the most ennobling influence on the development of the personality did not arise only as a result of his own pedagogical experience. It was suggested to A. S. Makarenko by the totality of socialist experience in which new social relations rest on foundations of collectivism, on the working and ideological solidarity of millions of working people. This conviction of Anton Semyonovich fully corresponds to the classic formulation by the founders of Marxism: "Only in the collective does the individual receive the means which permit the comprehensive development of his abilities, and thus only in the collective is personal freedom possible." [8]

"

In his *Book for Parents,* which after the war became the most widely distributed book on child guidance in the socialist countries, Makarenko viewed the family as a kind of collective in which the parents exercised their authority neither by patriarchal discipline nor by sentimental coddling, but by commanding respect through their example and their work in a collective of which all were proud: the factory, and beyond that, Soviet society. It was part of the school's responsibility to influence education in the family in the right direction. Makarenko was better at telling parents what they should do than at explaining how they should do it, however. Moreover, his direct experience was with homeless children, not with parents and in-

fants or preschool toddlers. Parents who tried to solve the
problem of authority simply by setting an example in their
personal life and their work for the public weal, as Makarenko
counseled, often found themselves in conflict with the school or
other institutions, of which they expected too much and which,
in turn, expected more of them.

Eventually the theory that environment could change man
overnight, and that criminality, prostitution, and neuroses
would disappear without special attention, had to give way.
Writing in the sixties, two Czechoslovak psychiatrists remarked
tactfully, in a book on legal psychiatry still used as a text by
university students: "Many years ago Makarenko aroused the
attention of the world with his ambitious educational experiment. He was a talented worker, devoted to his ideas, but he did
not have the theoretical and practical knowledge in the fields
of psychology and psychiatry which is at the disposal of workers
today. If the lag which has occurred is to be made good, it is
necessary to use and develop Makarenko's pedagogical experience still further."

Elsewhere in the same book they pay a reserved tribute to
Freud, whose theories regarding instinctive and unconscious
drives had earlier been banned as destructively pseudoscientific
and reactionary. His value, they wrote, is that he showed that
apparently meaningless phenomena, like dreams and mistakes,
are a motivated part of behavior, and especially "that the early
experience of the child has much greater importance for his behavior as an adult than was thought. He laid the foundation
for a detailed understanding of the connection between the
mental life of the child and his immediate surroundings, his
family." [9]

Freud received a degree of public recognition in Czechoslovakia in 1969 when a bust was unveiled in the small town of his
birth, Příbor in Moravia (formerly known as Freiburg). The
Moravian-born abbot, Gregor Mendel, who established the
basis for modern genetics in 1865 when he published his then-
neglected paper on the law governing the inheritance of dominant and recessive characteristics in peas, had received a similar
but more emphatic reinstallation in 1965. In that year UNESCO

celebrated the centennial of the publication of Mendel's work at an international symposium on genetics held in Brno, Czechoslovakia, and a statue of Mendel now casts its shadow on the site of his pea garden in the Brno monastery where he worked and taught.

Contact with developments in Western countries had been maintained unofficially by some individuals in several of the socialist countries during these cold-war decades. In the field of child care, many doctors and psychologists were conducting their own unpublicized investigations, having at their disposal the exceptional opportunities offered by various child-care facilities with their uniform policies and carefully kept records. They were familiar with the work of Spitz and Bowlby on "institutionalism" or "hospitalism" in infants, and had amassed considerable data of their own. Two psychologists, Josef Langmeier and Zdeněk Matějček, spent the decade between 1950 and 1960 studying all the available literature on hospitalism from both East and West, and had collected a bibliography of one thousand titles before they published their own study, *Psychological Deprivation in Childhood,* in 1963.

The Czechoslovak Pediatrics Society had discussed the psychological problems of childhood at a national meeting for the first time in 1961, previous congresses having been devoted wholly to medical questions. The actual breakthrough, if it can be pinpointed, had come in 1960 when Dr. Langmeier addressed the second national congress of psychiatry in Prague on sensory and emotional deprivation and its importance for mental hygiene in childhood. Although there had been critical studies published before this, he summarized the shortcomings of collective care and clearly formulated for the first time the objections to the official ideology that man prospers in a collective under all circumstances. The excitement caused in professional circles by this clear statement that problems of mental hygiene are not automatically solved by a change in the social system spread into the daily press, there to generate a spontaneous campaign for reform.

Langmeier and Matějček were not concerned primarily with day nurseries. What they were anxious to change was the whole system of institutional care which was built on the supposed benevolent influence of the collective. This had included the abolition of foster care in families in 1950, legal difficulties placed in the way of adoption, and, especially, a schedule according to which children who were orphaned or abandoned or whose parents could not care for them passed through institutions for infants, for toddlers, for preschool children, and finally for school-age children, thus experiencing a change in their environment and their caretakers four times in the first six years of life. Their book was a synthesis of results obtained at home and abroad since John Bowlby made his first study for the World Health Organization, *Maternal Care and Mental Health,* in 1951. The Czechoslovak medical community benefited from the delay in making this material public at least to the extent that they were spared Bowlby's first pessimistic conclusions regarding the universal and irreversible effect of psychological deprivation in children who lacked maternal care in infancy. Later studies showed that not all children institutionalized early in life suffered from serious personality disturbances, that severe damage was rare, that improved institutional care resulted in milder symptoms, and that preventive and therapeutic measures could be successful. For example, if a child was always cared for by the same nurse, who gave it individual attention and affection, this could to a certain extent compensate for the absence of a loving mother. Bowlby himself revised his original conclusions in the mid-fifties.

Czechoslovak observations distinguished four types of deprivation. Some children, they found, adapt relatively well to institutional life simply by adjusting their expectations; others become passive, withdraw into infantilism. Another type makes endless efforts to establish emotional contact with every comer, but lacks interest in all other aspects of life, is uninvolved; a fourth compensates with intensified antisocial and destructive tendencies. All have in common that their intellectual and emotional development is stunted. As they grow up they are unable to experience deep feeling or to establish satisfactory relationships. The fact that these reactions were found among children in all types of institutions and in children who had never known other than institutional life, which is relatively uniform, led to the conclusion that it was the effect of institutional conditions on the particular child's psychological makeup that produced the differences, and that hereditary background played a definite role but one that was difficult to define. Children admitted to institutions after months or years in their own families, (usually inadequate ones) exhibited the same type of behavior, although less frequently. Czechoslovak authors reported, on the basis of clinical experience, that emotionally deprived children were found not only in socially incompetent families (incomplete families, homes where one or both parents were alcoholic or mentally below par, etc.), but also in comfortably situated families where the mother took care of the child's physical needs but was emotionally uninvolved and uninterested.

Langmeier and Matějček were very careful not to confuse day care in nurseries with institutional care, and not to extend their observations mechanically. In their book they describe the nursery as an essential aid to employed women and a place where, provided proper psychological, pedagogical, and physical conditions are present, the child's normal development can be assured. The nursery can provide stimulation for the child and is a source of guidance for the mother. They mention many ways in which nurseries could be improved, including provision for more contact with men (there is an ironclad tradition that all nursery-school teachers are women); mixed age groups to create a family-like environment; and, above all, the proper selection and education of personnel. They warn that there will always be a certain percentage of children who will not adapt to even the best nursery. They emphasize, however, that a nursery is not a substitute for, but a supplement to, family care; and they observe that too often, in practice, families use them as a way to avoid their own responsibilities, while at the same time having confidence that the child will be well taken care of at minimum cost.

These potential dangers and disadvantages of collective care took on a much more concrete aspect when, in the campaign to reeducate the public, generalizations were translated into specific institutions and illustrated with living children.

The book had appealed to professionals. One of the most effective means of convincing the layman of the importance of the early emotional life of children was a documentary film, *Children Without Love,* made by the director Kurt Goldberger in cooperation with Langmeier and Matějček — a picture which won festival prizes and was purchased as a teaching aid by institutions in other countries. This film compared the life of babies and toddlers in model Czechoslovak children's homes, hygienic and full of toys, with attentive nurses, but with a stereotyped routine lacking in stimuli, with that of a child from a secure family who spent a few hours a day in a nursery. It caught the hunger of institutionalized children for demonstrations of affection and physical contact with a sympathetic adult, and the terror of a child suffering from psychological deprivation when faced with the unfamiliar — in this case a huge teddy bear — in contrast to the calm curiosity of a normal child.

The filmmakers also interviewed the director of an all-week, around-the-clock nursery from which children were taken home only for weekends. She regarded these institutions as an unfortunate necessity and hoped to see them cut to a minimum. "Every child should have a home where he belongs, with a family that belongs to him," she said. A week-long study later made in an all-week nursery school for the Pedagogical Institute of the Czechoslovak Academy of Science by a psychologist, Eva Vančurová, supported this point of view. Even children from what would be considered obviously inadequate homes revealed in their conversation a longing for home and mother. "I would rather be at home," was their constant refrain. Asked to draw a picture showing "Sunday at home," 70 percent drew either the family without them or themselves alone in a deserted house. Children in a control group who attended nursery school only during the day reacted quite differently: their pictures indicated that they regarded themselves as an integral part of the family, and showed them engaged in a variety of pleasurable activities.

In the documentary *Children Without Love,* babies were seen being trundled to the nursery in their carriages through a gray rainy dawn. Children were observed to become restless at four o'clock in the afternoon, while the commentator spoke for them. "We like it in the nursery, but when it gets to be afternoon we start to look forward to mother." And finally, the cameraman focused on the last little girl to be picked up, whose mother had been delayed or perhaps simply "forgot." "Maybe we will learn to live without tenderness," said the commentator as the audience looked at the child's wistful face. "We won't be capable of feeling it. At the moment it's still all right. We still know how to feel sad when you don't come."

This picture was shown in parliament and seen by the entire government. One result was a review of the whole system of children's homes and the introduction during the next decade of various types of substitute family care in small homes and children's villages. An increased number of children were given out for adoption; and, finally, in 1973 legislation reinstituting foster care was passed.

Regarding all-week nurseries and nurseries with continuous, round-the-clock service, the Ministry of Health reacted with a firm statement that these were to be regarded as social institutions for emergency situations; that mothers of small children should work morning shifts so that children could be in the nursery during the day; and that under no circumstances should nurseries be run on a shift basis, with children spending nights or days there depending on what hours their mothers were working. These round-the-clock institutions, originally established to free the mother for work at a time when collective education was given priority over individual care, and which accounted for 15–20 percent of all places in nurseries at the beginning of the 1960s, had by the end of 1968 been reduced to 3.8 percent of the total, and were caring for about 2,500 children.

Pediatricians and psychologists welcomed an atmosphere in which they could at least express their reservations about the value of collective life for children under one year, and many declared for two years as the earliest age at which a toddler might really profit from the society of his peers. One of these was Dr. Marie Damborská, director of one of Czechoslovakia's model homes for orphaned and abandoned infants in Luhačovice, the author of many studies of deprivation in children, and much sought after for her opinion. In one of her many articles,

after pointing to the fact that children under three who attend
a nursery are ill twice as often as those who stay at home, and
that paid and unpaid maternity leave already made it possible
for a mother to remain at home for a year, she wrote:

"

Is one year a favorable age for a child to enter a collective?
From my experience with children of this age I would be very much
in favor of at least another year at home. At 12–13 months the child
is most sensitive to strange faces and is afraid of the unknown. He
feels secure only with his mother or other permanent caretaker. I believe a two-year-old may be mature enough, but even at this age
eight hours in the society of other children make too great a demand
on his nervous system. Long hours in a group from which crying and
noise cannot be eliminated tire the child and weaken his nervous
system, leading to his neurotization.[10]

"

Rising early, especially in winter; divided authority between home and school; the importance of constant interplay
with an adult in learning to talk — these were some of the other
considerations she mentioned.

Writing on another occasion about "micro-deprivation" in
children growing up in apparently well-ordered homes, she
asked: "Does today's overworked woman and mother have time,
strength, and ability to create a good emotional atmosphere?
Indeed, with the present tempo of life is she not herself emotionally deprived?" She did not see the solution in women staying at
home, however, but in the proper evaluation of the mother's
importance by society, which should be expressed by improving
services to give her some of the six hours she normally spends
on housework, shopping, and cooking every day to spend with
her children.

Dr. Hanuš Papoušek of the Department of Preventive Pediatrics in the Institute for Care of Mother and Child in Prague,
on the other hand, declared that the question of the best time to
transfer a child from all-day care in the family to part-time care
in the nursery had not yet been thoroughly studied, and that
current hypotheses were based on nurseries as they were and
not as they might be. He considered that infants over six months

old might be admitted for four hours a day and children over a year old, for six hours. He saw the main dangers in the fact that children were introduced to collective life too suddenly, for too-long periods at a time, and were returned too soon after illness. He hoped to see experimental nurseries that would try out different combinations of family and collective care, and deplored the lack of funds for this purpose.

The physical illness of nursery children was the aspect that interested most pediatricians, although they also took note of such sources of frustration as being kept waiting in wet diapers or at feeding time, since nurses could not do everything at once. It was estimated that children enrolled in nurseries fell ill on an average of six times a year with a temperature of over 100.4 degrees, usually with illnesses of the upper respiratory tract — and some studies put the average for the youngest children at eight times a year. The incidence of infectious jaundice was reported to be five to ten times greater in nursery children than in those who stayed at home, and, of course, other infectious diseases were also more common. On a national average only 77 percent of nursery places were actually occupied on any given day, chiefly because of illness.

The establishment of "nursery hospitals" for slightly ill children had been tested and found to be impractical, a spokesman for the Ministry of Health told the public. The chief reason, she said, was that one could not tell at the beginning of a "mild" illness whether it would remain a sniffle or develop into measles. It would be necessary to isolate all such children immediately and to have qualified health personnel in attendance, and the cost of building and running such an establishment would be out of proportion to the benefits. Furthermore, she said, from the child's point of view, if he was mildly ill he was better off at home.

Baby-sitter services to care for ill children while mothers were at work foundered on the lack of suitable women — as most of these were already employed or taking care of their grandchildren — and on the high cost. One possible type of supplementary care was the micro nursery, in which a woman took care of three children in her own home. This, of course, required the training and inspection of the woman concerned if she was to be paid by the health authorities, and has not become widespread. Recently interest has been shown in this solution in Sweden, where it has been proposed to place such women under the patronage of the local nursery school, which will give them guidance and keep them from feeling isolated.

An international symposium on nurseries, held in Prague in October 1966 by the Czechoslovak Medical Society, the Ministry of Health, and the Department of Pediatrics of Charles University for delegates from the socialist countries of Eastern Europe was the first confrontation of its kind and revealed a lack of uniformity of opinion. All agreed that children's homes of the institutional type should not be expanded, and that more attention should be given to adoption and other types of family-like care. All had had similar experience with the high rate of illness among nursery children. Rumania reported good results with regular gamma globulin shots, while Czechoslovakia found them ineffective in children under one year and, moreover, reported that they reduced the infant's own immunity. Bulgaria had had some success with developing resistance by exposure to cool air, later to lukewarm water, and finally to cold baths.

The largest percentage of children under three who were enrolled in nurseries was reported from the Soviet Union; the figure given, 26 percent, was for the Ukraine only. In the German Democratic Republic, 16.8 percent of that age group was accommodated; in Czechoslovakia, 9.7 percent; in Poland, 8.3 percent; and in Hungary, Bulgaria, and Rumania, less.

In the Soviet Union the nursery was regarded as an institution beneficial to both mothers and children. Children were best admitted between the sixth and ninth month when they were not yet deeply attached to home, it was said. The nursery was not a substitute for the family, but, together with family life, could give the child everything it needed for its development, particularly the experience of collective life. A child could, of course, grow up without a nursery if its mother was at home, if there were other children in the family, and if the mother knew something about child-training.

Professor Schmidt-Kolmer of the German Democratic

Republic declared that the discussion reminded her of similar talk about nursery schools after the First World War; yet today no one doubted that nursery schools were a good thing and should be available to all children. In nurseries, collective education is carried out by experts, she said, and if we want to influence the character of the child, the second and third years of life offer a suitable opportunity. It is a question whether it is best to admit a child at this age, when it requires six months to adjust to nursery life, or whether it is not better to start the adjustment process in infancy. In any case, she added, in view of the shortage of labor in the German Democratic Republic, it is impossible to keep women home from work for such a long time.

Dr. Pomerska of Poland declared, however: "According to what we know today, the family without doubt provides the best environment. The socialist family is capable of and equipped for educating its children. If it cannot provide a proper upbringing I doubt that the nursery can, because who make up the personnel of nurseries? The same people. The necessity or the superiority of the nursery has not been proved."

The Czechoslovak delegates picked their way between the two extremes. A six-year longitudinal study of 126 Czechoslovak children who entered a nursery at various ages, and who were compared with children from similar families who were brought up at home, showed that in their physical development the two groups did not differ, nor were there marked differences in their neuropsychological development. However, babies brought to the nursery between the ages of six and nine months continued to have the highest illness rate of any group right up to the third year. Children who were entered between nine and eighteen months still had a high rate of illness and, moreover, were very slow to adjust; 60 percent fell ill during the first week. Those who started attendance at eighteen months quickly became used to their new surroundings and were ill no more often nor more seriously than those who stayed at home.

True, the nursery cannot replace the family; neither is it a necessary evil; but the concrete benefits to the child are not quite clear, said Dr. Papoušek. The relationship of the family to the collective under socialism has not been worked out. We do not have a clear conception of the respective roles of the family and society in the education of the child. In fact, we have no philosophical or sociological conception of the socialist family or of the position of women in society generally, he continued, expanding on a favorite theme.

If disagreement reigned in the ranks of the experts, confusion was compounded by the time the issue reached the general public. In spite of the care which had been taken to distinguish among them, children's homes, all-week nurseries, and day nurseries tended to blend in the public mind and to spell neglect and evasion of responsibility. This was balm to many older persons and unofficial keepers of the public morality who had "known it all along." Whereas mothers who had stayed home with their children in the early fifties had been the butt of public disapproval, those who now wheeled their children to and from a nursery often had to reckon with disapproving remarks and glances on the way. The survey mentioned earlier, made in 1968 and covering more than 1,100 women in the Liberec area working in industry, retail trade, and the professions, disclosed that 72 percent of mothers between the ages of twenty-four and thirty-nine were making use of nurseries or nursery schools, and, of these, 41 percent experienced a feeling of guilt because of it. The indecision resulted in a stagnation in nursery construction between 1966 and 1971, so that the net growth for that six-year period was only 1,033 places. Some pediatricians cried out in fear lest nurseries be closed, because through them it was possible to give adequate care during the week to infants and children who were not receiving what they needed at home.

A series of articles and discussions sponsored in 1967 by *Vlasta*, the women's weekly, attempted to answer the question Are nurseries for the benefit of mothers or the benefit of children? There seemed to be near unanimity that a good nursery could give even a small child values it could not get at home. Using UNESCO's formulation of a child's six basic "needs," Dr. Jaroslav Koch, a child psychologist known beyond the boundaries of Czechoslovakia for his demonstrations that the physical development of infants can be strikingly accelerated by appropriate training, pointed out that *love* and a *feeling of belonging* can best be given at home; this does not require the mother's constant presence, however; and not all love is equally beneficial. Both home and nursery can supply an adult *example* with which the child can identify. When it comes to *all-round development*, opportunities for *self-expression,* and a feeling of *self-confidence* — here the collective with a trained teacher and good equipment can give a child much he cannot get at home, and can also pass on to the family useful information and advice about the child's growth. The requirements most often mentioned for good nurseries that would operate successfully were: that mothers be persuaded to take full advantage of unpaid as well as paid maternity leave and to stay home with the child until it is a year old; that more delicate criteria be developed for deciding which children would not prosper in nurseries for health or psychological reasons, a project that would require better social services; and that groups be reduced to ten or twelve children to every 2 nurses instead of fifteen to every $1\frac{1}{2}$. Children should not be wakened early in the morning or left in the nursery too long or returned too soon after illness. The mother should be able to stay with her child until it is ready to remain without her. All this implies a much greater willingness on the part of women and employers to accept part-time employment for women with small children, and greater employer tolerance of absenteeism. There should be experimental nurseries to test various combinations of home and collective care.

Speaking of the ideal nursery, Dr. Koch foresaw the day when the nursery would be thought of as a necessary aid to family upbringing. "The nursery," he said, "will take over a larger share of the training of physical and mental abilities, while the family will devote itself more to the development of emotional life and interpersonal relationships. The modern nursery will educate not just the children but the family; it will help to improve the qualifications of the parents as educators both in theory and practice. . . ." Like nursery schools, nurseries will be pioneers in modern methods of education.[11]

The conflict seemed to be not between the home and the

collective but between the ideal nursery and the real one. Can the ideal be made the real? Not only the factory shift but the working day in general begins unusually early in Czechoslovakia, a habit probably dating from the nineteenth century when factory workers went home to work on their fields. Whatever the reason, there is no disposition to change it now. Everyone treasures those late afternoon hours after work. Women themselves are not enthusiastic about part-time work. A four-hour day at half pay with the same time lost in travel and four more hours spent with an exacting child is not necessarily an attractive alternative. A six-hour day for a mother at work still means as much as eight hours for a child in a nursery.

So much for time. As for personnel, Dr. Damborská complained in 1970 that the personnel plan for homes for abandoned or orphaned infants had not changed since the days when it was believed that the inmates needed only to be fed and kept warm and clean. One nurse, she pointed out, could not possibly give individual attention to babies when she had nine to dress, undress, put outdoors, bring indoors, feed, and change, not to speak of keeping records and caring for ill children. The same holds true in a day nursery. Moreover, the job is a highly responsible one with frequent critical decisions to be made on the spot, for the doctor visits only two or three times a week, and very few nurseries have a psychologist available at all times. The postgraduate education of these nurses in psychology and pedagogy — necessary because their original training is in a four-year secondary school for nurses — is still very irregular. A nursery teacher who has twenty two-year-olds in charge, and the help of a second nurse for only part of the day, can earn more and have fewer responsibilities as a saleswoman or a streetcar conductor or a mail-carrier. Because of the poor salaries and the demanding character of the work, the turnover of medium-grade health personnel is a major problem all over the world.

At this point society must answer the first question asked at the beginning of this chapter: What can we afford, and what are the priorities? What should the future be? Should all mothers eventually be paid to stay at home for two or three years while public funds are concentrated on the older children, with a limited number of nurseries for social cases and for the infants of highly qualified women who are needed on the job, who run the risk of losing their skills if they stay at home, and who are also able to pay more toward the care of their children? Such institutions could be model nurseries with experimental programs and well-paid staffs. One trouble with this idea is that nurseries, to be useful at all, must be widely distributed so that babies need not travel by public transportation.

In Czechoslovakia, the state (or, in about 18 percent of cases, a large factory) pays all of the original investment in a nursery and meets five-sixths of the operating costs; parents pay only one-sixth. The share of the daily cost of keeping a child in a nursery which is paid by the Ministry of Health (or the factory) is about equal to the sum now being paid to a mother for staying home, but in the latter case the entire original investment is saved. The present Czechoslovak plan is a compromise, however, because the allowance is paid only to mothers who stay home with the second child, and only until it is two years old.

In a situation where labor is in short supply, many branches of the economy — particularly clothing, retail trade, communications, and health, where women make up more than 60 percent of the personnel — would be hard hit if all women with children under the ages of two or three were to stay at home. The present intention is to expand nursery care, but it does not take much mathematics to figure out that, in view of the funds now being spent to permit mothers to be at home, it will not be possible to invest heavily in nurseries; and, in fact, it has already been indicated that it will be difficult to fulfill the plan for nursery schools, which are supposed to accommodate 65 percent of the children between three and six by the end of 1975.

Lenin's "simple, everyday means" of liberating women swell to enormous proportions as soon as one sits down with pencil and paper. It is no accident that the first Soviet *crèches* that caught the imagination of prewar liberationists were in agricultural areas right on the fields, where the mother could take time out several times a day for nursing. Running such a nursery was relatively uncomplicated. Today a nursery on factory grounds is helpful only to parents who live near the plant

— not usually a desirable location. Nurseries must be a part of every community and every new housing project, within easy walking distance. To meet modern child-care standards they need the services of pedagogical, psychological, medical, and dietary experts, cooks and cleaners, as well as a sufficiently large staff of trained nurses who like their work. As the ratio of children to personnel becomes smaller, the nursery appears to become an institution which frees one set of people by employing another. Sweeping generalizations about how socialism will take the responsibility for care of the child off the family's hands rarely take these details into account.

At the same time there are other important child-care aids to working mothers where the same investment may bring more substantial gains. Nursery schools for children over three are easier and less expensive to run. There is also, for example, the subsidized school lunch program, reserved for the children of working mothers in Czechoslovakia and actually used by only 48 percent of all children under the age of fifteen. There are supervised after-school facilities which many children are reluctant to visit because they are insufficiently attractive; they seem like an extension of school. Thirty-four percent of all Czechoslovak children between the ages of six and ten and 62 percent of all those between eleven and fifteen are without adult supervision after school. More funds are required to provide better facilities and programs, and personnel especially trained for this kind of work.

In 1969 Czechoslovak government payments for the benefit of mothers and children in cash (family grants, paid maternity leave, student grants); in the form of subsidies for children's clothing, and student fares on the public transportation system; and in the form of services like nurseries, nursery schools, school lunches, and free school books and supplies, amounted to 19,000 million crowns (22,000 million in 1973). This is exclusive of the cost of the school system, which is free (including university education), and the cost of the national health service and the pension system. Yet by themselves, these payments represent nearly 25 percent of all outlays from the central budget and the budgets of all local government bodies for social and cultural purposes, and more than 10 percent of all government expenditures, including investment in the national economy. These figures are cited to suggest how vast a job it is to satisfy only a portion of the demand, and that at a level considerably below expectations. Meanwhile, the other social services are in need of expansion and improvement: homes for the aged, for example, and outpatient clinics and hospitals, where plant and equipment are running a losing race with obsolescence, and the technological and scientific requirements (and costs) of good health care soar.

This is the experience of one relatively advanced country, which has almost one-third of its infants and children under the age of six in day-care centers. It is apparent that the real prospect for taking the responsibility for all care of children out of the hands of their parents in any urban society is remote. Recognition of this calls for a reevaluation of the importance of the family (not just the mother) to the child, and for a rethinking of the ways by which the family could be made an institution not for the enslavement of women but for their greater emancipation.

Langmeier and Matějček expressed the first half of this postulate in the mid-sixties.

"

It is not unthinkable that the basic needs of the child could be satisfied from other sources and in other conditions. Social change will certainly cause various further adjustments in the structure of the family and force certain transformations of relations between its members. In principle, however, the family remains the foundation of upbringing even under socialism . . . and other institutions must be considered as ancillary. In practice it is very difficult to realize anywhere else to such a broad degree and in such a natural way the necessary satisfaction of the basic needs of the child: warm emotional interest, permanent care by one individual, a dynamic and at the same time unified environment for the whole of childhood, which supplies the feeling of "home."[12]

"

The second aspect — a concept of the family which takes into consideration the new position which woman has won in spite of obstacles, as the preceding chapters have shown — has received no attention yet in the socialist countries, where change has been left to the spontaneous effect of woman's greater participation in work outside the home. The pioneer in this respect has been Sweden, which is trying to change people's attitudes before the problems reach the complexity they have assumed in Czechoslovakia, for example. In Sweden, the government has taken the position that no decisive changes can be brought about by measures aimed at women alone, but that the division of functions between the sexes must be changed in such a way that men and women have the same opportunities to be active parents and to be gainfully employed.[18] This makes of women's emancipation not a "woman question" but a function of the general drive for greater equality which affects everyone. The program to implement it includes equal education to wipe out stereotyped notions of male and female occupations, both on the job and in the home. One logical outcome is that the provisions for paid leave to care for a child are extended to fathers as well as to mothers, so that parents can really divide responsibility. Once this idea is accepted, the lack of a nursery no longer puts the woman at a special disadvantage; and, from the employer's point of view, "unreliability" (meaning ill children) is no longer a female characteristic. The care of children becomes a fact which society has to take into consideration.

No doubt this attitude is still far in the future, but at least it has a future; while as long as a woman is regarded as having two roles while a man has only one, women and men will never find themselves on an equal footing. To be successful, such a concept requires ultimately breaking down the accepted organization of the world of commerce and industry — in which woman is either an invader or a guest — and rebuilding it around the idea that it is not woman who is "different," but that each sex is different; and that both these sets of differences must somehow be taken into account.

CHAPTER NINE

"THE DEBT WE OWE OUR WOMEN"

The removal of "barbarously unproductive, petty, nerve-racking drudgery" from the home, and its transfer to the public sector, has been postponed in all the socialist countries until it has become a barely visible pinpoint on the horizon marked "communism." Engels's prediction that under socialism the state would take over the majority of domestic tasks has been replaced by the promise that improved services will gradually lighten women's load, and the emphasis is still on the word "women." It is doubtful whether anyone in Lenin's time had calculated what it would require to take housework out of the home and put it on an efficient, workable basis in an industrial society. In fact, this is a problem to which little attention has been paid, in practical terms, outside of Sweden, where the resolution to make complete services part of every new housing project has run up against many problems, but is nevertheless being given serious government attention.[1]

Theoretically, a socialist government should be able to do anything it wants; it is only a matter of assigning priorities. The socialist governments have so far given priority in the distribution of public funds for social purposes to health, education and culture, public transportation, social welfare services, and support for prices of some basic foods and other necessities, such as children's clothing. In Czechoslovakia the state has found it impossible to go through with its original generous plans for

191

supplying the majority of the population with low-cost housing.[2]

Common to all these public activities which have been subsidized with government funds is that they are services which families cannot perform for themselves. They are social by nature, specialized activities carried out by trained individuals for the community. They can be improved and expanded by technology, but they depend basically on personnel. They are coming to be thought of as human rights: the right to education, certainly; the right to health — and even to art, music, and the theater, to an increasing degree. Laundry and cooking belong to quite a different category, apart from the fact that "anyone can do them." Recognition of the right to have one's laundry done outside the home will have to be preceded by full recognition that men and women have exactly the same rights, including the right to neglect the housework.

The performance of services like laundry and cooking by society becomes truly effective only when manpower can be replaced by machines, and this has actually become possible only since the Second World War, although some social reformers recognized a century ago that it would one day become feasible. But the practical aspects are complex. It is true that an agricultural community with no shortage of labor could (and has) set up communal laundries without the use of elaborate technological equipment by hiring a number of unskilled women as laundresses and supplying at least hot running water, soap, mangles, and — later on, perhaps — some electrical equipment. This is certainly a boon to the peasant woman who was accustomed to scrubbing her wash on the rocks in the stream. Similarly, communal farm kitchens can probably supply better meals than those the peasant family would cook for itself after a day in the fields, and the inevitable noise and commotion may give the meal the air of a social occasion. But the expectations of the family in an industrial society are quite different. The housewife wants her wash done as well as she did it herself before she took a job, or as her mother before her did it, or she will not give it out. The laundry must either be within a few steps of her door or provide a delivery service. It must return the wash promptly, and its prices must be within the family's means. The alternative is a fully automatic washing machine in the apartment house or an easily accessible launderette.

The communal eating place must meet very high standards indeed to compete with even a simple meal served at home. Parents employed in industry, or even in an office, and surrounded by noise, haste, and physical or mental pressures, who have eaten their lunch in a works canteen or a restaurant, do not want to eat another meal there; besides, the children are waiting. They do not feel like shepherding children through the snow to another noisy cafeteria. The communal dining room must be near their home; offer the kind of food they are used to (which means it must supply a variety of meals); be quiet, clean, with quick service; and be no more expensive than eating at home. An alternative is the prepared meal which can be whisked into the home oven.

Launderettes and convenience foods imply a high degree of technology and a large output, if the services are to be reasonably priced. If, as a beginning, society can produce only ten thousand automatic washing machines, for example, they will be quite expensive. It is more effective to put these on the market as luxury "incentives," than to scatter one thousand launderettes about the country so that the demand for each creates waiting lines, the self-service principle has to be dropped, and the launderette becomes part of the poorly functioning municipal laundry service; while the public asks, "Why can't we have modern washing machines?" (This is, in fact, just what happened in Czechoslovakia when the first automatic washing machines were produced some years ago.)

Besides the question of meals and laundry there are the problems of housecleaning, dry-cleaning, repairs; and many other amenities like travel, recreation, and entertainment, which are no longer considered luxuries, but go to make up what industrial man expects in the way of a standard of living, and which provide the incentive for him or her to go on working productively. The less these services can be mechanized or automated, the more manpower they require, the lower their productivity, and the higher their cost of operation. Such services then have to be subsidized by the government to bring them within the reach of the average person, and again the question of priority arises. Even in a socialist country, everything that is subsidized by society has to be paid for by the production of new values, and the more things that are given away or sold below cost, the more efficient the production required in other spheres.

The development of effective services which can take housework out of the home depends on the ability of industrial technology as a whole first, to free manpower, and second, to make possible the mechanization of services so that these do not become and remain pockets of poorly paid (women, black, foreign-born) workers. The socialist economies, starting on a much lower level than the United States, did not have the manpower or the funds seeking investment or the technological equipment to make a dramatic beginning in the service (tertiary) sphere. What is more, although Czechoslovak authorities, for example, talked grandiosely of making housework a public industry, they did not appreciate that just to provide the minimum supplementary conveniences for the housewife would require a tremendous shift toward the "nonproductive" sphere instead of away from it. In fact, at that time, they considered the developments they saw taking place in the West proof of frivolous consumerism. The policy they actually did adopt systematically retarded the consumer goods industries so that the lag in their technology behind that of other industries was increasingly felt. The same lag was felt, in most cases to an even greater degree, in the other socialist countries.

At the point where the general level of industrialization might have made possible a real breakthrough in terms of beginning to provide communal facilities, investment funds and manpower were tied up — and are still tied up today — in a multitude of unfinished heavy-industry projects, in modernizing the neglected transportation system, and in trying to meet the housing crisis.

As far as communal dining is concerned, the number of restaurants has shown a tendency to decline in Czechoslovakia, and so has the number of factory dining rooms. Between 1963 and 1967 the number of main meals served in factory dining rooms dropped by 47 percent, and the number of these dining rooms was sharply reduced in favor of canteens selling chiefly cold snacks. At present only about 20 percent of Czechoslovak workers eat a main meal in a factory dining room, as compared with 47 percent in France (1964) and 45 percent in West Germany (1966). Originally these eating places were heavily subsidized by plant management. Measures taken since 1963 to put them on a paying basis have resulted in closing some and raising the prices in others.

Public laundries now take care of only about 5 percent of family wash; the goal is something like 10 percent by 1980. Cost is one reason for not sending the wash out, and quality is another; but most discouraging of all is the waiting time of two or three weeks, with an extra charge for more rapid service, and no deliveries. Dry cleaners have a somewhat better record, but here again there are complaints about quality and waiting time. "Express" service takes five days and the charge is one-third higher. The customer is asked to remove buttons, and not all establishments accept all fabrics. Self-service cleaners, a common sight in many Western European cities, are all but nonexistent.

Like the communal dining rooms, other services were put on a paying basis in the mid-1960s in order to enable them to modernize, mechanize, and pay higher salaries to their employees. It was announced in 1965 that the state would withdraw the tens of millions it was paying out in subsidies to services which were serving "only certain groups of people," since it could not afford to pay for everything.[3] This was followed immediately by the news that prices at laundries would rise by an average of 33.4 percent; at beauty parlors, by 31.5 percent; for clothing repairs, 10 percent; and for shoe repairs by 5.6 percent. Services as a whole recorded a retail price rise of 40 percent between January 1964 and the end of 1970. While their receipts rose in absolute figures in that period, their share in total consumer spending dropped from 31 percent in 1966 to 24 percent in 1970.

In Czechoslovakia the services have never recovered from the situation created in the 1950s by the nationalization of all the small craftsmen — the one- and two-man and family establishments of shoemakers, watchmakers, plumbers, electricians, mechanics, tailors, and others who had been supplying the consumer with hundreds of small repairs which no socialist enterprise was ready to provide. As there were no materials available for would-be do-it-yourselfers either, the results were catastrophic. The consumer in the German Democratic Republic has had a better time of it in this respect, since there the individual private craftsman was permitted to stay in business and today is still given "the fullest support of the Socialist Unity party and the state," even though larger private firms which were allowed to exist until 1972 have been taken over.[4]

Commenting on the stagnation of the service industries in 1967, Vlasta Brablcová, a Czech sociologist and economist who briefly held a government post, wrote that in view of the difficulties of automating services and the impossibility of expanding manpower in this sphere — and in the face of changing consumer preferences — it seemed likely that both socialist and capitalist countries would take the path of mechanizing domestic work through home appliances in the coming decades; this was in contrast to the conception held in the socialist countries "until relatively recently that gradually all domestic economic activity would be shifted from the family to society, which would insure the development of appropriate types of services."[5] In fact, by the end of 1973, 70 percent of Czechoslovak households had refrigerators and 85 percent had washing machines (considerably higher percentages than in Hungary or Poland). There were many complaints about the quality of these aids, however. Fully automatic washing machines were not generally available until 1972, and at the estimated rate of production it will be 1980 before half of Czechoslovakian homes have them. In 1971–72, ten thousand brand-new refrigerators refused to function, and the wait for servicing was usually three months.

It has been promised that expansion of the service industry will take place parallel with this process of supplying households with appliances, and the present Five-Year Plan (1970–75) calls for a 25–30 percent increase in volume. At the same time, as late as 1972, it was admitted by government officials most closely connected with the problem that a real analysis of needs and a realistic conception on which the desired reconstruction and expansion could be based were still lacking. "Services are in the real sense of the word part of the first line of struggle for the realization of the political line of the Party, the fight for a higher living standard and for the happy life of our people," wrote the vice premier of the Czech Republic.[6] At almost the same time, however, the single woman member of the Presidium of the Communist party of Slovakia pointed out that "research in this area directed at a substantial rationalization of household work is, at least as far as we know, minimal, not to speak of the fact that any existing proposals . . . find their way into practice very, very slowly." [7]

According to figures released in 1970 by the Council for Mutual Economic Assistance of the socialist countries (COMECON), it is estimated that by 1980 employment in the tertiary (services) sphere will account for 44 percent of the work force in Czechoslovakia and the German Democratic Republic, 41 percent in the Soviet Union, and so on down the list, ending with 35 percent in Rumania. It is difficult to make comparisons, since somewhat different complexes of services are understood under this heading in the capitalist and socialist countries, but generally speaking, if this aim is achieved the top three socialist countries (the GDR, Czechoslovakia, and the Soviet Union) will stand where the countries of the Common Market were, on the average, in 1970, and at the level reached in the United States (which now has 60 percent of its labor force in the service industries) in 1947 — at least as far as division of labor goes. Of course, these figures tell us nothing about the type and quality of the services, or the relative share of government-financed services (health, education, etc.) as against those paid for directly by the public.

No one who has followed the painful efforts to modernize socialist housework over the past three decades can fail to be struck by the way this is inevitably presented as "the debt we owe our women," as though women were responsible for all the wash that is dirtied and were the sole beneficiaries of clean windows and floors and ate all the potatoes that are lugged home. This convention is so convenient to men that they can hardly be expected to be anxious for a change. When Maj-Britt Sutherland, the author of the Swedish government's report on the status of women, which contained its program for a change in the traditional division of sex roles, presented her government's view to a United Nations symposium in Czechoslovakia in 1968 on problems of employed women, this view was received by the Czechoslovak participants as very interesting but "not in line with our traditions and not suited to our conditions at the present time." Socialist women themselves have not done anything in an organized way to combat the idea that woman's "right to be a mother" includes, as a free bonus, her right to do all the housework. As that great American convention-debunker, the columnist Heywood Broun, once remarked, "When Adam delved and Eve span, the fiction that man is incapable of housework was first established. . . . Probably a man alone could never have maintained the fallacy of masculine incapacity without the aid of women." [8] Although every poll of socialist women's attitudes suggests that they would welcome more help from their husbands, examination of this question has been limited to simple fact-finding; further, there is a lingering reluctance on the part of women themselves to press the issue. For example, Dr. Andrea Andreen of Sweden, a member of the Executive Council of the Women's International Democratic Federation — an organization in which the Soviet Union plays the dominant policy-making role — considered it a great advance when, in 1967, the Soviet members of the council were persuaded to incorporate in the program for discussion at the 1968 congress in Helsinki the idea of a more even division of work in the house between men and women. The controversial formulation ran, "The growing participation of women in economic and social life demands a new outlook regarding the division of family chores between husband and wife." [9] Explaining their reluctance, Dr. Andreen remarked, "Soviet women still want to rule in their kitchens."

Many socialist husbands have, of course, begun to help their wives in the house out of sheer compassion or necessity, and women's lack of free time and the actual division of tasks in the home have been the subject of numberless sociological studies. More recently, Lenin's long-neglected remarks on men and housework have started to appear in print. "Very few husbands," he told Clara Zetkin, "not even the proletarians, think of how much they could lighten the burdens and worries of their wives, or relieve them entirely, if they lent a hand in this 'women's work.' But no, that would go against the 'privilege and dignity of the husband.' He demands that he have his rest and comfort." [10]

There are no signs yet, however, that anyone is prepared to follow Lenin's advice and "root out the old slave-owner's point of view, both in the Party and among the masses." According to recent Soviet estimates, Soviet women on the average do 75 percent of domestic tasks themselves and divide the remaining 25 percent with their husbands. A Czech investigation conducted in 1966–67 of five hundred women holding managerial posts revealed that half of these women did all the housework themselves and about 35 percent divided it equally with another member of the family. As far as husband's help was concerned, 50 percent of the women said that he helped "rarely," 10 percent said "never."

International comparative studies are of limited value because they average out great differences in facilities and in ways of life within countries and between countries: an American four-member family may live in an eight-room house in Shaker Heights or a three-room shack in the Appalachians; a Czech family will most likely live in two or three rooms and a kitchen (70 percent of all dwelling units). Such studies do not reflect the fact that Americans entertain more than Europeans, or that some American housewives turn labor-saving devices into makework devices. Nevertheless, they show some interesting differences. According to a "multinational comparative time budget" made in 1965 of women in seven socialist and five Western countries, employed women have, on the average, a 75-hour week; men, a 68-hour week; and housewives, a 59-hour week, excluding child care. Both men and women work a longer day in the socialist countries: the highest figures for employed women were in Hungary and central Yugoslavia, where employed women put in 12.5 and 12.4 hours daily; while the shortest days were enjoyed by employed women in the United States and Belgium, where the average was 9.8 and 9.9 hours daily, respectively. The largest differences in length of the day worked between men and women were in the Soviet Union and Czechoslovakia; there women worked, on the average, two hours more, daily, than men.

The results correspond closely to results obtained in many time studies conducted in Czechoslovakia in the past fifteen years. The women executives mentioned above were found to spend an average of 3 hours daily on housework, one hour on shopping, and 2.3 hours on their children. In their hierarchy of values, free time occupied first place, before health, peace of mind, and far above recognition on the job. In a more recent survey of women's opinions on employment, household, and family, only 33 percent of the women felt they had enough time for themselves; 41 percent had enough time for their husbands; 22 percent, for near relatives; and only 19 percent, for their friends.

Thus, contrary to socialist theory, which holds that the economic functions of the family will be taken over by the state, the family in socialist countries retains and obviously will continue to retain for some time the important economic function of meeting the basic needs of its members. How does this correspond to what men and women in the socialist part of the world expect of the family? According to the UNESCO research mentioned in a previous chapter, women and men (and women more than men) in at least three socialist countries — Poland, Yugoslavia, and Czechoslovakia — hope that family ties will be closer in the future than they are today. What form they hope these closer ties will take is difficult to say, for very little basic research has been done on what the family might or should look like under socialism. In Czechoslovakia the sociology of the family has been recognized as a specific subject for theoretical study only since 1964, and much of the time since has been spent catching up with what has been done in Western countries. One of the few Czech scholars in this field, Vlasta Fišerová, noted in 1967 that it will take a long time before the failure to develop a sociology of socialist society is overcome and a Marxist theory of the family created.

At the same time a flood of surveys, polls, and investigations, many of which have been mentioned in this book, uncovered trends in Czechoslovakia very similar to what was going on in the West. Similar readings were taken in other socialist countries. The marked reduction in the size of families has already been discussed. Sex before marriage is widely taken for granted in Czechoslovakia. Young people marry early: about 50 percent of girls before they are twenty-one and 50 percent of boys before they are twenty-four. The divorce rate is rising: it climbed from 11.6 per one hundred marriages in 1963 to 21.6 in 1971. Yet marriage remains the institution in which people continue to seek permanent satisfaction. During the same period the number of marriages per one thousand inhabitants increased from 7.7 to 9. Since divorce is inexpensive, is refused only exceptionally, and can be obtained by one party without the consent of the other (since there is no "guilty party" and no alimony), it might be assumed that only happy couples would stay together. This is by no means the case, according to a poll taken by the Institute for Public Opinion Research in 1970. Asked if they thought that marriages in Czechoslovakia were, on the whole, happy, only 28 percent of men and 19 percent of women answered yes.

What causes disappointment? The reasons most often given by both men and women in divorce courts in 1970 were incompatibility and unfaithfulness, followed (in the case of the women's complaints) by alcoholism and rough treatment. What keeps families together? For the most part, practical considerations. More than seven thousand women and one thousand men returned a multiple-choice questionnaire published by the weekly *Vlasta* in 1966, in which they revealed what they expected of their mates. Women wanted their husbands first of all to be responsible for the financial security of the family; second, to help with the upbringing of the children; and third, to help in the household. Faithfulness was in fourth place, and "good lover" rated seventh. Less than 1 percent expected their husbands to act as the "head of the family." The men's picture of the ideal husband was almost the same, with only fourteen men expecting to be referred to as head of the family.

A much greater difference appeared between what men

and women thought women's role in marriage ought to be. "Motherhood" was assigned to first place by one-third of the men; care of the household held a strong second place in their list of values; "good lover" was seventh; and tenth and final place was given to woman's financial contribution through employment. But — a measure of their realism — women put their financial contribution in first place and motherhood in eighth, while they rated their obligation to be a good lover ninth. Like the men, they voted "care of the household" to second place.

In other words, there is plenty of room for disagreement, and happiness does not emerge from these results as the most important thing in family life. The Czechoslovak family is a unit which through joint efforts secures itself financially, maintains a home, and brings up children. The family with children which breaks up faces serious financial as well as emotional problems.

Consider the position of the divorced mother, for example. Unless her case is exceptional, the children will be assigned to her (although the law does not so specify), and under the divorce agreement the father will pay a certain monthly sum toward the expenses of the children. The woman is not entitled to claim anything for herself, however (except in cases of extreme need); it is assumed that she will work and contribute a share to the financial support of the children as well as care for their physical needs. But she is now maintaining a household of several people on one salary (inevitably the smaller one) plus the children's allowance contributed by the father; thus, her standard of living drops, and at the same time all the physical work and the responsibility fall on her. The difficulties which beset her if her former husband avoids making payments, and she must seek the help of the court in collecting, is an odyssey in itself. The husband's position is not enviable either; he must set up for himself (if he can find a flat) with his income cut by as much as one-third. There are great advantages to remarriage for both of them.

Unlike the free soul of whom Bebel dreamed, the woman who opts for children without a husband is in an even more trying position. Therefore, the overwhelming majority of unmarried pregnant women either marry the father of the child or take advantage of the abortion law. While pregnancies in unmarried women make up a growing share of total pregnancies, the percentage of children actually born out of wedlock has risen only slightly and is about 5 percent of the total. Some 20 percent of these children are placed in children's homes or given out for adoption.

Although there is no difference in the legal position of children born in and out of wedlock, the unmarried mother is at a great disadvantage. The woman who has been married and divorced benefits from a whole series of mutual legal obligations including the equal division of jointly acquired property and the equal duty to contribute to the upbringing of the child. The unmarried mother is entitled to a contribution from the father toward her expenses in pregnancy and confinement, and to regular contributions toward the support of the child. She has no other claims on him, and to obtain recognition of these rights she must either make a joint statement with the father declaring his paternity or go to court to establish it; a married woman's husband, on the other hand, is automatically the father of her children under the law. The unmarried mother usually has no home of her own and now finds it difficult to establish one. It is not surprising that the children of unmarried mothers have a lower birth weight, and thus a higher infant mortality rate, than those of children born in complete families. While the unmarried mother has certain advantages, such as a 35-week paid maternity leave and preference when it comes to placing her child in a nursery, and is entitled to special consideration from her employer, these do not balance the difficulties.

These were the kind of observations which caused those who took part in the first discussion on the family in socialist society, sponsored by the Czechoslovak Sociological Society in 1966, to observe that the very term "socialist family" was a misnomer, and that the "democratic nuclear family," with all its conflicts and paradoxes, was characteristic of all industrial societies. In the following years, a few persons attempted new theoretical approaches as the beginning of a socialist view of the modern family, although the number of practical problems crying out for solution made such discussions seem almost a luxury. While they must be regarded as preliminary excursions, these contributions do tell something about the type of conjecture which was taking place in Czechoslovakia in the late 1960s. As we have already seen, for sociologists and psychologists primarily interested in the child, recent information on emotional deprivation in childhood gave the family new importance as a socializing community which, by its small size and relative continuity, is uniquely able to transmit experience and provide models of behavior. One hypothesis, for example, put forward for discussion by Eva Vančurová, a child psychologist mentioned in an earlier chapter, is the primary importance of three levels of family interaction — intellectual, sensory, and emotional — for the child's receptivity in his earliest months and years. She stresses the fact that interaction in the family takes place not only on an intellectual and verbal level but, much more intensely than in any other group, on a sensory and emotional one, thus intensifying the learning process. She does not overlook the damage this same child might suffer as a result of pressures on him in a typical nuclear family, nor the inadequacy of this small unit as a training ground for the outside world; but to her these drawbacks do not constitute arguments for rejecting the family as an institution.[11]

Fišerová has gone further, making the point that parents need emotional ties with children as much as children need their parents' love, and she places these relationships within the family on a par with sexual love in importance — perhaps above it in importance for certain individuals or at certain times of life. She argues that it would be impossible for the family to fulfill its socializing function just because society demands it; the fact that the family continues to do so suggests, in her opinion, that love for children and the need of the individual to project himself into the future through a new life are continuing values in modern society. She doubts that Engels appreciated this aspect of the family, and considers that he used sexual love in too broad a sense. She does not agree that the family is going through a moral crisis, but thinks of it as experiencing a difficult process of rebirth connected with the loss of its patriarchal character. Love between men and women, she thinks, can develop better in an atmosphere of sexual freedom, and the demand that love should be liberated from fear of the consequences — unwanted conception — has been met by contraception. Consequently, one of the arguments advanced by Engels for giving the responsibility for the upbringing of children to the state no longer applies.

The separation of sex from myth has freed the family for the realization of other experiences, in her opinion. She believes that the importance of the adult-child relationship will grow, and that it can become a factor enabling man to think beyond himself and his own future, thus making possible Marx's concept of the fullest realization of the individual. The conflicts and tensions under which people live, she believes, cannot be resolved by doing violence to the family; on the contrary, the family can, potentially, satisfy man's deep and long-term hunger for understanding, friendship, and criticism. Thus, she regards both the "free-love" experiments in abolishing the family in the Soviet Union in the 1920s and the reaction away from them — the attempt to impose the concept of an "ideal 'socialist' family" in which "there was no place for any violation of traditional Christian norms" — as deformations of Marxism. Of course, she adds, the family is not designed to be a refuge from society. On the contrary, it places great demands on the ability of the individual to adapt to reality. If the family is used as an escape, it is because "few people realize that everyone must carry his personal portion of loneliness himself."[12]

Ota Klein, whose work was cut short by his accidental death, was one of a handful of Czechoslovak sociologists who, in the 1960s, began to concern themselves with the socialist style of life — something which Klein believed society was a long way from being able to define. In the fragments of his work which have been published, he makes a central point of man's frustrated search for love in industrial society. He points out that psychologists tend to regard the character of the relationship between mother and child or family and child as given. But, he argues, this relationship has undergone great changes since preindustrial society as a result of the recognition of the "right to love" and the concentration of all emotions in a small family group.

Klein identifies not a crisis of the family but a "crisis of emotionality." The intensity of the modern mother's emotion arouses expectations in the child which later experience cannot fulfill. The result is frustration, and this is, he believes, one explanation for increasing divorce and suicide and for the common feelings of nonparticipation and alienation which are a cause of growing delinquency.

He does not view the "consciously collective" society as an alternative to the family in an industrialized world, however — either in the form attempted in the 1948–58 decade in Czechoslovakia or in the communes developed in Israel and China. The Czechoslovak attempt, he says, suffered from a duality of concept — "emphasis on collective education combined with the slogan 'the family the foundation of the state,' taken over from the individualistic structure of capitalistic society" — and at the same time lacked sufficient boldness to carry it through. This is fortunate, he adds, for neither the theoretical nor the economic conditions were present for such an ambitious reconstruction of the way of life, just as they were lacking in the much bolder and more significant experiments which took place earlier in the Soviet Union. Both failed to create the collective-minded man, he thinks, because this "concept of collectivism does not correspond either to the inner or to the external social requirements of the modern individual." All such experiments seem to Klein to be a "romantic criticism of civilization," an attempt to return to simple, preindustrial relationships at a time when Western mankind is conditioned by two centuries of development to something quite different. His solution is to put creative fantasy to work to find ways of consciously limiting man's emotional fragility, to shift his emotional equipment in the direction of greater intellectualization, an undertaking which would require great investment in pedagogy and psychology, and the freeing by technology of many more people to take part in the socialization process.[18]

Attempts like these to find theoretical solutions to the conflicts which disrupt the family in socialist countries, by viewing them as part of a general crisis of industrial society, received only very brief encouragement. At the present time they are rejected as part of an unfortunate flirtation with Western ideas, and the "ideological consolidation" of sociologists themselves is considered to be sociology's first task. "Exaggeration of the influence of industrialization on society led to the conclusion that the process of industrialization in socialist society creates a series of universal characteristics common to the family under capitalism and socialisms. Indeed these opinions in the case of many theoreticians even led to the denial of a socialist type of family, and the substitution for this term of others like the industrial family, etc.," the Slovak journal of sociology said in 1973.[14]

The sense of this criticism is that socialist industrialization is not just any industrialization, but that technological progress is realized quite differently by the capitalist and socialist systems. It has been argued that due to a failure to take full advantage of the possibilities offered by a socialist economy these differences are not so obvious as they will be with the advance of the "scientific and technological revolution." At the same time it is acknowledged that so far very little has been done to clarify the differences in the public mind.

Socialism has created a highly industrial society and a demand for the consumer goods that make it possible to live in it; at the same time, however, a real vacuum exists in the thinking about the future of the family and woman's position in it, and, in fact, about the whole style of life socialism might aim for in a world where science and technology are expected to open up limitless possibilities. Having but one life to live, and that in the here and now, the socialist family of today has filled the gap by accepting the only model that presents itself. This is, of course, the consumer society of the West, which has gained widespread and uncritical acceptance in the socialist countries; there it is judged chiefly on the basis of exported products, since other aspects of Western life are rarely encountered. This fascination extends not only to manufactured goods, which are demonstrably better than those made at home; and to films, books, and plays, which are often more entertaining and stimulating than those being produced in the socialist countries; but also to the advertisers' views of woman: both eternally being kissed by moonlight (or wearing blue jeans and a T-shirt and driving her own car), and eternally admiring the shine on her kitchen linoleum. Everyone in a socialist country knows that consumer goods are held in contempt only by those who already enjoy them. In conflict with the realities of her life, socialist woman attempts to exorcise the unresolved and at present unresolvable conflict, between her rights and the limited possibilities of exercising them, with dreams of a model home, a model kitchen, and the glamor which she believes or pretends to believe surrounds women in the West.

For she is a split personality, expected to ride two horses at once. She was brought up to be economically independent, wants to be economically independent, and often finds satisfaction in her work, or at least in her contact with the larger world. Yet in her conflict between her job, where she must still compete with men on an unequal basis, and her home, where she is considered irreplaceable, who can blame her if she favors the role in which she can prove her superior qualities, and if she even has ambivalent feelings about sharing that role with men? It is not surprising if she still realizes herself through her family and the satisfaction of its desires, if her chief reason for working is first, to help furnish a flat and clothe the children; later, to help buy a car, a summer cottage, her daughter's trousseau, her son's cooperative apartment, or her grandchildren's real blue jeans.

The abolition of private ownership of the means of production does not bring about the end of the single family as the economic unit of society, nor the transformation of private housekeeping into a social industry. Even when the best intentions are present, there must also be an economic base sufficiently strong and well-organized to assume these economic functions. At the same time there must be a theoretical concept and a plan of action. So far no socialist country has met these conditions.

CHAPTER TEN

CAN WOMEN BE FREE?

The experiences described in the preceding chapters leave no doubt that socialism has not yet succeeded in making women free and equal. Some of the reasons why this is so have been suggested. But, in spite of shock and ridicule and with many sacrifices, this painful and laborious effort to put into practice a revolutionary concept of the position of women has kept alive for more than one hundred years ideas which are now common currency among women's liberationists. Among these are the dehumanizing influence of property relations and patriarchal attitudes on the family, the liberating effect on women of economic independence and productive work outside the home, the mind-destroying, exploitive character of housework and the need to make it a public industry, and the idea that even very small children can be cared for at least part of the time away from their parents.

Although most women in socialist countries are not realizing their potentialities and are not always even sure that they want to be working, the vast majority of them have emerged from the narrow confines of home. Millions of them have proved to themselves and to men that they are capable of doing any job a man is capable of doing, and under far more difficult circumstances. Although they have not achieved positions in proportion to their numerical strength, there are few fields which they have not entered in sufficient numbers to show that they are not just the exceptions that prove the rule, and that there are no talents which are exclusively male. In this sense they have acted as an advance guard, and deserve admiration.

Today, they take the right to economic independence, their legal equality, and their social benefits for granted, and expect an equal voice with their husbands in the family and in the household. Their husbands accept this too, even if reluctantly, and the atmosphere that has been created has a feedback effect. Women are brought up and educated to expect that they will work outside the home for a large part of their lives. Although they soon discover that it is not true that all doors are open to them, the idea of taking an active part in the business of society has become a natural one, and for many women with a better than grade-school education — and particularly for those with a higher education — there is satisfaction in the work and prestige, in addition to social contacts and financial reward. An enormous number of these women have shown — even if at great cost to themselves — that a job is not just something a woman can do before she has children and after the children leave home; that it is possible, with society's assistance, to work and at the same time to bring up children as successfully as women who devote full time to mothering.

The socialist experience has also shown that formerly semi-feudal, semifascist, relatively backward states, as well as those with an industrial and democratic tradition, can almost overnight clear the books of archaic legislation and lay the basis for full legal equality; and that even relatively poor countries can institute social policies which recognize the individual's right to health, security, and education, without which full equality cannot be achieved. That individual laws cannot always be enforced, or may have unforeseen side effects, and that good social policies are not always well administered, is another story. This makes it all the more inportant for women elsewhere who are dedicated to the idea of liberation to learn both the advantages and shortcomings of family law, the social security system, and the health service in socialist countries.

But all this does not add up to full equality for women.

A final contribution made by socialist experience with the

"woman question" — and that is what this book has really been about — is the revelation of the true depth and enormity of the problem. To resolve what Engels called the "conflict between the sexes" requires a social upheaval at least as great as that required to resolve the conflict between wealth and poverty, capital and labor, black and white, although it may not take such dramatic forms. The abolition of private property does not necessarily bring this about even after fifty years, experience has shown. The early proponents of Marxism evidently did not realize that a lag in consciousness is involved which is more difficult to overcome than it is to win recognition for the rights of labor or the rights of blacks or other minorities or oppressed nations, because belief in women's inferiority is older and more deeply ingrained, and involves the total population, since woman sees herself in the mirror man holds up. Thus, in every victory won by labor, women workers remain worse off than men workers, and in every concession exacted by blacks or oppressed peoples women remain worse off than men. While the conflicts between capitalism and socialism, between the haves and the have-nots, oppressed races and oppressing races, are considered the burning problems of the day, requiring far-reaching solutions, the "woman question" is everywhere regarded as peripheral, something that can gradually be solved by individual measures like accepting qualified women for jobs previously held by men, by teaching father to diaper the baby, or by allotting funds to nurseries.

Yet exactly what the socialist experience proves is that these measures by themselves do not really liberate women. If proportionately more Soviet women are found in unusual or responsible jobs than are Czechoslovak or East German women, it is not because Soviet women have proportionately better services or more household appliances at their disposal, or because technology has provided better protection on the job, for in fact this is not the case. It is not simply because the Soviet Union has had twenty-five more years in which to break down male prejudices, either. If this were the reason, it is reasonable to suppose that prejudices against male participation in housework would also have diminished considerably, but this has not happened. Women did not have to compete with men for these jobs, because a critical manpower shortage opened up the positions to women and actually put pressure on women to fill them. The same situation occurred temporarily in the United States during the Second World War, when Rosie the Riveter became famous.

In all the socialist countries women still do most of the low-skill, poorly paid work, and the majority of women do work of this kind. Although there are also more women in medium-grade positions of responsibility than in other countries, there is no built-in guarantee that this process of penetration will grow naturally until women receive full equality. Quite the contrary, given a normal male-female balance in the population, the gradual mechanization and automation of some unskilled jobs, and fears for the birthrate such as the socialist countries are experiencing today — it is inevitable that there will be the kind of brake on the advancement of women which can now be observed in the socialist countries, unless a more realistic approach to the problem is found.

At the end of the 1960s, Libuše Háková, writing in the Czech journal of sociology, called attention to a "crisis in the concept of the social function of women" in Czechoslovakia, and recalled that for long years the "woman question" had been considered solved by the change in the social order and the introduction of legal guarantees of equality. She pointed to the complete stagnation of theoretical work in the field of women's emancipation. The official Marxist model, as presented in numerous speeches and documents, was unrealizable and had therefore never gained real acceptance, she said. According to it, socialist woman works not only from economic need but also from internal conviction and interest, and is, moreover, aware of the social usefulness of her work. She is active in community life — or at least takes a lively interest in public affairs — and at the same time brings up her children; with the aid of services and other members of the family, she takes exemplary care of her household and is also an equal partner with her husband in all things. Underneath this proclaimed version, the old traditional model of the woman whose chief function is in the family retains deep roots, but this too is unworkable. A new model is needed, she wrote.

This new model, she continued, would have to take into consideration — in agreement with both Simone de Beauvoir and Marx — that what are considered woman's natural role and her essentially feminine qualities are a product of history and culture, and also that her biological function, already greatly diminished in terms of its part in her physical life, could still undergo radical changes in the future. It would require acceptance of something like the Swedish concept of the equal division of roles between men and women in the family and in society (here given serious attention for the first time in the whole Czechoslovak discussion around women's position). "No progress in the emancipation of woman as a human being can be achieved without changes in the structure and function of the family which take account of the entire *complex* social function of woman," she declared, adding, "A Marxist analysis of the contemporary family can contribute . . . significantly to speeding up this process of change." [1]

She warned that in the struggle from which she expected a new attitude toward the woman question to emerge, together with a new model of the social function of women, there was "danger that in this clash of forces, where the business interests of enterprises, the population interests of the state, the political interests of parties and organizations, and the economic needs of individuals meet, the result could easily be a compromise, utilitarian model of woman and her social function and roles." [2] Her statement of the problem, which should have been a signal for the beginning of a new discussion, in reality simply put the final period to the old one. Although investigations of women's difficulties have, if anything, increased in Czechoslovakia since then, they have only confirmed earlier findings. No creative thinking has taken place (at least not publicly), and Háková's warning has proved well founded.

The socialist countries tried to make of the observations and proposals offered by Marx, Engels, and Lenin — far-reaching in their implications but still touching on only certain aspects of woman's total problem — a complete theory of emancipation to which nothing could be added and from which nothing could be taken away. They have combined this theory with the form of the family which is characteristic of mid–

twentieth century industrial society — the democratic nuclear family with diminishing but still noticeable patriarchal over-tones — which happened to be emerging in the socialist countries and was therefore ipso facto the socialist family, to form their picture of the framework in which woman will be liberated. They have belatedly realized the irreconcilability of this theory with certain realities of life, but because they do not feel able to change the theory and cannot change the realities, they are forced to perpetuate the myth that the two can be successfully synthesized, and that this is, in fact, what liberation means: to make it possible for woman to combine her role as wife and mother, as the dominant figure in the home, with her role as worker. In this concept, one less-skilled, less-rewarding, less-prestigious job plus homemaking contains the same potential for equality as one better-paid, more interesting, or at least less tedious, job by itself (or else "equal" means different things to men and women because they are different). But this is not so, and cannot be so, as we have seen.

This is the theoretical impasse in which the socialist countries find themselves. It is maintained that eventually socialist production relations will, through the advance of science and technology, make it possible for woman to be both man's equal in the outside world and a successful housewife and mother, to carry two responsibilities and execute both jobs as well as man does his one. Within this dual-role conception, the way is open to practical discussion to find ways of ameliorating woman's condition, but this has been shown to run in an endless circle. Once the precarious mathematics of the dual role are accepted, there are more special privileges and protection for women on the job, more women are discriminated against by employers, more women find it difficult to compete; they have less time for and interest in acquiring qualifications, and they give in to the demands of their homemaking functions.[3] Men cannot be ex-pected to give up more than a minimum of their "better paid" time to help in the home or with the children. Technology is used first to raise productivity in the more important men's fields, and, where it mechanizes women's jobs, women tend to be replaced by men who supervise the machinery. A shortening of the working day, either for women alone or for all workers, gives women more time to spend on the house and children and men less reason for having to help. There is no crash program to improve services or establish ideal nurseries because women are being given time, and even housewives' allowances, to do the work at home, and the need for these facilities is not felt by the predominantly male policy-makers who allot funds. There are always (and always will be) enough other projects which seem more vital to the economy and which need money. Patchwork solutions alleviate particular conditions — for example, when women decide to resolve the conflict by not having children — and shift the problem to another plane, there to simmer until the social consequences are such that someone — the child psychologist, the population expert, the physician, the educator, the rationalizer of industry — rings an alarm.

Implicit in the present socialist position is the idea that in socialist society vestiges of bourgeois prejudice in the minds of men will gradually be overcome and men will voluntarily give up more of their free time, take over some of the housekeeping and child-care tasks for which they have not been prepared by tradition or training, and free women to take over a substantial number of skilled jobs and positions of power for which they have somehow managed to become better qualified than the men who previously held them. But how is this piece of consciousness-raising to be performed? Men believe they have enough trouble without looking for any more; and why should they when they have already been told that the responsibility for the children and the home is primarily women's, and that this is not inconsistent with equality?

A huge women's organization with half a million members out of an adult female population of five million is not in a position to undertake this educational task in Czechoslovakia, for example, because its members are still waiting for theoretical enlightenment themselves. The first theoretical education of women on the "woman question" since World War II is scheduled to take place in 1975. The Union of Women has announced a study program for its members to begin in that year, in which they will gradually be acquainted with excerpts from the works of Marx, Engels, and Lenin relative to women which are contained in a small anthology edited in the Soviet Union.[4] This is a step forward, certainly, but there is every probability that this instruction will be in line with the article by the Slovak sociologist Jarmila Šimuničová which appeared in 1973. This author, reflecting the prevailing line of thought, expresses the belief that the impending "scientific and technological revolution" will make it possible to solve the problems of women's qualifications, their free time, and their fair remuneration, and will insure facilities for child care and take housework out of the home. "All this would," she continues, "create optimal conditions" for woman to realize herself both professionally and politically. "The final result would be to enable women to formulate their own criteria for their equality. Thus, existing barriers erected by prejudice, and inappropriate criteria for women which men have created over generations, would be overcome, and the privileges which men have had up to now would be eliminated; for all these privileges are really only the appropriation of the freedom of others." [5]

This is, of course, a masterly piece of cart-before-the-horse-manship, because while the "scientific and technological revolution" may make a variety of things possible, which of these possibilities will be realized will depend on the criteria which society has already adopted and toward which it is working. As Engels astutely pointed out in *Origin,* it was modern industry which made it not only possible but necessary for woman to emerge from the home and take part in production, and this source of her dual exploitation was also the source of her potential emancipation. Technology makes it possible either to plan children or not to have them, to establish communal services, to employ women in jobs they could not otherwise safely undertake; but the mere possibility does not guarantee that technology will be used in that way. Even if the millennium should arrive and society have plenty of resources for everything, choices would still have to be made between conflicting policies.

Theoreticians of women's liberation who need not work within any such rigidly prescribed formulas will be right in drawing the conclusion that the time to start raising man's

consciousness is now, and the emphasis is on man. Consciousness-raising, when it comes to changing the attitude of men
toward women's condition, is a bootstrap operation which has
no parallel. Political agitation has been men's province down
through the centuries, and men have always persuaded other
men to act in a particular way *in their own interests.* In any
conflict between nations, or within nations between parties,
races, or classes, men have been won over to one side or another
because the existing situation was intolerable and the benefits of
a change seemed clear. When men are asked to participate — in
fact to take the lead, since it is they who still control political,
financial, and ideological power — in a redivision of the roles in
the family and society, they are being asked to give something
up, whether they are white, black, working-class, middle-class,
intellectuals, capitalists, or socialists. The ultimate benefits of
such a redivision to men are hard for them to perceive.

During the between-the-wars struggles of the working-class
movement for women's emancipation this was not as obvious as
it is now. Then it was not a question of fighting for women to
be executives but for the right of married women to work as
teachers and bank clerks or even, in times of economic crisis, for
women to work at all. The children were hungry and didn't
have shoes; women needed jobs, and if this created problems
men workers did not mind demanding a solution from the
capitalists. Now, of course, socialist captains of industry have to
pay for the solutions and put up with the inconveniences themselves. Consequently, even in countries where women's equality
has been an officially stated goal for decades, woman's "natural
function" remains the convenient and honestly believed-in rationale for not admitting her to man's world on an equal basis,
or at least for postponing this prospect until after the technological revolution — a new version of pie in the sky.

Men as well as women must be convinced not only that
roles in the home must be changed, and the child's right to its
father and the father's right to the child accepted as equally as
important as the mother-child relationship, but also that the
need for women of the outside world of industry, politics, science, and culture is on a par with its need for men. This means

that the differences between men and women will be looked upon as differences in each sex, and not as female deviations from the norm, and that not only the home but the working-place must be reorganized accordingly. It requires an end to the assumption that men's jobs are necessarily more important than women's. Only the creation of a mentality which acknowledges this, and approaches questions of nurseries and services as problems which touch all of society, will make it probable as well as possible that men will actually share that inevitable portion of housework and child care which will remain in the family for the foreseeable future, and that boys will really choose jobs as hospital nurses and girls, as airplane pilots.

This will take more than one generation to achieve, for even if it were to be universally accepted as a principle of education, the teaching would still be done by men and women who cannot escape the weight of their own traditions. This makes it urgent that women who already believe that humanity will benefit from equality of the sexes should not confine their consciousness-raising to their own sex but should put it on a coeducational basis beginning in the cradle, where possible. Every mother who expects her daughter to do the dusting while she herself washes out her son's drip-dry shirts, or who does not encourage her small boy's interest in babies or cooking or the washing machine, or who does not consciously help her little girl develop nontraditional interests, is postponing the dawn.

Even if there is a more equitable distribution of wealth, it will not be until this new consciousness dawns that real equality will be possible, because it will take a radical reallocation of society's resources to finance adequate nurseries and communal services, and to alter working conditions and pay scales so that the same criteria apply to men and women in all industries and professions. And that is not all that is necessary. Formal equality granted in conditions of inequality results in more actual inequality. Because woman has been held back for so long, like a newly freed colonial nation, she will take some time to grasp her new identity. Since, in addition, she will undoubtedly continue for some time to perform the biological functions of motherhood, society will need to invest in a gigantic Headstart Program

for women. Girls need more attention than boys in their formative years to divert their interests from the conventional
channels into which society will, perhaps in contradiction to its
own consciously expressed aim, continue to encourage them for
a long time. Women need special training opportunities to
qualify them for better jobs and to make up for time lost during
pregnancy, childbirth, and nursing, as well as the legal guarantees to make these jobs available to them. They need time and
strength to avail themselves of such opportunities, and massive
doses of encouragement. Women who still prefer to devote
themselves to the home will have to be granted that option
without being made to feel that they are disgracing the sex. The
society that is able to do these things will be able to say that it
has liberated women.

Meanwhile a tremendous amount of study needs to be done
by both men and women on such questions as how much child
care can really be entrusted to nurseries, and what kind of nurseries and what combination of institutional and individual care
is really best for a child; what services can really be done economically on a community basis, and how can they be organized
and financed; how girls and boys should be educated to break
the circle of cultural conditioning — these are only a few of the
practical problems that need to be solved.

Support must be obtained for experiments in family arrangements and thought given to the social policies that might
influence various kinds of personal relationships; for all experience to date everywhere tends to support the belief that the
much-abused family — in the sense of a more or less stable relationship between members of the opposite sex, formalized by
law or custom, and involving the upbringing of children — will
neither be "abolished" nor continue to exist in exactly the form
in which any of us are experiencing it now. There is no "theoretically correct" form of the family, and the search for it leads us
into a blind alley. The family will continue to change under the
influence of many complex interacting influences which are not
yet fully understood, and it will do so slowly. People and institutions do not change overnight; but it is a good thing that they
do not, because a world without tradition and continuity is as

unthinkable as a world without change. Even if the economic factor is seen as Engels saw it, as the finally determining driving force behind the driving force, it does not follow that economic change will be or must be immediately or clearly reflected in the form of the family. The final result will depend on the intervening gear wheels as well as on the original driving force. Whatever form of the family — or absence of it — exists in a given place at a given time will also change in part in response to the effort to use it to emancipate women.

These seem to me to be the lessons to be learned from the socialist experience and the perspectives it holds out for the future.

NOTES

(Names of Czech and Slovak articles are given in English translation only; the titles of periodicals and newspapers in which they appear are given in the original only. Titles of foreign-language books are given in the original with the translation in parentheses.)

CHAPTER ONE

1. Jiřina Brejchová, Božena Holečková, and Vlasta Košňarová, *Women in Czechoslovakia* (Prague: The Czechoslovak Women's Committee, 1963), p. 19.
2. These were agriculture, industrial communications, retail trade and restaurants, public transportation, post and telegraph, municipal services, housing administration, health and social welfare, education, and banking and insurance.
3. Jaroslav Kohout and Jaroslav Kolář, "Complex Sociological Research at Tesla Pardubice," *Sociologický časopis*, no. 4 (1966), p. 547.
4. Miroslav Hora, director of the methodological center of the ČKD apprentice training plant, in a round-table discussion sponsored by the Czechoslovak Union of Women, reported under the title, "Into the Ditch with the Girls?" *Mladá fronta*, May 1, 1968.
5. "Women, Qualifications, and Equality," *Rudé právo*, November 16, 1964.
6. Jaroslava Kaliberková, "Woman, an Economic Problem," *Hospodářské noviny*, no. 49–50 (1968).
7. Jaroslava Bauerová et al., *Problémy zaměstnaných žen* ("Problems of Employed Women") (ČVTS Pardubice, 1971), p. 123.

8. *Education*

	average monthly earnings in crowns (May 1968)	
	men	women
elementary school plus apprentice training	1,995	1,424
elementary school plus on-job training	1,925	1,266
elementary school only	1,934	1,255
complete secondary school (academic course)	2,000	1,323
vocational secondary school	2,127	1,396
university or technical college	2,579	2,067

9. Bauerová et al., op. cit., p. 104.
10. "What Shall We Do With Them?" *Vlasta*, July 20, 1966.
11. V. Wynnyczuk, "Woman and Education in the Light of New Demographic Information," *Rudé právo*, March 8, 1968.
12. "All activity aimed at orientation and consultation in the choice of employment was basically stopped in our country in the middle of the 1930s," wrote V. N. Shubkin in the Soviet journal, *Voprosy filosofii*, no. 5, 1965, reporting on job placement of young people in Novosibirsk (reprinted in part in the Slovak weekly, *Predvoj*, no. 32, August 12, 1965).
13. *Práce*, March 2, 1972.
14. "They Are Outstanding Workers," *Rudé právo*, March 1, 1972.
15. "Women and Leading Jobs in Industry," *Hospodářské noviny*, December 21, 1973.
16. Eva Bártová, "Attitudes to the Problem of Woman and the Family," *Sociologický časopis*, vol. 8, no. 1 (1972), p. 49.
17. "Misplaced Consideration," *Rudé právo*, February 1, 1971.
18. Editors' note in *Sociológia*, vol. 5, no. 3 (1973), p. 196.
19. Jolana Jančovičová, "Increasing the Participation of Women in the Direction of Society," *Sociológica*, vol. 5, no. 3 (1973), pp. 211–12.
20. "We Want Youngsters But Not Girls," *Práca*, March 17, 1970.
21. "The Worries of Women in Agriculture," *Zemědelské noviny*, June 17, 1969.

CHAPTER TWO

1. Frederick Engels, "The Condition of the Working-Class in England," in *Karl Marx and Frederick Engels on Britain* (Moscow:

Foreign Languages Publishing House, 1953), pp. 176–79.

2. Karl Marx and Frederick Engels, "The Communist Manifesto," in *A Handbook of Marxism* (New York: International Publishers, 1935), p. 42.

3. Karl Marx, *Capital* (New York: Modern Library, 1936), p. 536.

4. Frederick Engels, *The Origin of the Family, Private Property and the State* (Moscow: Foreign Languages Publishing House, 1948), p. 93.

5. Ibid., p. 94.

6. Ibid., p. 102.

7. Ibid.

8. Ibid., p. 230.

9. Ibid., pp. 253–54.

10. Ibid., p. 106.

11. Ibid., p. 105.

12. Ibid., p. 108.

13. Robin Fox, *Kinship and Marriage* (London: Penguin Books, 1969), p. 18.

14. George W. Stocking, Jr., *Race, Culture, and Evolution* (New York: The Free Press, 1968), pp. 228–29.

15. David F. Aberle, "Matrilineal Descent in Cross-Cultural Perspective," in *Matrilineal Kinship*, edited by David M. Schneider and Kathleen Gough (Berkeley: University of California Press, 1962), pp. 658–59. For a recent discussion of some of the pitfalls of making and assessing such studies, see Eleanor B. Leacock's introduction to Engels's *Origin of the Family, Private Property and the State* (New York: International Publishers, 1972). She arrives at what is probably the maximum reconciliation possible between Engels and the results of modern anthropological research.

16. Margaret Mead, *Male and Female* (London: Penguin Books, 1964), p. 44.

17. August Bebel, *Woman Under Socialism* (New York: Schocken Books, 1971), p. 30.

18. Juliet Mitchell, *Woman's Estate* (London: Penguin Books, 1971), p. 77.

19. For example, Kate Millett, *Sexual Politics* (New York: Doubleday, 1970), and Shulamith Firestone, *The Dialectic of Sex* (New York: Bantam Books, 1971). Firestone, who reluctantly comes to the conclusion that the family, miserable as it is, is probably as good as any of the experimental alternatives that have been tried, makes the pertinent point that without the development of a feminist consciousness prior to the initiation of the experi-

ment, the communes "merely extend the family structure to include a larger number of people" (pp. 220–25).

20. Wilhelm Reich, *The Sexual Revolution* (New York: The Noonday Press, 1969), pp. 161–63.
21. D. Chesnokov, *Historical Materialism*, English translation from Russian (Moscow: Progress Publishers, 1969), p. 261. Prof. Chesnokov is head of the Department of Historical Materialism, Philosophical Faculty, Moscow University.
22. Engels, *Origin of the Family* ... (Moscow, 1948), pp. 117–18.

CHAPTER THREE

1. Marx and Engels, "The Communist Manifesto," *Handbook of Marxism*, pp. 42–43.
2. Frederick Engels, *Anti-Dühring* (New York: International Publishers, 1939), p. 284.
3. Quoted in Philip Foner, *The Labor Movement in the United States* (New York: International Publishers, 1947), p. 385.
4. Klára Zetkinová, *Z dějin ženského proletářského hnutí v nemecku* ("From the History of the Women's Proletarian Movement in Germany"), Czech translation from German (Prague: Státní nakladatelství politické literatury, 1961), p. 86. This collection of articles by Clara Zetkin, some written in 1905, others in 1928, was published for the first time in 1958 on the basis of material in Moscow archives by Dietz Verlag in East Berlin, with the title *Zur Geschichte der Proletarischen Frauenbewegung Deutschlands.*
5. Bebel, *Woman Under Socialism*, p. 191.
6. Ibid., p. 343.
7. Ibid., pp. 347–48.
8. Gustav Bareš, introduction to Bebel's *Žena a socialismus* ("Woman Under Socialism") (Prague: Státní nakladatelství politické literatury, 1962), p. 5.
9. Zetkinová, op. cit., pp. 88–89.
10. Bebel, op. cit., pp. 4–6.
11. Zetkinová, op. cit., p. 156.
12. Ibid., pp. 164–65.
13. Clara Zetkin, "My Recollections of Lenin," in *The Emancipation of Women, from the Writings of V. I. Lenin* (New York: International Publishers, 1966), p. 97.
14. "The Programme of the Communist International," in *Handbook of Marxism*, pp. 997–98.

15. All of these comments by Lenin are according to Zetkin's recollections (see note 13 above). The same booklet contains Lenin's correspondence with Inessa Armand concerning a pamphlet which she intended to write but never did.
16. In 1937 the natural increase in the population per one thousand inhabitants was 19.8 in the Soviet Union, 3.2 in Czechoslovakia, 0.3 in France, 2.7 in Great Britain, and 5.8 in the U.S., according to *Statistická ročenka ČSSR 1972* ("Czechoslovak Statistical Yearbook for 1972"), pp. 563–64.

CHAPTER FOUR

1. "We are all Hussites without having been conscious of it," wrote Luther in 1520. "Yes, Paul and Augustine are literally Hussites" (quoted in R. W. Seton-Watson, *A History of the Czechs and Slovaks* [Hamden, Conn.: Archon Books, 1965], p. 87).
2. Premier Zápotocký's speech, together with the text of the law on the First Five-Year Plan, appear in English in *The Czechoslovak Economic Five-Year Plan* (Prague: Orbis, 1949).
3. For an account of the Truman Doctrine and its effect on postwar Czechoslovakia, see D. F. Fleming, *The Cold War*, vol. 1 (London: George Allen & Unwin, 1961), pp. 433–503.
4. Compare these figures for Eastern and Western countries at the beginning of the 1960s, compiled by a Slovak writer, Blanka Svorenova-Királyová, mostly from International Labor Organization studies, in *Žena 20 století ve světě práce* ("Twentieth Century Woman in the Working World") (Prague: Práce, 1968):

	Year	Percentage of working female population	Percentage of women in total work force	Percentage that are women of all agricultural workers
USSR*	1959	41.5	53.7	54.0
Poland	1960	40.6	44.3	54.7
Rumania	1956	52.7	45.3	53.6
Bulgaria	1956	45.7	42.0	50.5
German Democratic Republic	1963	38.8	46.0	47.1
Czechoslovakia	1963	38.9	44.0	52.5
Hungary	1960	32.3	35.1	36.9

	Year	Percentage of working female population	Percentage of women in total work force	Percentage that are women of all agricultural workers
Denmark	1960	27.9	30.9	9.4
Sweden	1960	25.7	30.4	8.7
U.S.A.	1962	25.9	34.1	17.6
Canada	1964	19.8 (1961)	28.3	6.9
France	1962	27.5	34.2	32.6
Great Britain	1962		35.6	15.6

* According to Norton T. Dodge, *Women in the Soviet Economy* (Baltimore: The Johns Hopkins Press, 1966), employing Soviet census figures for 1959, 49 percent of all Soviet females were employed in that year, and women in agriculture accounted for 55.3 percent of all Soviet working women (p. 37 and p. 45). However, he includes women employed in private subsidiary agriculture.

In 1966 Czechoslovakia derived 14 percent of its GNP from agriculture, Denmark, 10 percent; France, 7 percent; Great Britain and the United States, 3 percent; but Bulgaria, 35 percent; the Soviet Union and Poland, 22 percent—all according to the "Czechoslovak Statistical Yearbook 1969," pp. 543–44. In that year 22 percent of employed Czechoslovak women were working in agriculture.

5. Quoted in the booklet *The Right to Social Security in Czechoslovakia* (Prague: Orbis, 1957) (in English), pp. 9–10.
6. *The Constitution of the Czechoslovak Republic* (Prague: Orbis, 1958) (in English).
7. Details of the Social Security program may be found in English in the booklet mentioned above in note 5; also in Bohumil Erben and Jaromír Mařík, *Social Security in Czechoslovakia* (Prague: Orbis, 1957), and *Social Security*, third revised edition (Prague: Orbis, 1962); and in "Social Security in Czechoslovakia," *Bulletin of the International Social Security Association*, vol. 13, no. 3 (March 1960). None of these is completely up-to-date, however.
8. A letter from Dr. John M. Thomas of Omaha, Nebraska, published in *Medical Tribune*, June 10, 1967, is typical: "The proposal . . . that 'every family be given a cash allowance for each child irrespective of income' is madness. Just who is going to put up the cash? Johnny Q. Taxpayer, as usual. This sort of

socialist scheme would only encourage people to be less self-
reliant."

9. Senta Radvanová et al., *Žena a právo* ("Woman and the Law")
   (Prague: Orbis, 1971), p. 213.

10. *New Family Legislation in Czechoslovakia*, published as a pam-
    phlet by the Ministry of Information and Public Culture and
    the Ministry of Justice in 1950 in Prague, contains the provisions
    of the Family Law of 1948 and Minister Čepička's speech in
    English.

11. Dorothy W. Douglas, *Transitional Economic Systems* (New York:
    Monthly Review Press, 1972), p. 256. This book, originally pub-
    lished in 1953, gives a picture of the economies of Czechoslovakia
    and Poland before the war and of some of the mechanics of
    planning and economic transformation in the immediate post-
    war years. The story is brought up to date in George Shaw
    Wheeler, *The Human Face of Socialism* (New York: Lawrence
    Hill & Co., 1973), which discusses the economic problems which
    led to the crisis of the 1960s.

CHAPTER FIVE

1. Zetkin, "Recollections of Lenin," p. 110.

2. *Prague News Letter*, vol. 15, no. 15, Prague: Orbis (July 25, 1959),
   p. 1.

3. *The Constitution of the Czechoslovak Socialist Republic* (Prague:
   Orbis, 1961), p. 10.

4. Unlike the situation in some of the other socialist countries,
   sociological research could not be said to have been interrupted
   in the Soviet Union because no tradition in this field had actually been created. In the mid-1960s Soviet theoreticians still considered Marxist sociology to be adequately covered by historical
   materialism, and did not recognize specialized sociological fields
   such as the sociology of the family, although they were actually
   devoting research to them.

5. The discussion was published in abbreviated form under the title
   "The Position of Women in Socialist Society" in the bulletin of
   the Czechoslovak State Population Commission, *Zprávy státní
   populační komise* (hereafter referred to as *ZSPK*), no. 4 (1965),
   pp. 32–46.

6. Proceedings of the Twelfth Congress of the Communist Party of Czechoslovakia, *XII. Sjezd KSČ* (Prague: Ustřendí výbor *KSC*, 1962), pp. 34–35.

CHAPTER SIX

1. Milan Kučera, "Employment of Women and Reproduction," *ZSPK*, no. 2 (1965), p. 33.
2. Marx enunciated the principle of remuneration according to work done in the first stage of communism, known as socialism, in his *Critique of the Gotha Program* (1875), in order to counter what he considered unrealistic ideas about the desirability of distributing rewards to all alike once the means of production were taken over by the workers. All the socialist countries have experienced difficulties in arriving at wage differentials which reflect differences in diligence, ability, and responsibility and at the same time do not create an elite.
3. "Troubles with Women," unsigned lead article in the Slovak weekly, *Predvoj*, August 18, 1966, p. 1.
4. In a poll of a sample of two thousand persons conducted for the Union of Women by the Public Opinion Research Institute in 1968, 45–55 percent of men and 60–70 percent of women said that they did not think Czechoslovak women had achieved real equality. In reply to the question What steps do you think the Union of Women should take to help women? the answer given most frequently by both men and women was, "Raise men's pay so that women can stay at home" (33 percent of Czech and 26 percent of Slovak men, 20 percent of Czech and 14 percent of Slovak women).
5. Radoslav Selucký, "Emancipation or Equality?" *Literární noviny*, March 6, 1965.
6. Marie Sulková, "Concerning Some Ideas on the Position of Women," *Rudé právo*, May 20, 1965.
7. Libuše Háková, "It's Women's Turn," *Kulturní tvorba*, August 26, 1965.
8. J. Prokopec and V. Wynnyczuk, "On the Employment of Women, Concretely," *Hospodářské noviny*, January 8, 1965, p. 6.
9. Jiří Švejkovský, "The Economic Effect of the Employment of Women," *Rudé právo*, September 1, 1965.
10. Letters quoted here appeared in *Rudé právo* for September 28, October 12, 19, 26, November 9, and December 8, 1966. The

article, "No New Policy," was published February 8, 1967.
11. Anna Tučková, "What Do We Really Want of Them?" interview with Vladimír Wynnyczuk, *Kulturní tvorba*, no. 5 (1966).
12. Senta Radvanová et al., *Žena a právo*, p. 104.
13. Jiřina Lišková, "A Woman on Women," interview with Magdalena Sokolowska, *Mladá fronta*, July 14, 1965.
14. Soviet weekly *Nedelya*, no. 20 (1968).

CHAPTER SEVEN

1. Engels, *Origin of the Family*, p. 14. Even this formulation gave too much importance to biological reproduction as a determining factor in social development to please Stalin, and during his lifetime all Soviet editions of *Origin*, including the English-language one used here, carried an editor's preface correcting Engels's "inaccuracy," and quoting Stalin to the effect that the principal determining factor in society is always the "mode of production of the material values necessary for the existence of people and the propagation of their species." Engels was formally exonerated on this point at a conference of Soviet social scientists in 1962.
2. Bebel, *Woman Under Socialism*, p. 370.
3. V. I. Lenin, "The Tasks of the Working Women's Movement in the Soviet Republic," speech delivered in September 1919. Included in *The Emancipation of Women*, p. 69.
4. Prof. Karel Kácl, "The New Legislation on the Interruption of Pregnancy," *Svobodné slovo*, December 20, 1957.
5. *Tisková informační služba ministerstva zdravotnictví*, vol. 11, no. 11 (March 16, 1962), vol. 12, no. 5 (January 18, 1963).
6. Henry P. David, *Family Planning and Abortion in the Socialist Countries of Eastern Europe* (New York: The Population Council, 1970), p. 58. The Soviet study is by N. S. Sokolova, "Statistical Analysis of the Outcome of Pregnancies" (originally published in the Soviet journal *Zdravookhranenie Rossiiskoi Federatsii*, vol. 14: 38–40). A condensed report appeared in Patricia G. Steinhoff, "Abortion Data from the Soviet Union," *Abortion Research Notes*, ARN Supplement no. 3, November 1972.
7. Dr. Miroslav Vojta, "Suggestions for Improving the Work of the Interruption Commissions," *ZSPK*, no. 2 (1968), p. 18.
8. Věra Hájková and Anna Tučková, "Pillory or Aid" *Kulturní tvorba*, June 17, 1965.

230 DOES SOCIALISM LIBERATE WOMEN?

9. Prof. Alfred Kotásek, Chairman of the Czech Gynecological Society, interviewed in the health workers' weekly, *Zdravotnické noviny*, June 19, 1969.
10. Prof. Karel Vácha, "The Activity of the Interruption Commissions," *ZSPK*, no. 2 (1968), p. 15.
11. Jiří Prokopec, secretary of the State Population Commission, *ZSPK*, no. 2 (1968), p. 9.
12. These findings from studies conducted at the University of Hawaii are given in Milton Diamond, James A. Palmore, Roy G. Smith, and Patricia G. Steinhoff, "Abortion in Hawaii," *Family Planning Perspectives*, V (1): Winter 1973, pp. 54–60; and Milton Diamond, Patricia G. Steinhoff, James A. Palmore, and Roy G. Smith, "Sexuality, Birth Control and Abortion: A Decision-Making Sequence," *Journal of Biosocial Science*, 5:1973, pp. 347–61.
13. Helena Svarcová, *Populace* ("Population"), (Prague: Státní nakladatelství politické literatury, 1966), pp. 38–39.
14. Prof. Jan Horský, "The Status of Contraception in the World and Its Perspectives," *ZSPK*, no. 2 (1970), p. 24.
15. There is no way of knowing from this study how these children would have turned out if they had been "wanted." A study in which "unwanted" children, born a decade ago in Prague to women whose applications for abortion were rejected both by local commissions and by an appeals commission, have been paired with "wanted" children of the same age, sex, and background, has been completed by a research team in Prague with World Health Organization support, but the results have not yet been made public. If there proves to be a significant difference in the way the two groups of children are developing, it should have important implications for future abortion legislation.
16. Švarcová, op. cit., p. 170.
17. Frederick Engels, "Outlines of a Critique of Political Economy," published as an appendix to Karl Marx, *Economic and Philosophical Manuscripts of 1844* (Moscow: Foreign Languages Publishing House, no date), pp. 198–200.
18. Marx, *Capital*, pp. 692–93.
19. *Politická ekonomie* ("Political Economy") (Prague: Státní nakladatelství politické literatury, 1960). p. 658.
20. Quoted in Alfred Sauvy, *Fertility and Survival* (New York: Collier Books, 1963), chapter 23.

21. J. N. Gusevati in *Mysl* (Moscow, 1971), p. 404, quoted in O. Schmidt, "Trends in World Population Development," *Hospodářské noviny*, January 5, 1973.
22. Milan Kučera, "The Present Population Situation in Czechoslovakia," *Rudé právo*, March 5, 1968.
23. Radvanová et al., *Žena a právo*, p. 32.
24. In October 1973 Hungary announced new restrictions on abortion which will permit the legal interruption of pregnancy in married women for nonmedical reasons only if they already have three children, except in unusual cases. In 1972 there were 117 legal abortions in Hungary for every 100 live births, and Hungary led Europe in figures for "spontaneous abortions." The government has raised all children's and family allowances substantially as of 1974.

CHAPTER EIGHT

1. "Granny, Keep an Eye on Her," *Rudé právo*, February 8, 1972.
2. The distribution between urban and rural districts and among the individual republics is very unequal. Details will be found in Dodge, *Women in the Soviet Economy*, Chapter 5. This comprehensive statistical study, referred to also in note 4 to Chapter Four of this book (p. 225) is based primarily on official Soviet sources.
3. Quoted by Bruno Bettelheim in *The Children of the Dream* (New York: Avon Books, 1970), p. 19.
4. Bettelheim's review of *Children in Collectives: Childrearing Aims and Practices in the Kibbutz*, edited by Neubauer and Thomas, appeared in the *New York Review of Books*, October 6, 1966, p. 12.
5. Lenin, *The Emancipation of Women*, p. 64.
6. George A. Miller, *The Science of Mental Life* (London: Penguin Books, 1966), p. 212.
7. At an historic meeting of the Lenin Academy of Agricultural Sciences of the USSR, held July 31–August 7, 1948, Lysenko declared: "Darwin himself, in his day, was unable to fight free of the theoretical errors of which he was guilty. It was the classics of Marxism that revealed those errors and pointed them out. Today there is absolutely no justification for accepting the erroneous aspects of the Darwin theory, those based on Malthus's theory of overpopulation with the inference of a struggle pre-

232   DOES SOCIALISM LIBERATE WOMEN?

sumably going on within species. . . . The materialist theory of the evolution of living nature necessarily presupposes the recognition of hereditary transmission of individual characteristics acquired by the organism under definite conditions of its life; it is unthinkable without recognition of the inheritance of acquired characteristics" (from the verbatim report, published in English as *The Situation in Biological Science* [Moscow: Foreign Languages Publishing House, 1949], pp. 14–15).

8. A. S. Makarenko, *O výchově dětí v rodině* (Prague: Dědictví Komenského, 1950), Czech translation of a Russian edition of *A Book for Parents,* containing an introduction by Prof. Kolbanovsky.

9. Ferdinand Knobloch and Jiřina Knoblochová, *Soudní psychiatrie pro právníky a lékaře* ("Legal Psychiatry for Lawyers and Doctors") (Prague: Orbis, 1965), pp. 109–12.

10. Marie Damborská, "Facing Employed Mothers' Dilemma," *Prague News Letter,* April 30, 1966.

11. Jaroslav Koch, "Whom Do Nurseries Serve?" *Vlasta,* January 25, 1967.

12. Josef Langmeier and Zdeněk Matějček, *Psychická deprivace v dětství* ("Psychological Deprivation in Childhood") (Prague: Státní zdravotnické nakladatelství, 1963), p. 227.

13. For the Swedish view, including the government document on the position of women submitted to the United Nations in 1968, see Edmund Dahlstrom et al., *The Changing Roles of Men and Women* (Boston: Beacon Press, 1971).

CHAPTER NINE

1. See, for example, "The Status of Women in Sweden," in Dahlstrom et al., *Changing Roles* . . . , p. 265.

2. The government still underwrites 60 percent of the cost of cooperative apartment building (which accounts for 44 percent of all new housing) and of privately built homes (25 percent of the total). The share of housing actually built by the government wholly at its own expense has dropped from 57 percent in 1960 to 15 percent at present. The remaining 15 percent of new housing is built by socialist factories and other organizations for their employees.

3. Czechoslovak President Antonín Novotný in a speech to outstanding workers in the uranium industry, *Rudé právo,* November 20, 1965.

4. "Private GDR Firms Go Socialist," *Democratic German Report*, Berlin, May 17, 1972.

5. Vlasta Brablcová in *ZSPK*, no. 3 (1967), p. 22.

6. Ladislav Adamec, "A Question of the Structure of Services," *Hospodářské noviny*, no. 43 (1972).

7. Elena Litajová, "Woman in Socialist Society," *Sociológia*, vol. 5, no. 3 (1973), p. 195.

8. Heywood Broun, "Holding a Baby," in *Fifty Great Essays* (New York: Bantam Books, 1964), p. 45.

9. See the official Women's International Democratic Federation magazine, *Women of the Whole World*, published in East Berlin, no. 4 (1967).

10. Zetkin, "Recollections of Lenin," p. 115.

11. Eva Vančurová, "The Socio-psychological Basis of Interpersonal Relationships in the Family with Reference to the Socialization of the Child," *Sociologický časopis*, no. 5 (1970), p. 477.

12. Vlasta Fišerová, "Notes on the Theory of the Family," published as a postscript to Engels's *Původ rodiny, soukromého vlastnictví a státu* ("Origin of the Family . . ."), (Prague: Mladá fronta, 1967), p. 164, and "The Relation of Basic Civilization Variables to Changes in Family Behavior Patterns," *Sociologický časopis*, no. 5 (1970), p. 423.

13. Ota Klein, "The Crisis of Emotionality," *Sociologický časopis*, no. 2 (1969), pp. 129–49.

14. Jarmila Šimuničová, "Woman and the Family as a Subject for Research in Socialist Society," *Sociológia*, vol. 5, no. 3 (1973), p. 202.

CHAPTER TEN

1. Libuše Háková, "A Contribution to the Understanding of the Social Function of Women," *Sociologický časopis*, no. 5 (1970), p. 446.

2. Ibid., p. 443.

3. The inevitability of conflict inherent in this concept of women's emancipation is further illustrated by the fact that in 1973 87.5 percent of Czechoslovak women between the ages of 15 and 54 were employed, in conformity with the economic plan; in that same year a new handbook on legislation protecting pregnant women and mothers, referring to paid and unpaid maternity leave, stated categorically: "Medical research has shown that up to the age of three a child benefits most from direct maternal

234 DOES SOCIALISM LIBERATE WOMEN?

care, for which there is no substitute of equal value," suggesting the direction in which social policy is moving. See Vladimír Vitásek, *Pracovní podmínky těhotných žen a matek* ("Working Conditions of Pregnant Women and Mothers"), (Prague: Orbis, 1973), p. 107.

4. Marx, Engels, and Lenin [in Czech], *K ženské otázce* ("On the Woman Question"), (Prague: Nakladatelství Svoboda, 1973); and [in Slovak], *Žena a spoločnost* ("Woman and Society"), (Bratislava: Nakladatelstvo Pravda, 1973).

5. Šimuničová, "Woman and the Family . . . ," p. 205.